LEARNING TO SEE

A PHOTOGRAPHER'S GUIDE

FROM ZERO TO YOUR FIRST PAID GIGS

DAVID MOLNAR

HARPER HORIZON

Learning to See

Published by Harper Horizon, an imprint of HarperCollins Focus LLC.

ISBN 978-0-7852-5367-9 (ebook)
ISBN 978-0-7852-5366-2 (HC)

Library of Congress Control Number: 2022934085

Printed in Canada

22 23 24 25 26 TC 10 9 8 7 6 5 4 3 2 1

To my beloved wife, who believed in me before I learned to see

Contents

PART 4: DEVELOP

PART 5: EARN

Author's Note

AS A SPECIAL THANK-YOU FOR BUYING THIS BOOK, I'VE RECORDED AN accompanying video lesson for each chapter to illustrate the more technical aspects of the material we cover. It's a completely free resource for you, but I apologize ahead of time for all the puns and dad jokes in the recordings.

Throughout this book, you'll see examples of how to apply the concepts we explore, but in some cases it's just easier to watch a step-by-step video tutorial. I've also included a list of the latest gear, resources, and tools I recommend (since those are changing faster than the publisher can print paper).

▶ To get free access, all you have to do is go to PhotoMentorship.com/LTS. Enjoy!

Introduction

I WAS NEVER SUPPOSED TO BE A PROFESSIONAL PHOTOGRAPHER. IT'S amazing how almost dying can change the course of your life forever, though.

My creative career began on a crisp December 24 when I was driving ninety minutes to reach the nearest mall for some last-minute Christmas shopping. My 1981 mustard-yellow, rusted-like-crazy Volvo station wagon with the white fur seat covers (don't ask) was affectionately called "Marva," and she was old enough to buy beer.

I, however, was not. Having just turned eighteen a few months before, I had gotten my private pilot's license and was on my way to becoming an airline pilot.

The plan was simple: Finish senior year of high school as an undefeated wrestler, win the state championship, and accept one of the many scholarship offers from the universities that were courting me. Then, leave my sleepy little town in North Carolina, get a bachelor's degree in *something*, and work my way up the ranks until I could fly planes for a living.

But that day, all those dreams came to a crashing halt.

Driving sixty-two in a fifty-five, I saw something out of the corner of my eye drifting toward me, and to this day I still don't know what happened. One moment I was cruising down the highway. The next, I woke up in a hospital with the nurses telling me it wasn't my fault.

There had been a head-on collision in which the closing speed between me and the other driver was well over 120 miles per hour. When I came to, my legs didn't work, my whole body ached, and I knew I would never wrestle again.

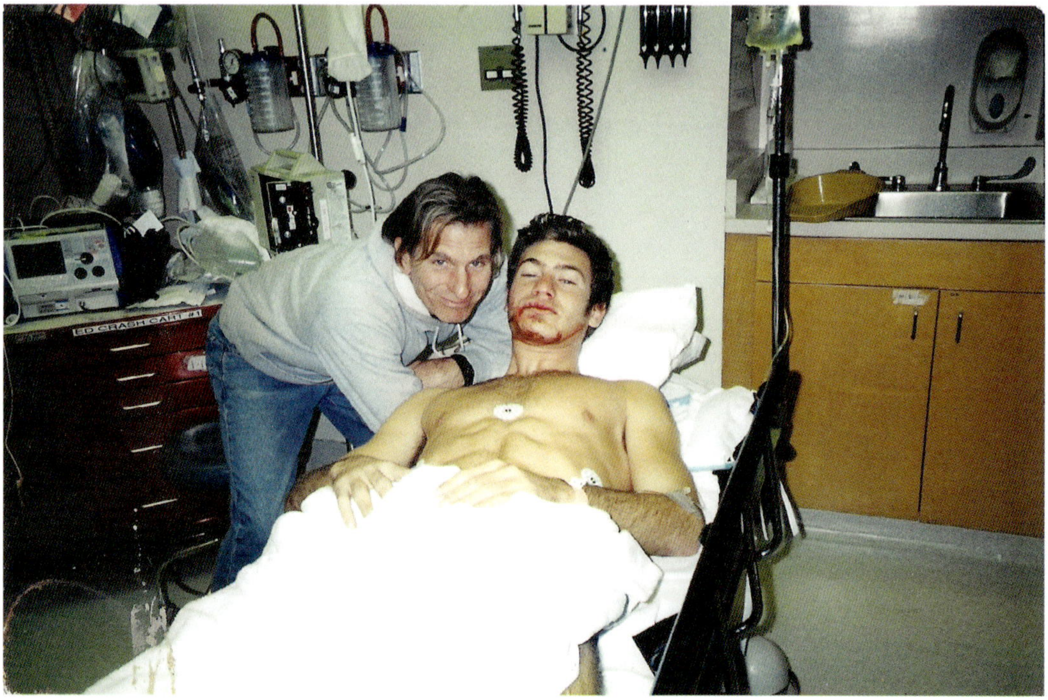

My dad and me in the hospital on Christmas Eve 2002

My world was turned upside down that day. I found myself at a point in life where everything I thought was going to happen did not. I was not going to college, not on scholarship or for any other reason. I would not wrestle again. I would not become an airline pilot. The life I had envisioned just would not *be*. The irony of that accident, however, was that it gave me eyes to see another life that was not only possible—it was necessary. I had to get a new vision for the future since the one I had was no longer possible. I would one day start to see it come together, but that was still a long way away.

As I dug my way out of a minor depression, a new path started coming into focus—not as a wrestler or a pilot but as a photographer. We'll come back to all that, but for now, all you need to know is that life doesn't always go the way we expect—and that's where some of the best stuff can be found.

When you fail, whether in photography or in life, you can always refocus on what's important and take another shot.

Why I Wrote This Book

My journey toward becoming a professional photographer started in struggle. I remember all too well what it was like to hustle through a decade of work, using painful trial-and-error to stumble my way through to eventual success.

My dad gave me his old Nikon 35mm film camera so I could take Photography 101 in high school. After graduation, I begged a nonprofit to let me volunteer as a photographer for their organization. During this time, I began to tackle the basics of how my camera worked. I also started fumbling around with editing.

Next, I worked with my godfather, Billy Diggs—a professional surfing photographer and contractor—to help him build a website for his construction company. I learned some techniques from him and even made my first twenty-five dollars from a magazine as a surf photographer. Unfortunately, I never made another dime off surfing photography.

For a brief three-month stint the following summer, Biff Jennings gave me a job shooting beach portraits of tourists on medium-format film cameras. It was fun, and I learned about posing and lighting and how every family must wear khakis and white polos on the beach. On one shoot, I managed to insult a lady's weight completely by accident and almost got beaten up by her husband. Needless to say, they didn't order any extra prints. Sorry, Biff! Clearly, beach portraits weren't the long-term focus for me.

Then I moved to Nashville and asked other professional photographers to let me assist on their shoots. I ended up cleaning toilets, carrying sandbags, making lots of coffee runs, and setting up far-too-many-to-count lighting rigs. My role in these shoots was something like a cross between a housekeeper and a Sherpa. I would pick up clues here and there but still had to spend years assisting others only to learn a fraction of what I needed to know.

While I was an assistant to other photographers, I began shooting low-budget weddings. To make these shoots, I'd often have to drive all night to another state—getting only a few hours of sleep in a crappy hotel room—then photograph all day before driving home back to my life and work in Nashville. In between gigs, I spent thousands of hours trying to edit my photos. Sometimes, I would delay delivering my work to clients because I was unsure if it looked good or not. Determined to succeed, I spent years struggling to make ends meet.

As I developed my skills as a wedding photographer, I became proficient and slowly started raising my prices, which allowed me to travel more and attract a higher-end clientele. Eventually brides started flying me in to shoot weddings from LA to NYC and many domestic locations in between. My wife was able to quit her job and join me shooting full time as we traveled internationally to exotic destinations like the Alps in Switzerland and the emerald waters of the Greek islands. Our wildest dreams were coming true. Except for one: shooting album covers.

Once I was established, I was able to transition to building a commercial photography portfolio. I dreamed of shooting album covers for bands that millions of people would see, but first I had to learn studio lighting and build my portfolio. I shot my musician friends for free and experimented with cheap studio lighting. I was trying to figure out how it all worked. Working my way up to indie bands with small budgets, I began attracting some small record labels to become clients.

I caught a big break when Zach Kelm believed in me enough to take a risk and pitch me to shoot my first major record label gig. I poured my heart and soul into the job. The album cover *Awake* for the band Skillet went on to sell more than two million copies. Suddenly the labels and advertising agencies knew who I was; my phone started ringing off the hook.

It all seemed to happen so quickly, but the truth is that I was not an overnight success. I had worked my rear end off for almost a decade at this point. Nonetheless, what happened next never ceases to delight this surfer boy who didn't go to college and lacked any formal training. Eventually my photos appeared in *People* magazine, in the *New York Times*, on twenty-eight million Pepsi and Mountain Dew cans, on bestselling books, and on billboards across the country. Flying all over the world, I was charging what previously felt like ridiculous amounts of money to do what I loved. I stumbled through the dark, and with God's grace and the doors he opened—and a lot of persistence—I found a way to achieve my biggest dreams.

I feel blessed to be doing what I love and am so thankful for the life that photography has enabled me to live. I love every part of the work I get to do: the challenges I've overcome, the types of clients I've worked with, and the chance to provide a lifestyle of freedom and prosperity for my family. Photography has made all these things possible!

But I never forgot what it was like to start out.

When I began, nobody told me the exact steps to become a professional photographer. All too often, I felt like an imposter, like I was going to be discovered any minute as a fake. And more times than I care to admit, I wanted to quit. I remember thinking that if only there was a clear path to success that someone could show me, I would have gotten there much sooner and with a lot less heartache. The whole time, I just wanted to know how to become a legitimate photographer, to know that I was good enough to go pro. But there is no bar exam for photography. You just have to figure it out on your own. I don't regret any part of struggling through those ten years, but I also don't wish them on anyone.

It was around this time that a new dream began to arise. *What if*, I thought, *I could help* other *photographers pursue their dreams? What if I could become the mentor I never had?* I became obsessed with figuring out a way to help others do what I had done—only better and in less time. Realizing that camera manuals and photography classes are confusing and convoluted, I thought that there had to be a better way to simplify the process of learning to be a photographer.

As I tested my theories through teaching other photographers to use their cameras, I learned a lot. That said, my first attempts were pretty bad. But that's when I told myself, inspired by the capricious Barney Stinson, "Challenge accepted!" I became obsessed with how to simplify the process so that anyone could understand what it took to use their cameras well. I wanted to teach people simple practices and avoid confusing them with irrelevant science and math.

Instead of focusing on the fractions and decimals, I used analogies and simple visual displays to show people how their cameras actually worked. The result? Tens of thousands of students learned how to master their cameras and began taking incredible shots.

After years spent coaching new and budding photographers, I discovered something else: not only did my fellow photographers need help mastering their cameras, they also wanted to learn what it took to go pro. As it turns out, I learned that there *was* a clear path to doing this—a path, earlier in my journey, I wished someone could have laid out for me. This is exactly why I started a worldwide community of photographers called The Photo Mentorship. In The Photo Mentorship, my team and I teach the five steps to photography success that can help you go from having never picked up a camera to growing a six-figure business in no time.

So why write a book? Why share all this backstory? Because I want to help as many people as possible without holding anything back. All the secrets we teach in The Photo Mentorship, I'm going to reveal here, as best I can. Of course, you can always join us at The Photo Mentorship if you want step-by-step videos of photography training programs and get your questions answered by photography experts so that you can expedite your learning. Nonetheless, I'll be as thorough as possible here, because I want every photographer to see how simple this work can be. It's not rocket science! At least, it doesn't have to be, and that's something I wish someone would have told me many years ago.

In this book I want to take you on a journey of learning to take great pictures. You will learn to set up the shot and edit like a pro, and even explore making money in this industry that all too often feels like a mystery to those just starting out. I'll share more of my own story, as well as the stories of countless others who have become great photographers—and how their lives and work changed as a result. My goal is to take the guesswork and confusion out of photography, and with your permission, become your personal photography mentor—the one I never had.

Whether you want to take better photos in your everyday life or make a full-time income as a photographer, the framework taught in this book will work for you. This book contains a proven process to become a successful photographer. If you use it, it will shave years off the learning curve I had to go through.

How This Book Can Help You

Nata Salvatori was born in Brazil but came to the United States as a nineteen-year-old college student on a volleyball scholarship. At the time, she had only thirty dollars to her name and didn't speak more than ten words of English. By the time we met, she had put herself through school to become a doctor of physical therapy. Her photography journey began when she wanted to take pictures of her kids after she became a mom. Nata signed up for one of my classes and decided to pursue photography with everything she had.

Within a few months of taking that first class, she had devoured all the training and began to develop her skills as a portrait photographer. She picked a name for her business, built a simple website and initial portfolio doing free shoots for friends and family, and then was able to book her first paid gig. After that first shoot, she booked another . . . and another. Soon her clients were referring work to her nonstop, and she was able to book more shoots than she knew what to do with. As a result, she had to keep raising her prices. Within her first twelve months as a professional photographer, Nata booked 140 gigs. In her second year of business, she made over $100,000—and that was only the beginning.

Clearly Nata is a very special person, but a huge part of Nata's photography success is due to her discipline in following a clear path laid out for her. She knew where she wanted to go and blazed a trail to get there. Unlike me, who had to fumble my way through the dark over the course of a decade, Nata found nearly instant success due to her focus, allowing her to quit a full-time job and make a great living doing what she loved. The difference between Nata and me is that she followed a simple five-step framework that I've been teaching online for years and that we will go through in this book.

In the work I get to do, my team and I hear stories like Nata's all the time. As disciplined and focused as these photographers may be, anyone can do what they've done—if they're willing to do the work. What I've learned as a photographer and mentor to others is that this system works.

"Okay, okay," you say. "So *how* does it work?"

There are five simple but important steps to becoming a successful photographer, and those steps will make up the major parts of this book. They are *see*, *shoot*, *edit*, *develop*, and *earn*.

We start our work as photographers by learning how to *see*. Being a professional photographer isn't about having fancy equipment. Foundationally, it's about seeing a certain way—having a vision for your shot and being able to execute that vision. You have to understand what moves people emotionally and how to use what you see with your naked eye to capture that. That's why our framework begins with that first essential human ability: sight. We have to learn how to see ourselves, our subjects, and our work differently. We have to see like a photographer.

The second part of the framework covers what most people think of when they think of photography: *shoot*. This is the most technical part of the book and where people commonly get hung up. But it doesn't have to be scary. I'll use a simple analogy and in fifteen minutes you'll understand your camera.

The third part of the framework is *edit*. Editing is an important part of any photography workflow and helps recreate the emotion you and your subject felt on the day of the shoot. I'll introduce a simple editing process that you can make your own.

The fourth part is *develop*. After you've learned the three foundations of *see*, *shoot*, and *edit*, then it's time to really start developing as a photographer in the area that you want to focus on. Before you can have an official photography business, you need to know who and what you're shooting. If you aim for everything, you'll end up capturing nothing. Pick a niche and make it clear, and your ideal clients will come to you. You might not know yet exactly what you'd like to specialize in, but that's okay. We will figure that out together. As you begin to move in a specific direction, you'll learn more about your interests and strengths as you go.

And the final part is *earn*. This is about finally getting paid for your art. This step is completely optional for those of you who want to shoot just for the love of it. Feel free to skip that part of the book if making money is not your goal with photography. I've included it because over half of my students aspire to make a part-time or full-time income off their photography. But, of course, that's not for everyone.

Once you've learned to *see*, *shoot*, *edit*, and *develop* your skills, you should be taking professional-quality images worthy of compensation. At this point, it's finally time to start charging for your work—but not before. If you follow these first few steps well, it really is only a matter of time and a little business savviness before people are willing to pay you. There is a lot about starting a photography business that is confusing, hidden, and just plain not talked about in the industry. In the *earn* section we will explore how to book your first clients, price your services, and build a successful business. It's the part I imagine some of you may be most excited about, and it could be a big reason why you picked up this book. But it's important to remember that the four steps before this one are crucial. Do not start charging before you've completed the fourth step.

This framework is the secret sauce—the road map to not just going pro but becoming a world-class photographer. My hope for you by the end of this book is that you come to believe in yourself, whether you want to go big-time or just hone your craft as an artist. I hope you can not only call yourself a photographer but begin to act like one. I hope you learn to see, because in the end, that's what a photographer does. They notice what other people often miss and understand how to capture those things in a masterful way.

So let's start there.

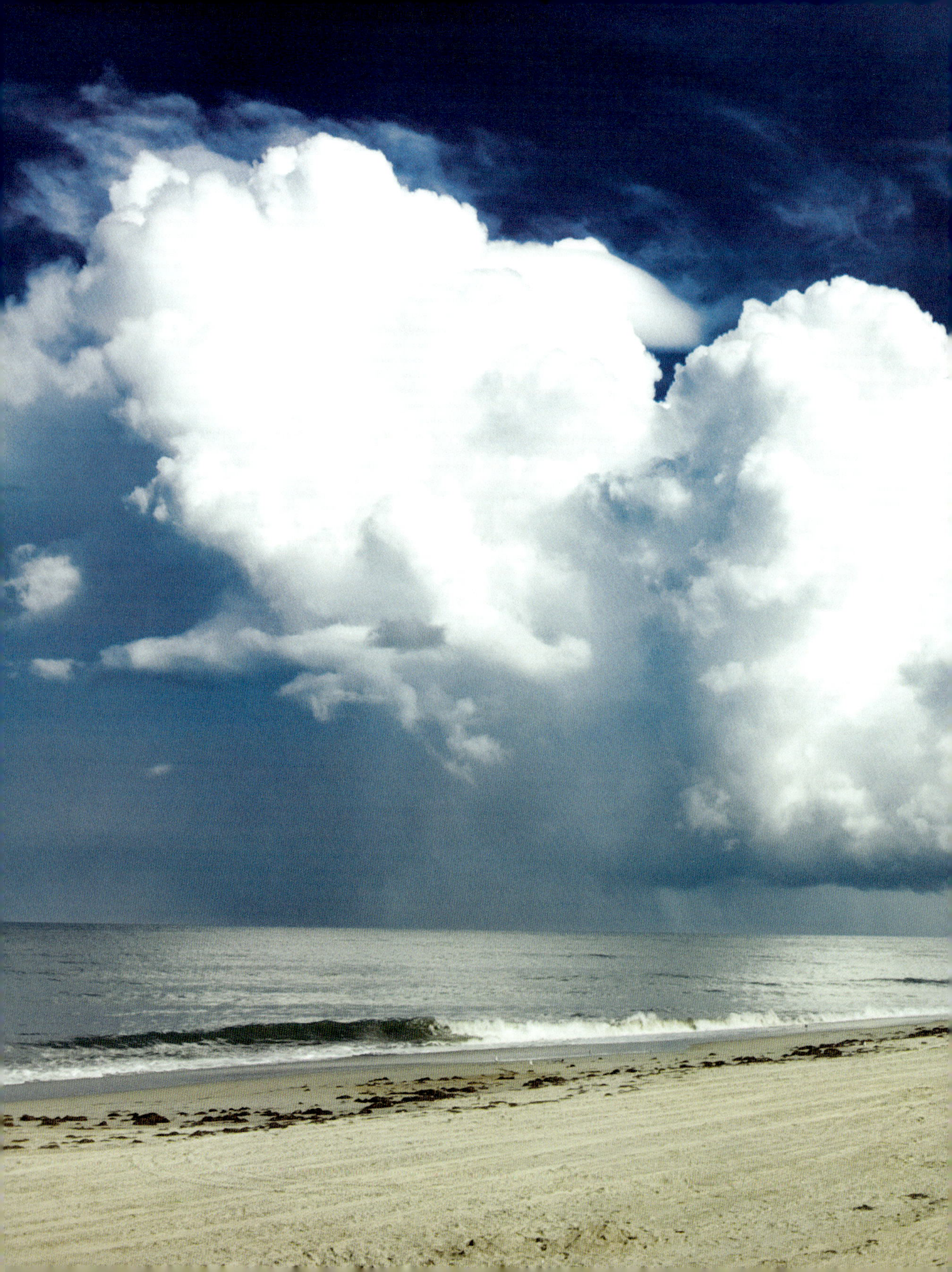

PART 1

SEE

In this first part, we are going to explore what it takes to see like a photographer. Before you can shoot truly great photos, you first have to know what to look for. Here, we will explore secret formulas that took me years to learn—tricks professionals know but rarely disclose. We'll talk about composition, what lenses to use, and a lot more. We'll explore how to create photography magic and why every magic trick helps you avoid a common rookie mistake. All this is preparation for what's to come: mastering your camera so you can start taking photos you'd be proud to share with the world.

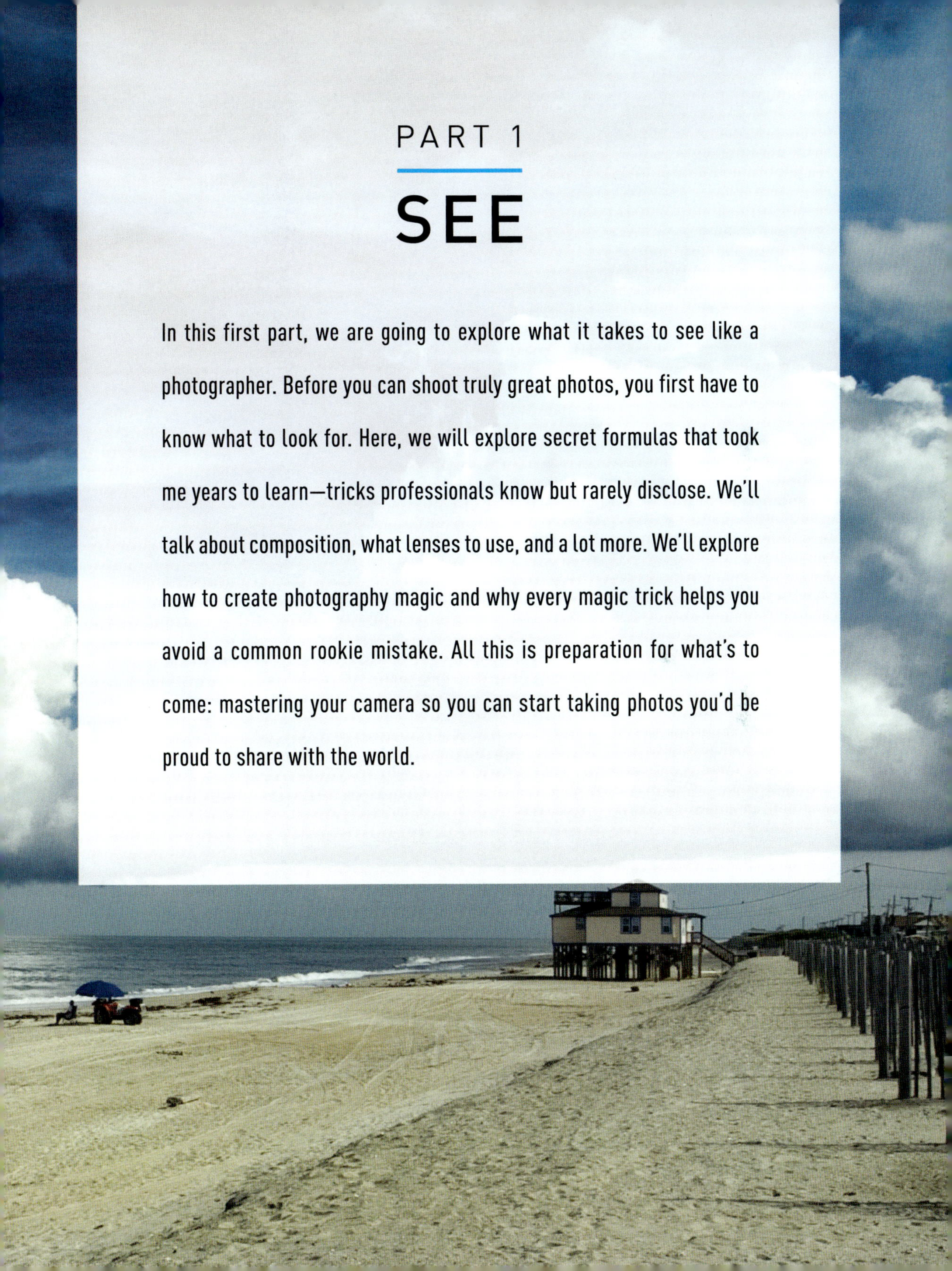

CHAPTER 1

Start with How You See Yourself

THE OUTER BANKS OF NORTH CAROLINA WAS A GREAT PLACE TO GROW UP. My friends and I surfed in hurricane swells, fished from canoes in the waters of the Albemarle Sound, and snorkeled and spearfished on the many submerged shipwrecks that make up the Graveyard of the Atlantic. We started our mornings watching dolphins jump and ended our days melting into beautiful amber sunsets

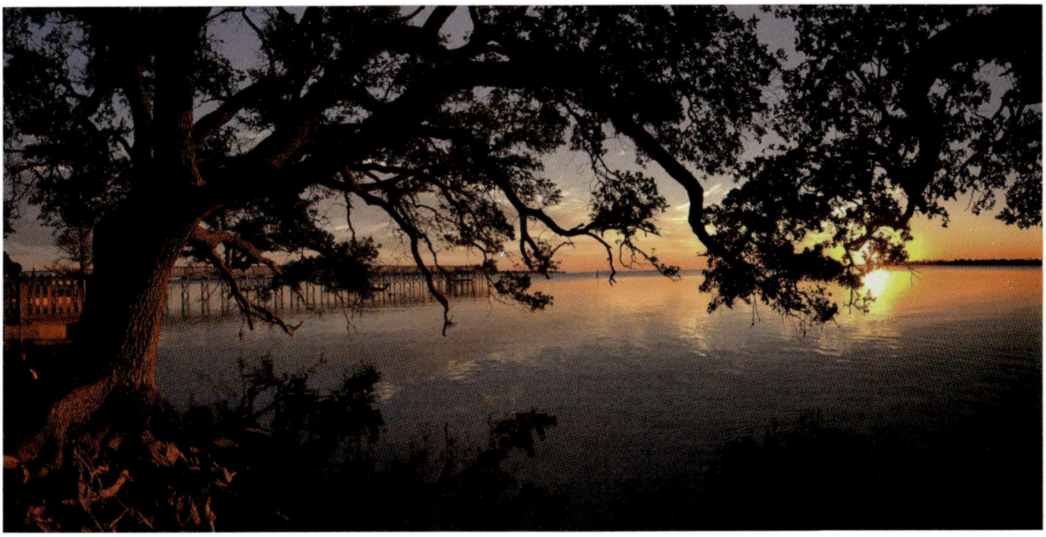

burning over the brackish waters of the sounds. It was an idyllic lifestyle that could easily seduce you into settling for a relaxed kind of mediocrity.

I wanted more than that, though—more than a carefree, comfortable life. My mom and dad always told me that God had a plan for my life, that I could be anything I wanted to be when I grew up, and that I was destined for great things. And I believed them. I didn't know exactly what it was, but I knew there had to be *more*. Getting a college education seemed to be the best way forward, but I couldn't afford to go to school unless I took on major school debt. My ticket to a better life, then, was to use my skill as a wrestler to get a full-ride athletic scholarship to the college of my choice.

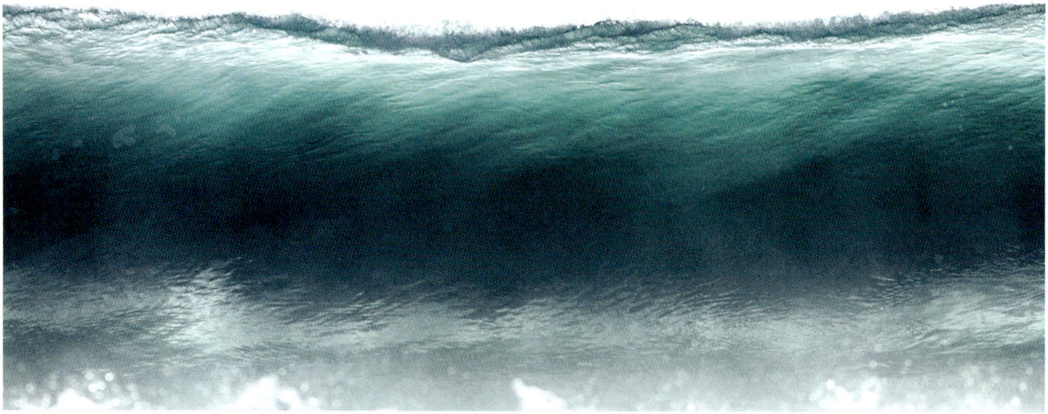

Wrestling may have been my meal ticket, but photography was my first love. I didn't take it seriously as a vocation, though, because I didn't think such a thing was possible. My perception of photographers was that they all seemed to be struggling, and I really didn't want that. It wasn't a viable option for me, since I was on my way to bigger and better things.

In high school I wrestled all four years and placed fifth in the state in my junior year. During my senior year I was undefeated and expected to win the state championship—until that fateful Christmas Eve when I woke up in a hospital bed after surviving a head-on collision with another car, requiring surgeries in both my knees. I would not compete in the state championship. I would not get a scholarship from any of the six colleges that were interested in me. I would not achieve my dream. My ticket out of that sleepy little town vanished in an instant. The only wrestling I did after the accident was with anxiety, loss, and depression. I spent the remaining two months of the season in a wheelchair, watching my teammates compete, experiencing the agony of seeing the wrestler I had previously beaten go on to win the state championship.

During this time, though, I had more free time than I knew what to do with. I already had enough credits to finish high school after the accident, which was good because I needed the time to recover. I dropped an extra class in my final semester so I could learn to walk again. Between physical therapy appointments for my legs and slowly working more and more in my dad's cabinet shop, I found my mind often wandering to what I really wanted now that my dream had been taken away from me.

I remembered four years earlier, when I had signed up for Mr. Binkley's Photography 101 class, using my dad's camera and learning things like darkroom techniques and how to develop film. I had no idea what I was doing, but it was fun, and photography became an obsession after that. Eventually other people started to take notice, and I was asked to take pictures for the school yearbook. It was a hobby that helped me see my life and hometown differently.

Ever since I was a young boy, I had been obsessed with the seascapes and surf culture all around me. With not much else to do, my obsession only grew: I studied surf magazines and fell in love with shots of crystal-clear water, underwater scenes, volcanic mountains, and the surfers themselves. Suddenly this sleepy little town was inspiring—to me, at least.

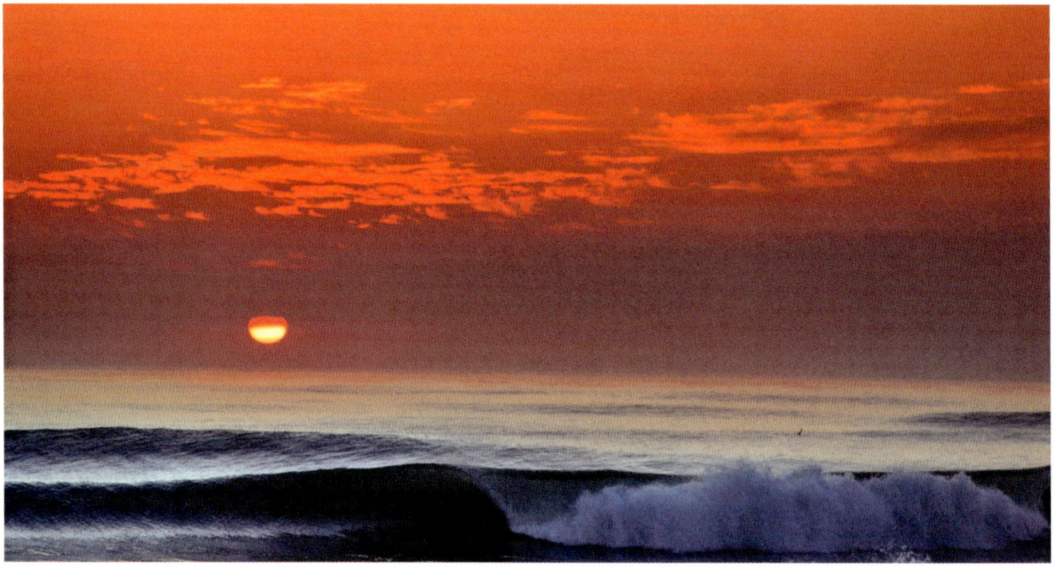

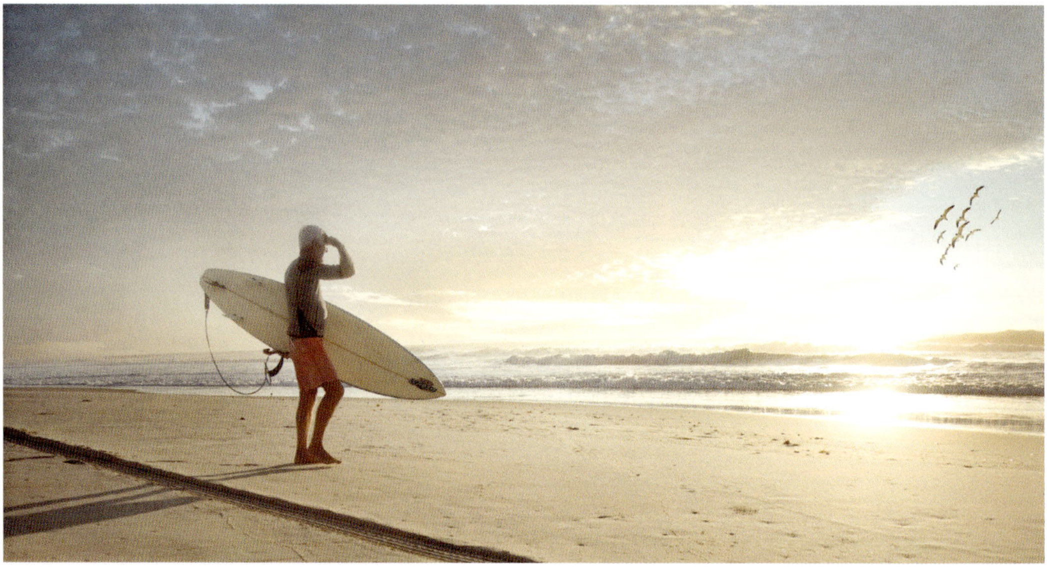

After the accident, I had to quit the yearbook gig because I was incapacitated for a while, and then I had too many doctor and PT appointments to get to. But I thought about photography a lot. *Maybe I could do this. Maybe it could be more than a hobby.*

Maybe I could get paid for it and make a greater impact with my life. Maybe I could even travel the world doing this. I wondered about all these things.

I had other voices in my head too: *I'll never make it. I'm not a real photographer anyway. Who would pay for that? I'll never be good enough.* I knew I was capable of more than working on the Outer Banks in construction for the rest of my life, but I still didn't believe I could pursue this new dream. I kept hearing, "Go to college. Get a corporate job." Because that's what meant *success* where I grew up; it's how people created something better for themselves. Something else was developing in me, though: an idea I was too embarrassed to say out loud but felt deeply in my soul. I wanted to be a photographer but wasn't yet ready to go all in.

Instead of going straight to college and getting into debt—since all my potential scholarship opportunities were off the table—I applied for a yearlong internship at a nonprofit organization in another state. There, I would spend a year working with other interns putting on Christian youth events. It was essentially one part pep rally, one part rock concert, and one part church service. I actually wasn't that excited about the idea, but I felt a nudge inside that it was what I was supposed to do. I went down for an interview and was offered the internship. The idea started to grow on me to take a gap year, so I took it.

When I arrived in East Texas, I was placed with the creative department, spending my time photoshopping flyers and banners for events. That was fun to learn but absolutely not what I wanted to do with the rest of my life. I kept asking if I could take pictures instead, and my bosses kept telling me they already had someone for that. But that wasn't good enough for me. If I was going to be volunteering there for a whole year—in fact, paying to be there—I wanted to at least focus on something enjoyable. So I started volunteering to shoot for the organization.

I became friends with the official photographer and started tagging along on her shoots. As my skills improved, the organization started using some of my photos on their website, which was viewed by hundreds of thousands of people. They started sending me out on bigger jobs shooting huge events, sometimes with fifty thousand people in attendance. I started shooting bands onstage and backstage, and some of them even used my shots in their promotional materials. I was getting a ton of practice: shooting in manual mode, learning on the fly, and figuring out why some of my pictures were blurry and some were crisp. I would make adjustments and do a little better each event. It was trial by fire.

I was also learning how to edit the photos to look and feel like the concerts looked and felt, and to recreate the emotion. I was basically developing into a concert photographer. I was excited to be making so much progress, but I was still immensely insecure and didn't feel worthy of being paid yet. But, as we'll discuss later in the framework, I was advancing in the area of photography I wanted to specialize in: concert photography. I had developed the fundamentals of seeing like a photographer, shooting in manual mode, and was even halfway decent at editing. In a few short months I had rapidly advanced through the first four steps of this process, and I was approaching the fifth: compensation.

My First Big Break

As my confidence grew, I started taking bigger risks. When I heard my favorite band, Switchfoot, was playing in a city just five hours away, I decided to go for broke. They had just released the album *The Beautiful Letdown*, which I'd already worn out in my CD player. (You may have to google what that is.) Their music had helped me through one of the darkest seasons of my life, and I wanted to photograph them.

I didn't care if I made any money. It was the most audacious goal I could think of at the time: I was going to photograph Switchfoot and pray to sweet baby Jesus that they liked my pictures. I was looking for validation. I wanted someone to pick me, to tell me I was a great photographer. This felt like a chance to make that happen.

The organization I worked with booked lots of bands and speakers, so I thought someone there could get me access to Switchfoot. I started telling people I *was* going to photograph the band, trying to manifest the experience into existence, but no one had a connection. Nonetheless, I kept asking, and eventually my friend Lacey said, "You know what? I don't know Switchfoot, but my boss has worked with them in the past, and I think she keeps in touch with one of the guys. I could ask her."

I nervously thought, *Her boss is that older, gorgeous girl I was introduced to in the hallway who heard me stuttering in front of her.* If I messed this up, I'd not only embarrass myself but also Lacey, her boss, and potentially the entire organization.

Lacey told her boss, Tammy, that she really believed in me and that I was an amazing photographer. For some reason, Tammy agreed and called the band's guitarist, Jerome, to ask if I could come down to shoot their concert. He said it was fine and that he'd put my name on the guest list. I begged my sister, Melody, who was on staff at the nonprofit, to let me borrow her car. When the time came, I jumped in the car with some friends and started the five-hour road trip. We were young and poor, and her car made weird noises the entire trip. I honestly wasn't sure we would make it, but I was determined—even if it meant having to up my plasma donation from one to two times per week to fix the car when it exploded.

Fortunately the car made it. When we got there, I went to the will call window where my ticket was supposed to be waiting for me. After standing in line for what felt like forever, I arrived at the window and gave the woman my name. She looked and looked, and as the minutes went by, I became increasingly nervous. Grimacing, she eventually broke the news to me that she couldn't find my name on the list.

I knew it! They found out I'm not a real photographer.

What was I supposed to do now? I had driven all this way and was moments from achieving my dream but couldn't get past this stupid ticket person. I wanted to cry. There was only one option left: call Tammy, that gorgeous girl I was nervous to talk to. She had already helped me so much, and now I had to ask for more. I was humiliated, but it was the only way. Fortunately one of my friends had given me her number just in case something happened, so I made the call.

When she picked up, I frantically told her, "My name isn't on the list." I was thinking, *They must not want to waste their time with a fraud.*

As my confidence went into a downward spiral, Tammy said, "Here's what I want you to do. Stay on the phone. Walk to the back door, hold the phone to your ear and stay on with me, act confident with your head held high, like you're supposed to be there. Believe that you're supposed to be there. Walk straight to the backstage door and tell them you are David Molnar, *the photographer.*"

But I'm not a photographer! I thought, terrified. *I'm just some kid who ended up here!*

I was more nervous than I'd ever been in my entire life. I didn't know what to do. I thought about quitting. I felt physically sick with tears of anxiety welling up. It felt like I was about to have a nervous breakdown. I was a nobody, a nineteen-year-old kid borrowing a camera from a nonprofit to shoot the concert, *pretending* to be a photographer. The self-doubt was suffocating.

I'm a fraud, I thought. *Who do I think I am?*

It was the biggest moment of my life, but I didn't know it at the time. What stopped me was this: I was still waiting to be picked. After everything I'd gone through to get there and all my experience that told me, "Yes, you can do it," I still didn't believe in myself. I didn't see myself as the world-class photographer I wanted to be. The pain of continued failure didn't seem worth the cost of pushing further.

But before I could convince myself to jump ship, my legs kept moving on autopilot, just like I had trained my hands to do when operating a camera. The three-hundred-pound security guard sitting at the door by the entrance came into view, and life began moving in slow motion. Still on the phone, I thought again of how embarrassed I'd be if this failed. I had told all my friends and family that I was going to photograph Switchfoot. I had even blogged about it on my Xanga site! (Yikes.) But I kept moving forward, with Tammy on the phone as my coach. If she believed in me, maybe I could believe in myself.

"Hey," I said to the security guard, Nokia brick cell phone still pressed against my ear. I mustered all the confidence I could. "I'm David Molnar . . . *the photographer*."

My heart was pounding as the guard scanned the sheet of paper in his hand for my name. It's almost as if I blacked out. To this day, I still can't remember if he asked any questions, if he miraculously found my name on that sheet, or if somehow this false bravado worked, but here's what I do know: I got in.

I just strolled by, not waiting or wavering. *It worked!* I had never felt such relief in my life.

He pointed me in the direction of the VIP room. As I climbed the stairs, I felt like

I was ascending to a bigger, brighter future. I knocked on the door, and as the door swung open, a warm glow flooded the dark hallway. I stepped in.

When It All Just Clicks

My favorite band was sitting right in front of me. Graciously they greeted me, introduced themselves, and carried on as usual. We spent some time hanging out backstage before the show. They played cover songs to loosen up while I sat and listened, even chatting with the front man, Jon, a little. Truth be told, I was having the time of my life. Then they walked downstairs and out onto the stage to perform.

I watched the entire show through my camera and poured my heart into the work like I had never done before. Sweating in the Texas heat and in my tight, emo black skinny jeans, I dodged, ducked, and weaved on the stage and did my best to see the potential shots like a photographer and anticipate their movements. I did my very best to expose the camera manually to capture crisp moments and freeze the motion of their rock and roll.

I felt like I knew what I was doing. The hundreds of hours I had poured into practicing at previous events made shooting this concert a breeze. All my practice was paying off, and I felt like everything was clicking. I was on cloud nine.

When I got back to my intern desk, I edited the photos to recreate the emotion the audience and I felt when we were immersed in the concert. With sweaty palms, I shipped my work to their manager via FedEx. My CD burner failed four times while trying to write the images to the disk. I was praying it wouldn't get scratched and the band wouldn't hate the images. I waited patiently.

A few weeks later, the band's manager told me they *loved* the images and wanted to use them on their world-tour T-shirt and on the inside of their next album. I was ecstatic! To top it off, they insisted on paying me, even though I kept telling them it was free. They gave me $400, which at the time might as well have been a million. At nineteen years old, I had just achieved my biggest goal, met my personal heroes, and now had a small fortune in the bank.

The best part of that experience, though, was that I finally became a photographer. Not because I was taking pictures; I'd been doing that for a while. Not even because I had been paid, because that doesn't make it real either. I became a photographer the moment I told that guard I was David Molnar, *the photographer*. I saw myself for the first time as a photographer, and after that, there was no going back.

I started telling people that I took photos for a *living*. I was a photographer. A professional. Nobody picked me. *I* picked me. I saw myself as a professional, and that changed everything.

Oh, and remember Tammy, that gorgeous girl who helped me see myself as "David, the photographer"? Well, I married her. My whole life clicked into place that day, and I didn't even know it.

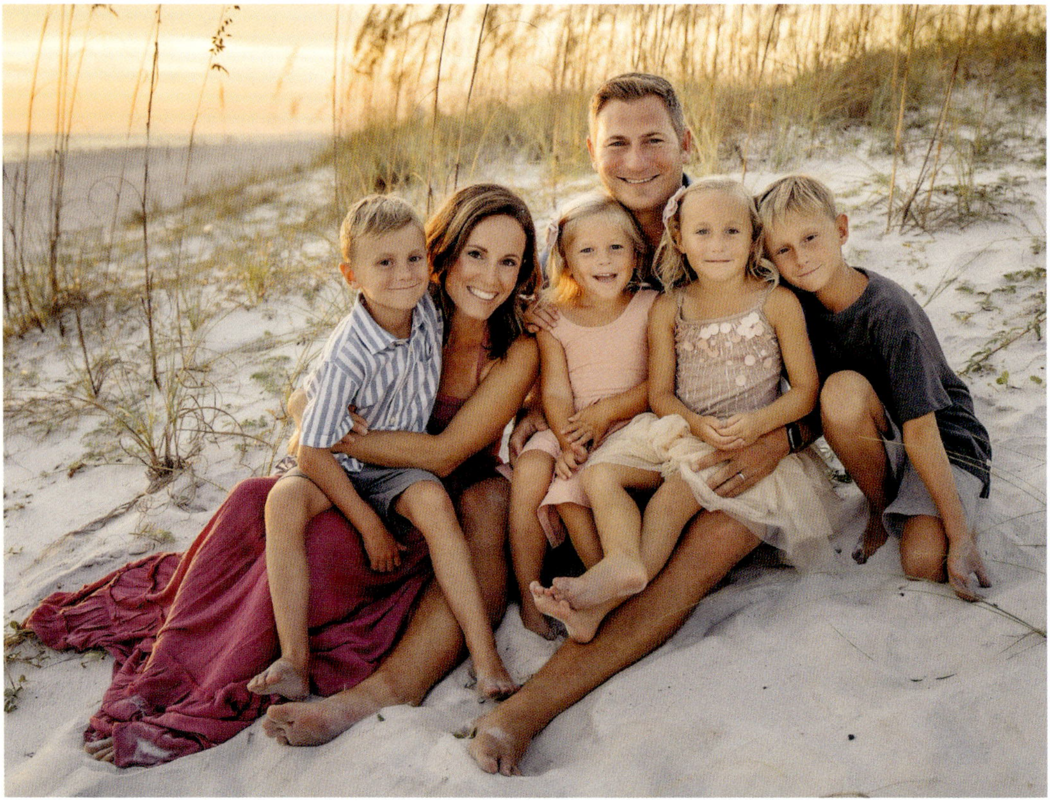

Credit: imagesofgracephoto.com

Seeing Starts with You

The journey to becoming a world-class photographer begins with how we see ourselves. These days, we all take photos, but not all of us are photographers. If you've ever seen a sunset or watched a concert or observed your children playing in the yard and wanted to capture that moment as you experienced it, then maybe you, too, have longed to be a photographer. But if you really want to begin, you have to put down the camera and look in the mirror. You have to start with the decision to start calling yourself a photographer.

The art of photography is about learning to see, which we'll explore together. We'll talk about shutter speed, aperture, ISO, and so many other technical concepts—editing, culling, lighting, and more. But before you can see like a photographer, you first have to look at how you see yourself. Being a photographer is one part functional and one part mental. It's a mind game, and if you don't see yourself as a photographer, you're not going to be able to take the kind of photos you want to take. So consider this your first challenge from your friendly neighborhood photography mentor: You might have what it takes to become a world-class photographer, to be truly great. But are you willing to believe that you can do this? Can you start seeing yourself as who you want to be instead of what you've been? The simple but scary decision to own the identity of a professional photographer changed my life. If you follow this path, it will change yours as well—maybe even in ways you can't imagine.

CHAPTER 2

Borrow Someone Else's Eyes

"WHAT KIND OF CAR DO YOU DRIVE?"

I was twenty-one, living in Nashville, pursuing a full-time career in photography. This was my second shot at life: I was recovered from my accident and newly married, and my latest professional interest was not going well. Having done photography for a few years at this point, I began calling local photographers to offer my services as an assistant. I was cocky, having experienced a few small wins along the way, but I figured a little bit of practice couldn't hurt. My friend Velvet Kelm had introduced me to a successful photographer who was willing to let me intern a bit, but she was so busy it was hard to get ahold of her. One day, however, her assistant answered my call. I said I was looking to assist with shooting if they ever needed any help, and that's when she asked about my car.

"Um, a 4Runner," I said.

"Can you fit equipment in the back, like light stands?" she asked.

"Yes . . ." I said, confused.

"Can you be here in twenty minutes?"

"Yup."

This was how it began—my apprenticeship as a photographer. Off I went, rushing to a very sketchy part of town. I parked right next to a group of homeless people, handed one of them the change in my pockets, and walked through the door to the photo studio. With no idea what I was walking into, I was thrust right in the middle of a high-profile, Hollywood-caliber shoot for a Taylor Swift–type country singer. I had never seen anything like it: a makeup artist, a wardrobe stylist, a hair stylist, lighting technicians, and at least twenty people were on set. It was quite the production to get an album cover photo of just one person, and the whole experience captivated me.

The photographer that day was Kristin Barlowe, and as I watched her work, the images that popped up in the back of her camera amazed me. Unable to take my eyes off them, I wondered, *How can she take pictures that are so beautiful?* I had no idea how to do what she did: to look at the same set she was viewing and know exactly what to shoot, how to fix something that wasn't working, how to create photos that looked *that* good. My mind was blown. It was as if we were looking at completely different scenes. I saw a big room with a young woman and some random accessories. But on the back of the camera I saw absolute magic.

When I used to look at magazine covers, I thought the lighting must have been perfect the day the photos were taken. Maybe the person was having a good hair day, or the light was just right, or she just naturally posed in the angle that accentuated her curves. Until that moment, I thought photos were simply a thing to be taken, not a gift you could give the viewer. I never knew what could be created if the photographer only knew how to see it. That is, until I saw Kristin shoot.

At that moment, I realized I did not know how to be the photographer I wanted to be. I wasn't seeing what she was seeing. I did not know what it took to be a professional—someone had to show me. The set seemed like total chaos, but there was, I realized, a hidden order to it all. There was a reason Kristin did everything she did, and as I watched her that day, I realized she knew exactly what she was doing. Humbled and hungry to learn more, I knew I had a long way to go. I needed a teacher and a mentor—someone who could help me see what I was missing.

So I went in search of one.

My First Teacher

Roger Gibbs, the first assistant on the shoot, helped get me more assisting gigs. He told me, "If you continue to bust your butt like you did today, I will recommend you to other photographers." He made introductions and told me who to call, which led to assisting a few other photographers. At first, these experiences were exciting. I thought of all the questions I was going to ask and everything I was going to learn—all the things these masters would teach me after taking me on their shoots and giving me the insider info. Quickly, though, I realized these photographers didn't see our working relationship that way. They had work to do, and I was their gopher, only there to grab things and move them from place to place. I carried light stands and sandbags, cleaned the studio toilets, fetched coffee for celebrities, and picked up food for the whole crew. Anything you could think of, I did it. For a year, this went on, and it wasn't what I'd hoped. Most photographers barely let me carry their cameras, so it was out of the question that I take any pictures on their shoots. They weren't there to teach me.

One time I was on the set of a big commercial shoot with a famous photographer. The photographer was asking his boss-for-a-day—the big-shot art director—which direction he thought the camera should be pointed at for the next shot. Immediately I thought, *This is my moment!* Being a diligent understudy, I, of course, knew the answer, so I proudly said out of turn: "What if we shoot it that way with the beautiful scenery in the background . . . instead of in the direction with the horse manure!"

This was the obvious answer. Anyone who was paying attention would have been able to put this together—and that was the problem. What happened next was insane: the photographer blew a gasket and threw a light stand at me! This was both scary and impressive—because those things are *heavy.* I had to do a slow-motion, *Matrix*-style, bullet-dodging Keanu Reeves move to avoid being hit by it. But why did he blow up at me? It was, after all, the correct response. It wasn't the answer that was the problem but rather the fact that *I was the one giving it.*

The savvy photographer was asking the client questions that I, the newbie, thought were pretty obvious. Not understanding that he was trying to involve the client by getting them to contribute something, I chipped in with my own ideas. That's when I was very thankful for my two years in gymnastics as a kid, which saved me some major physical scarring. As a bonus, I finally got inner healing from the fifth-grade boys chanting, "Cartwheel Ken, do it again" at recess. Anyway, like I said, it's hard to find a mentor in this business.

I was having to learn things the hard way, because no one told me the assistant shouldn't verbally give ideas in front of a client. I was being taught a lesson by that photographer—that you keep your mouth shut, speak only when spoken to, and let the professional talk to his clients without your interference. To learn, I had to make a mistake—a mistake that embarrassed me. It would have been nice if I could have learned some lessons without having to endure the threat of physical violence, but such is the life of a fledgling photographer.

Still, it's curious. What if the photographer had taken me aside and had a private conversation before the shoot started instead of throwing a light stand at me? What if he had said, "Hey, I'm going to be having a 'dance' with the art director on this shoot, carefully massaging and subliminally directing his opinions to get him to come up with the exact ideas I want to shoot anyway"? What if he had let me in on the trick? He might have continued, helping me understand, "So I'm going to ask him obvious questions. Keep your mouth shut so he looks like a genius for coming up with the idea." Ah, okay. Got it, chief!

No one had told me this is how the business works, that most photographers don't like being asked questions, and they certainly don't like explaining how and why they do the weird things they do. That photographer was there to work; he wasn't there to explain things to me and help me out. My job was to assist. If I was told to change the lighting to F-8 and I asked why, the answer would have been something like, "Just do it." If I was going to learn, it was going to happen through keen observation, not someone patiently instructing me. However, often I was holding lighting across a field and couldn't see what the photographer was doing. I was so busy assisting the photographer, I didn't really have the opportunity to learn.

Sometimes, after shoots, I'd ask photographers if I could take them to lunch or coffee to ask questions and learn a few tricks of the trade. Many seemed open to it but would then immediately stop returning my calls or texts. I don't know if they saw their hard-earned knowledge as *theirs* and didn't want me to get it the easy way, or if nobody cared enough to help me learn, but I was disheartened either way. To me, it made sense that they'd want to help me. If I knew more about why I was doing what I was doing, I could be a better assistant. Nonetheless, a good mentor proved hard to find—almost impossible.

Professional photography is a mysterious industry. The successful people tend to hold their information very close to the chest. It was a rough first few years trying to figure it out on my own, but eventually, I did. And now, the technical stuff that took me two years to learn, I could explain in fifteen minutes. It's not overly complicated; it just has to be explained correctly. After decades of doing this, I have the same hard-earned knowledge as those other professional photographers, but one thing sets me apart: I never forgot what it felt like to *not* have a mentor. When I'm on shoots these days, I do my best to explain to my assistants why we're doing what we're doing. And so far, I have never thrown a light stand at them.

What Seeing Looks Like

Despite my somewhat traumatic beginnings in my own photography journey, I did end up finding some good teachers along the way. Michael Gomez, Kristin Barlowe, Biff Jennings, Russ Harrington, and Jeremy Cowart all taught me important lessons and took the time to answer my questions. They taught me about lines, composition, lighting, and storytelling—all topics we are going to cover in this book. They taught me what to look for as a photographer, how to notice things I never would have been able to spot otherwise.

There are some things in life you can't see until you "look" through someone else's eyes. I'm thankful to those guys because they were a huge part of my learning to be the photographer I am today—to see the way I see now. In those early days most people weren't helpful. I had to patch together my knowledge of photography, learning a little here and there as I went. I see so many people struggling to find the kind of guidance they need in their photography careers—I was the same. I know how hard it is to find a mentor who is willing to share with you what they know so you can start to see as they do. For the rest of this book, I am going to share with you exactly what I learned. I hope it helps you see the world, yourself, and this craft differently.

Now, let's get into it.

CHAPTER 3

Telling Stories with Photos

EVERYONE THINKS THEY'RE A STORYTELLER. WHO HASN'T BEEN AT A DINNER party or overheard someone going on and on about something that happened, never actually getting to the point? We've all been there. On the other hand, we have all heard a story that astounded us. People love great stories, but few know how to tell them well. As it turns out, masterful storytelling is an essential skill for all successful photographers and a craft you will have to discipline yourself to learn.

Storytelling, when done well, is powerful. When we tap into this power, we can change the way other people see and treat us. Although it takes time and energy to learn how to tell a great story, we each have the potential to develop this skill, if we want. Unfortunately, few people ever take the time to learn how to tell a good story, and as a result miss out on the power of such an ability. Photographers, in particular, have an advantage of pairing stories with images that illustrate what they're trying to communicate. How you use this ability is up to you, of course. You can choose to tell stories that aren't true or are, at best, slightly exaggerated to make you look better—or you can use your power for good and tell tales that are authentic, believable, and powerful.

Snapshots Versus Crafted Stories

Here's what I mean. Take a look at this image of the mother lion biting the head of her cub. It's pretty horrific, right?

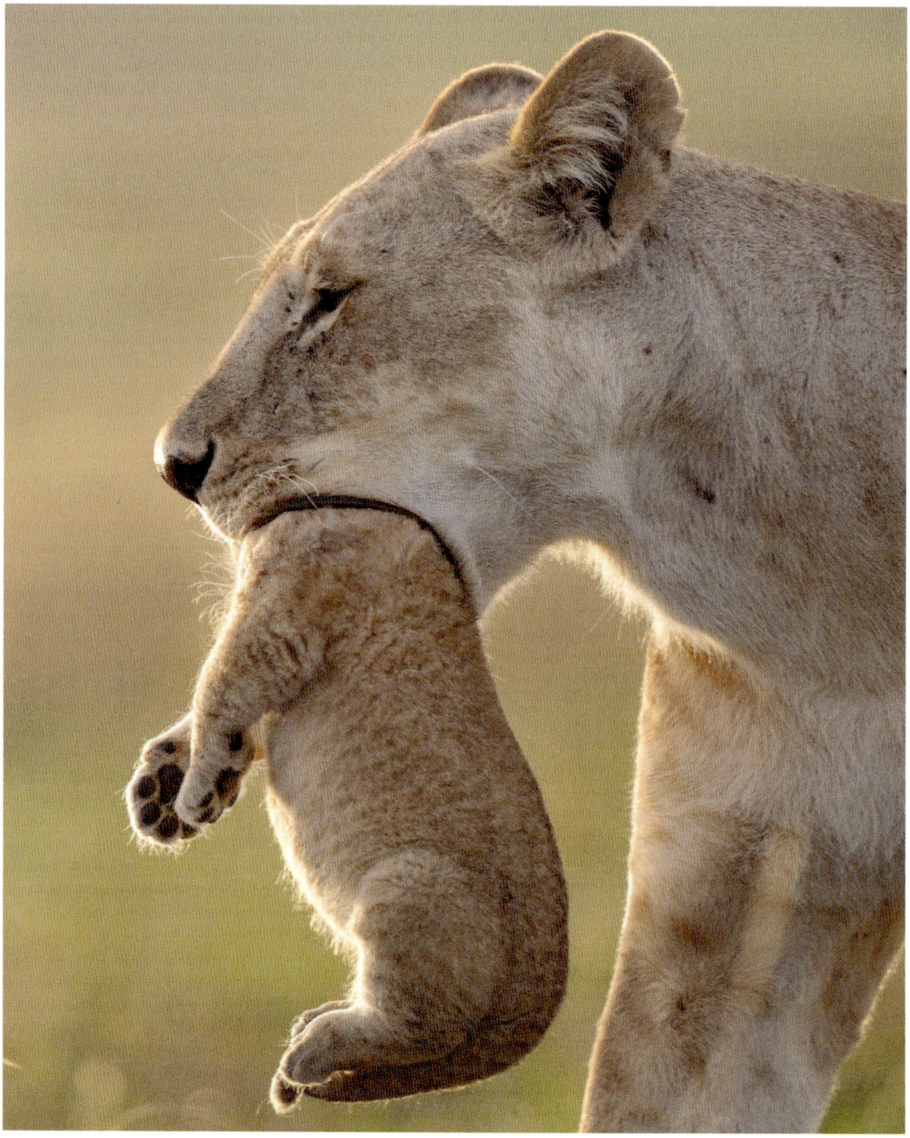

What if I told you that the image wildlife photographer Andreas Hemb was actually capturing was of a much gentler moment? The true story here is not the murder of a lion cub; it's of a mother carrying her child in a sweet, beautiful way. Perspective matters.

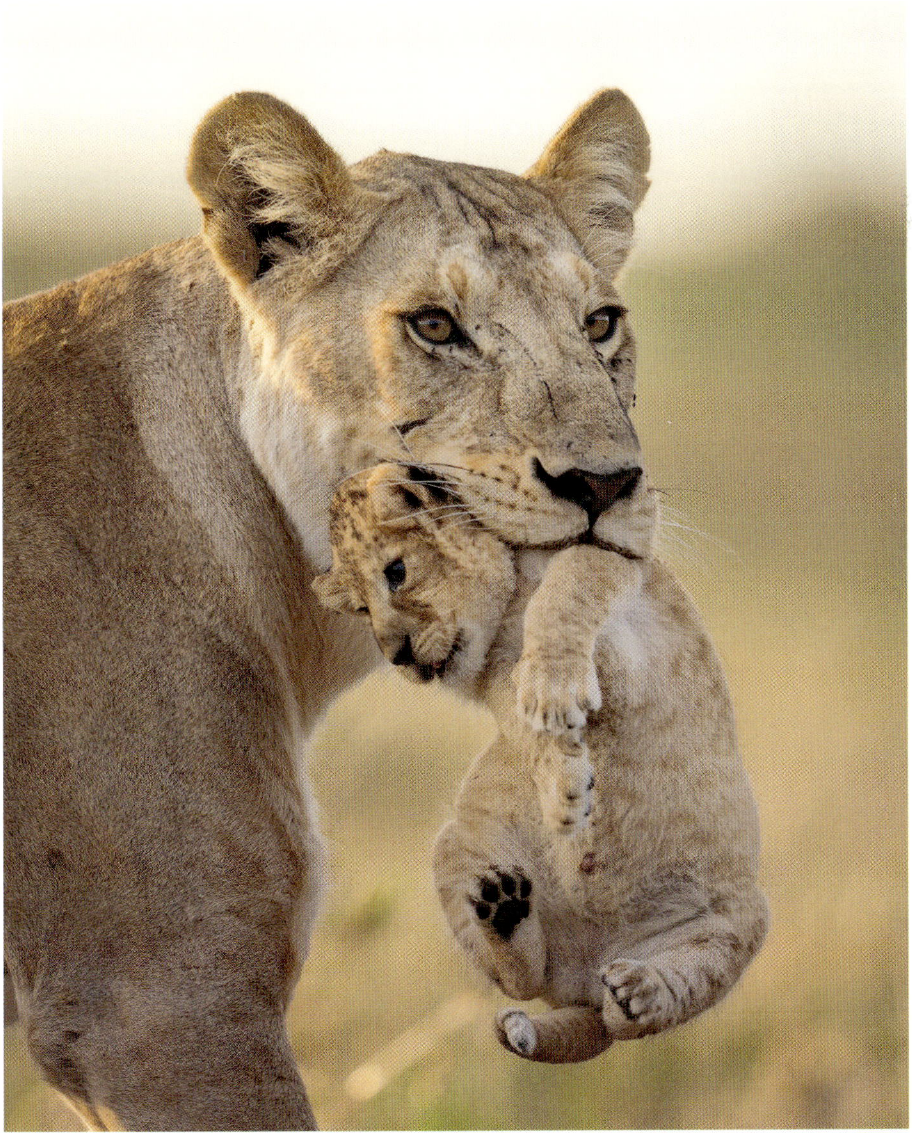

Both images tell a story. Both convey completely different ideas and emotions. So what story do you want to tell? Our job as photographers is not just to take a snapshot of a moment. Our job is to craft a story. Anybody with an iPhone can take a snapshot. But someone who sees themself as a photographer—someone like you and me—can tell an amazing story with the photos that come from that little device. That's because it's not the gear that makes the photographer; it's the way we see ourselves and our subjects. A maxim often attributed to Ansel Adams states that the single most important component of a camera is the twelve inches behind it. It's the brain—your brain—thinking through what's important in the story you're trying to tell. When we learn to see what's important in the picture, that's when we can create magic. Only then can we tell stories that have the power to move people.

So ask yourself: *Do I want to use my superpower to take snapshots or tell crafted stories?* If you learn to see yourself as a photographer, you'll learn to see that the real magic is in the story. Now, let me teach you how to craft a story you want to tell.

The Five Steps to Masterful Storytelling

Great storytelling means more than sharing an anecdote; it's about creating and managing tension and resolving it in just the right way. Anyone can do this, but few are willing to take the time to get it right. There are five sequential steps to successfully crafting a photographic story. Be mindful that if you skip any of these five parts, you most likely won't get the photo you want. Each step is valuable and works with the others to tell the story you want to share.

STEP 1: DOCUMENT THE FLEETING MOMENT

Step 1 is the quickest and easiest, but it's not to be rushed or skipped over. Moments are fleeting, and it's our job as storytellers to capture them. The moment you want to shoot can change quickly: the eagle flies right by, the kid stops smiling, the laughter ends. That's why it's important to document the story as you see it happening, even if it results in a snapshot (i.e., an off-the-cuff, unplanned image that captures a single moment) at first.

Of course, we'd all love to take the perfect, world-class image every single time, but we know that's not realistic. We owe it to ourselves, to our subjects, and to the stories we want to tell to capture the fleeting moments and preserve them in time. You may not get a second chance to get that story on film. And if you don't, you'll be kicking yourself when you realize you missed it. Or worse, you'll let your client down—because you can't get the moment back. Trust me, I know from experience. Even a crappy snapshot of the father of the bride dancing will be cherished if the father unexpectedly passes away. Take, for instance, the first kiss at a wedding.

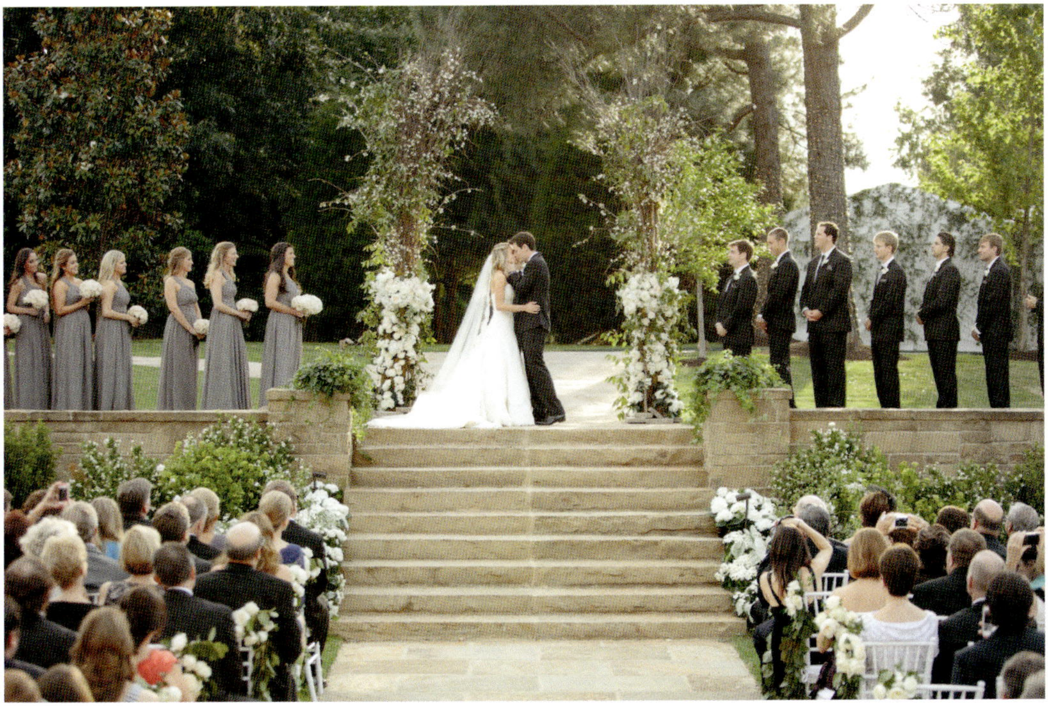

As the photographer, you know that kiss is an integral part of the couple's story. Of course you're going to think ahead, anticipating the angles and considering what variables might impact the scene. But if you find yourself waiting for the perfect light, the perfect frame, or the perfect shot, you'll probably miss the moment. Instead, immediately document the moment to make sure you have it preserved. From there, you can start crafting your story.

STEP 2: IDENTIFY THE ESSENTIAL STORYTELLING ELEMENTS

Step 2 is identifying what's essential to the subject of the story—because more than just your subject contributes to the story you're trying to tell.

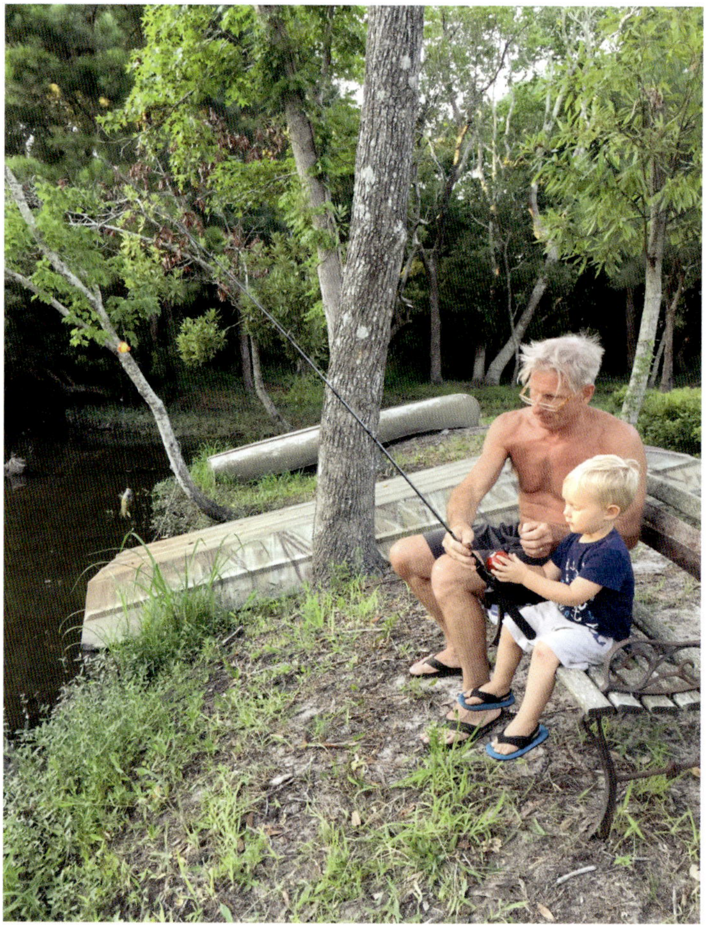

Let me share with you a photo of a moment I love and will forever treasure. It's a picture of my dad teaching my oldest son, Judah, how to fish. It sounds simple enough, right? But in this scene you'll also notice a bunch of clutter: two old boats, some mossy trees, and a lot of leaves. Then you see Judah, my dad, and—if you look hard enough—the fish Judah caught.

Taking all that in, here's the question: *What's the story I want to tell, and what's important to that story?* For me, the story is the moment in which a grandfather teaches his grandson to fish. So that makes the subjects my son and father—the grandson and his grandfather—and the object of their attention the fish. What we don't need is what isn't important to the story: the boats in the background, all the trees and grass, even the lake. Those details don't matter as much, not when compared to the boy, his grandfather, and the fish. Yes, those elements are part of the snapshot, but they don't serve any purpose in the story I want to tell. What's important is Judah holding the fish, the smile on his face, and the pride of his papa. (We'll show the revised picture with those prioritized shortly.)

Those background details *might* matter if the story was about something else. In other scenarios, the boats and trees and grass and even the lake could be important—for example, if they had personal significance to us. Every story, after all, is different; it just depends on which one you're trying to tell. This one, though, is centered on my dad teaching my son to fish. Everything else that doesn't help me show *that* is just getting in the way.

Judah was elated when he caught the fish, and my dad was so proud. But in the initial snapshot, you can barely see the fish. Your eyes are drawn to the distracting elements, like the boats, the tree, and all the different things happening in the background. In reality, the first image isn't telling a compelling, powerful story at all. Or rather, it's not telling the story *I'm* trying to tell. If I was trying to tell a story about a boat or a tree, it'd be different. To help shift this from a snapshot to a story, we have to find what's important. The fish, my son, and my dad. Those are the three essential pieces of this story.

STEP 3: REMOVE DISTRACTIONS

That brings us to step 3, which is to identify the distractions. Here, we want to eliminate what's causing the story to get lost in the image. That means removing the boats, the trees, and whatever else isn't serving the story—anything that's not an essential element to the story. Cutting them out helps you, the viewer, focus back on the fish and the looks on my son's and dad's faces.

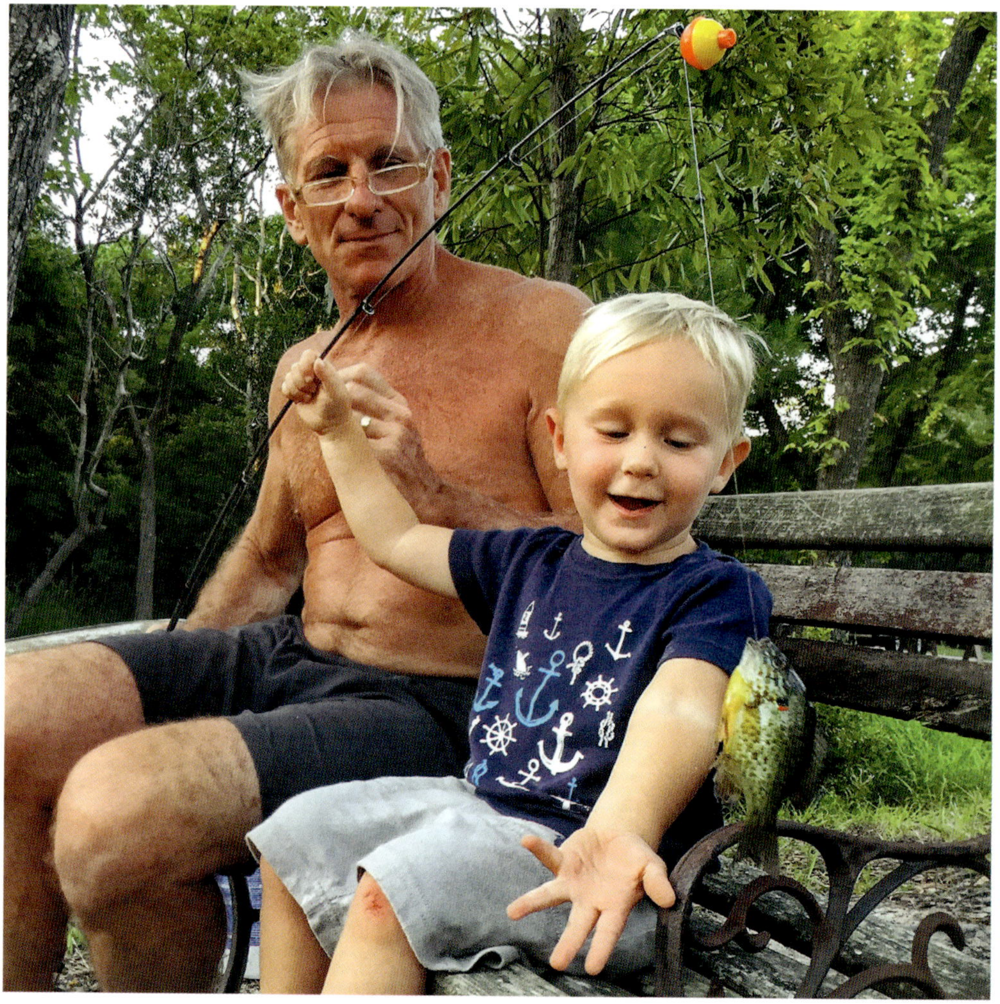

In hindsight, I'm so glad I captured this, because at the time I was worried the fish would fall right off the hook and back in the water. Even with distractions, at least I caught the moment. You might be able to fix a snapshot, but you can't relive a fleeting moment. We'll elaborate on this more in part 3 of this book, because there are certain things that editing *can't* fix. And what it absolutely cannot fix is a picture that was never taken, however imperfectly.

STEP 4: FIND THE LIGHT

The fourth step is to focus on the light. You want to use light to aid in telling your story and not distract from it. If you're shooting portraits, I suggest looking for soft, even light that isn't spotty. I also recommend avoiding direct sunlight most of the time, so the light and shadows are not harsh.

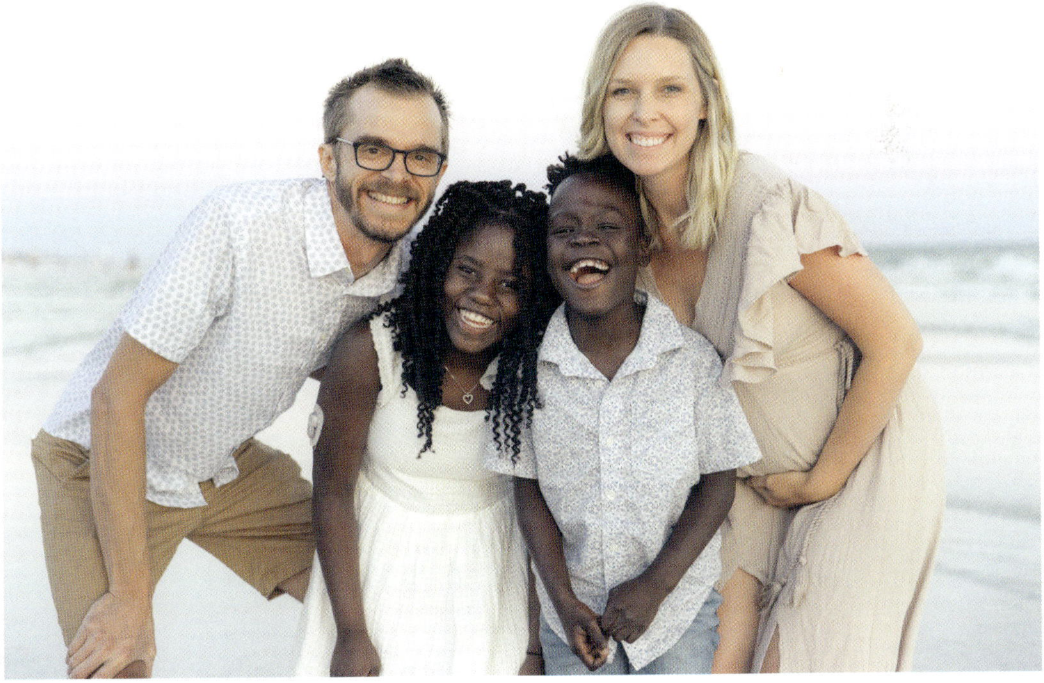

Look for the right light to evoke the emotions you're trying to convey. Think about how the harsh or soft light will make your viewers feel. Will awkward, shiny spots on the subject's face distract the viewer? If you make the shot too bright, does it convey the somber mood that you might want?

Notice the light; control how bright it reads in your image; even move your subjects to more desirable light. Step to the side so the sun flare is in or out of your frame. We'll talk more about lighting tricks in the next couple of chapters, but I just wanted to give you a sense of how to start thinking like a photographer. Understand that this isn't about right or wrong. This is about you taking control of how the light is recorded in your shot and going with what feels good to you. Below are two images that were taken literally ten seconds apart from each other. Lighting can make a photo feel completely dull or full of life. It's all in how you use it.

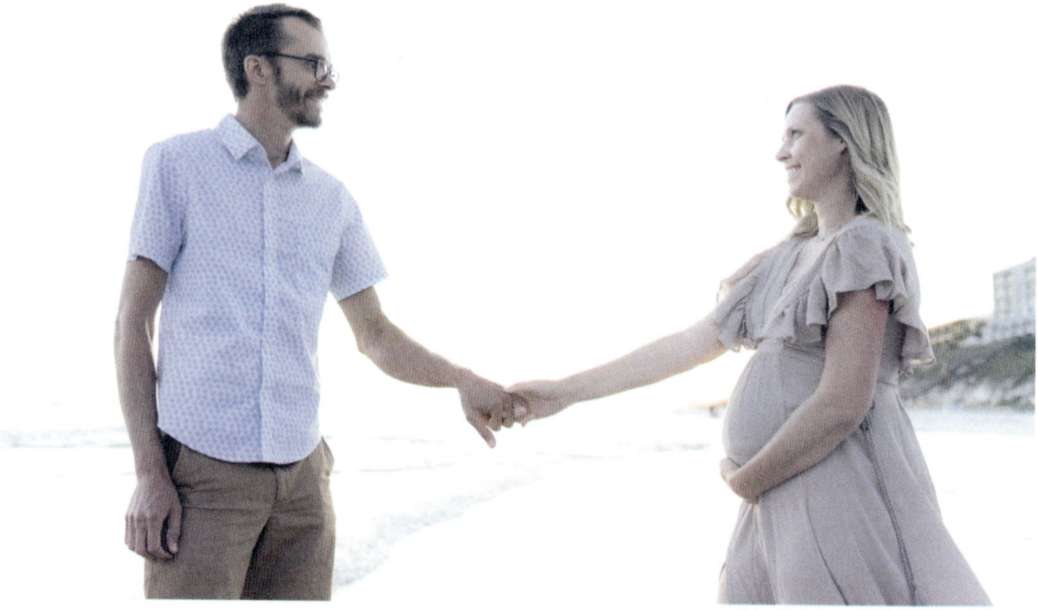

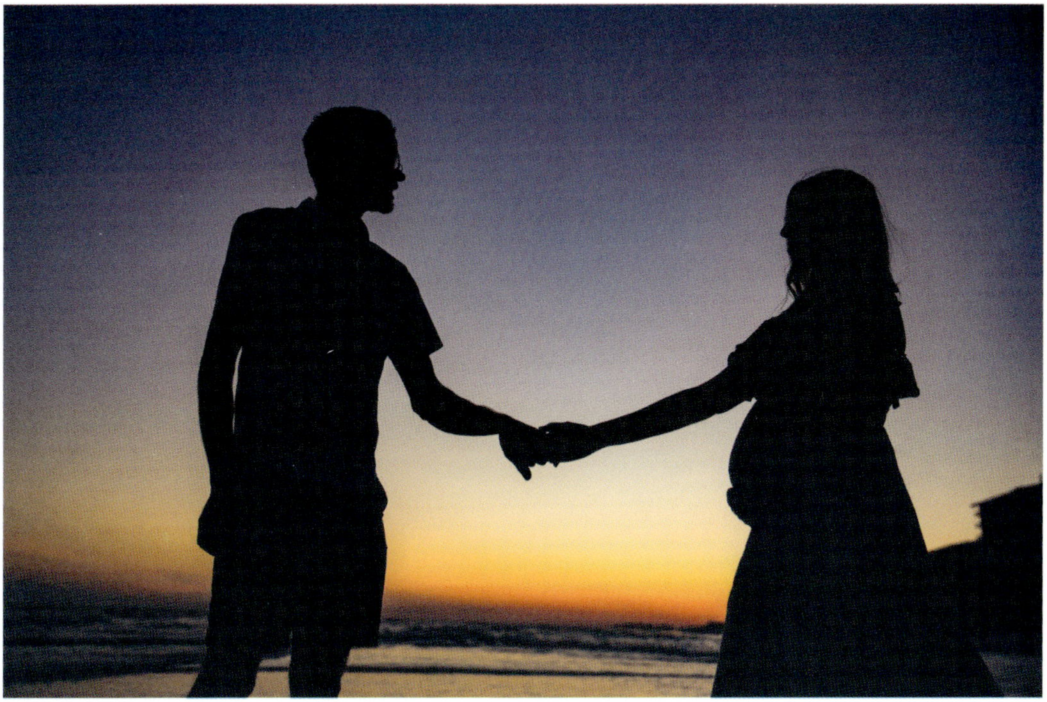

STEP 5: BRING THE STORY TOGETHER

The final piece of this formula that brings your story together is the composition of your shot. This is where we bring together all the elements of shooting the photograph. It's about whether or not you're zoomed in. It's about your lens choice. It's about your angle. It's about your perspective. It's about the way you crop. It's about how you frame the shot. It's about how much or how little is in focus. It's about what you keep in the shot and, ultimately, in the story. Composition is what you actually see and how it looks in the image itself.

Let's go back to the revised version of my dad teaching my son to fish one more time. You'll immediately notice that the general composition of the shot is a lot tighter. I zoomed in to exclude a lot of the cluttered background that you saw before. Notice the fish is held out in front of my son. That closer perspective makes it look bigger, because whatever is closest to the camera will appear larger and more prominent in the frame. In this situation I'm telling a little white lie about how big the fish actually was. In the previous shot that fish looked really small (because it was), and it impacted our ability to see it as the object of their attention and an essential storytelling element. This new, up-close perspective changed that.

Now you can also see the smile on my son's face; the joy of catching his first fish isn't lost here, as it was before. You can also see his grandfather looking on proudly. Your eye is drawn to their expressions because we've changed what's showing in the frame by recomposing the shot. We cropped in closer and rid the picture of distractions. We've blocked additional parts of the distracting boat in the background by lowering the angle of the shot. By framing and emphasizing only what's essential, we're able to draw the viewer's attention to exactly what we want them to see. Composing does that; it brings all the essential storytelling elements together to create a story. We'll dig more into composition in the next chapter.

What I love about this formula is that it isn't about the gear. This shot was taken on an old iPhone. Whether you're shooting with a Canon, a Nikon, a Sony, or an iPhone, you can use this formula to craft a story with your images. These storytelling techniques work for *anyone* who has learned to see like a photographer. And when you put them to use in your work, you'll tell much better, more compelling, and more powerful stories with your images.

When you begin seeing like a photographer, you'll start to notice stories everywhere. You won't be able to see a sunset without trying to catch the light just right. You will never experience a moment with your loved ones the same way again. As life is happening around you, you'll begin seeing not just fleeting snapshots but potential stories waiting to be captured. You'll be thinking about the finished product in every story you find. But to get there, you have to start practicing. To develop the eye of a photographer you must hone your instincts, visualize the finished images of the narrative, and start crafting the story you want to tell. A little time and experience can go a long way in helping you truly tell stories—and that's when photos can change lives. So use your new superpower for good.

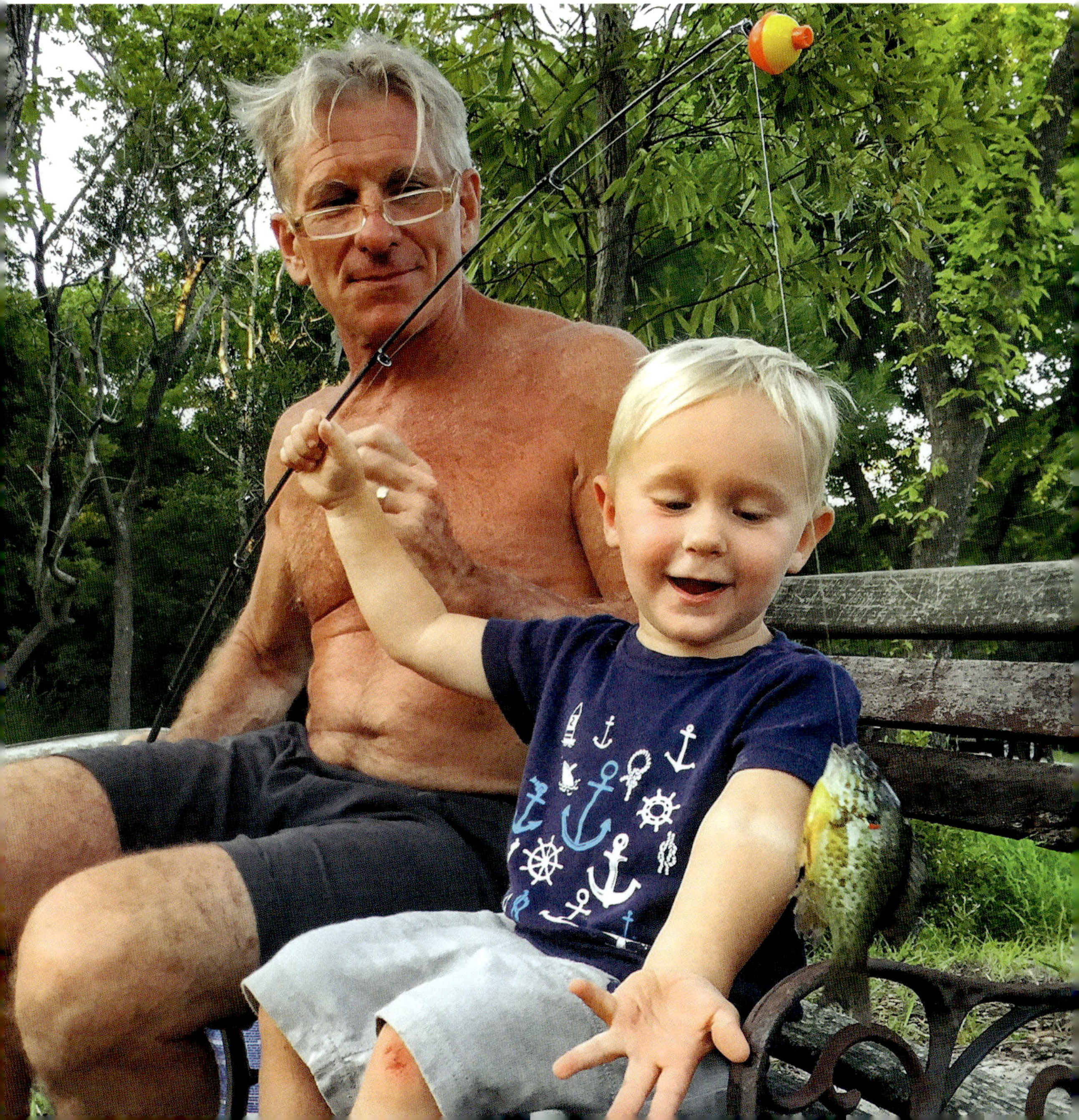

CHAPTER 4

Composing a Story with Your Camera

EARLY ON IN MY CAREER, I MADE A LOT OF MISTAKES ON IMPORTANT PHOTO-shoots. You can fix certain things in editing, but the way you've framed your subjects usually cannot be undone. And when you mess this up, it makes everything harder. Hopefully this chapter will spare you the early frustrations I had in learning the skill of composing stories.

If you remember from the previous chapter, composing your shot was the final step in the Five Steps to Masterful Storytelling. Now we bring all the elements of shooting the image together. Put simply, composition is what's in the picture before you edit it. The final composition is what shows up in the image based on the decisions you've made before and during shooting: the high or low angle you shoot from, where you stand, what's in the background, what's in the foreground, and how much is in focus. Composition is about how you frame the shot. In general, it is what you see and how it looks; but more specifically, it's what you let your *audience* see. When composed properly, an image doesn't just show them something; it *says* something. Composition is how we masterfully set up the story.

How you compose your shots can make or break an image. There's nothing more frustrating than getting home after a long shoot only to realize what you thought was a great setup was . . . not. As you approach the story you want to tell, you need to learn to see the shots before you take them, and that really comes down to composition.

The next section gives examples of what you can do to compose a better story. Sometimes, you'll use many of these ideas in a single image; sometimes, you may use only one. This isn't about the right or wrong ways to take photos. It's simply a list of ideas you can think about while crafting your visual stories. Photography is an art form, and no single principle applies to every situation. Of course, these guidelines are important when you're getting started, but as you understand the principles behind them, you realize that everything is situational. There are no absolutes that you must always follow, and if anyone tells you otherwise, don't listen to them. There are fun and inventive ways to break the rules. But before you do that, you have to learn what works.

Composition Guidelines

You know you have to make some decisions about what should be in the photo and what shouldn't, but how do you actually do it? How do you accomplish what you want? What does it look like? This is where you can use some composition guidelines to properly compose your shot. Below are some factors to consider.

LENSES

Different lenses can massively affect the composition of your image. If you are shooting with a wide-angle lens, for example, you are going to see a lot more of the background (and possible distractions) than if you are zoomed in with a telephoto lens and see only your subject's face.

WIDE-ANGLE LENS (16 MM)

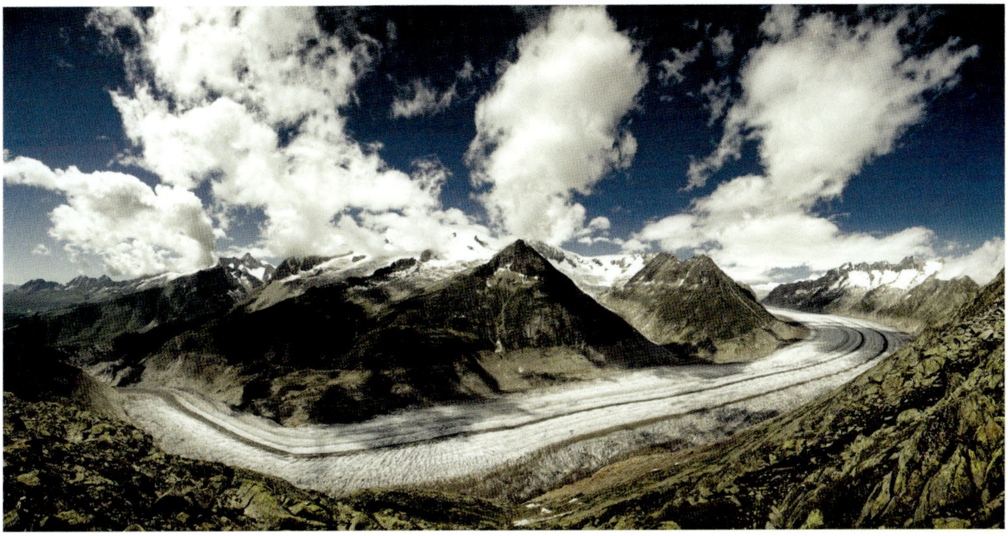

ZOOMED-IN TELEPHOTO LENS (200 MM)

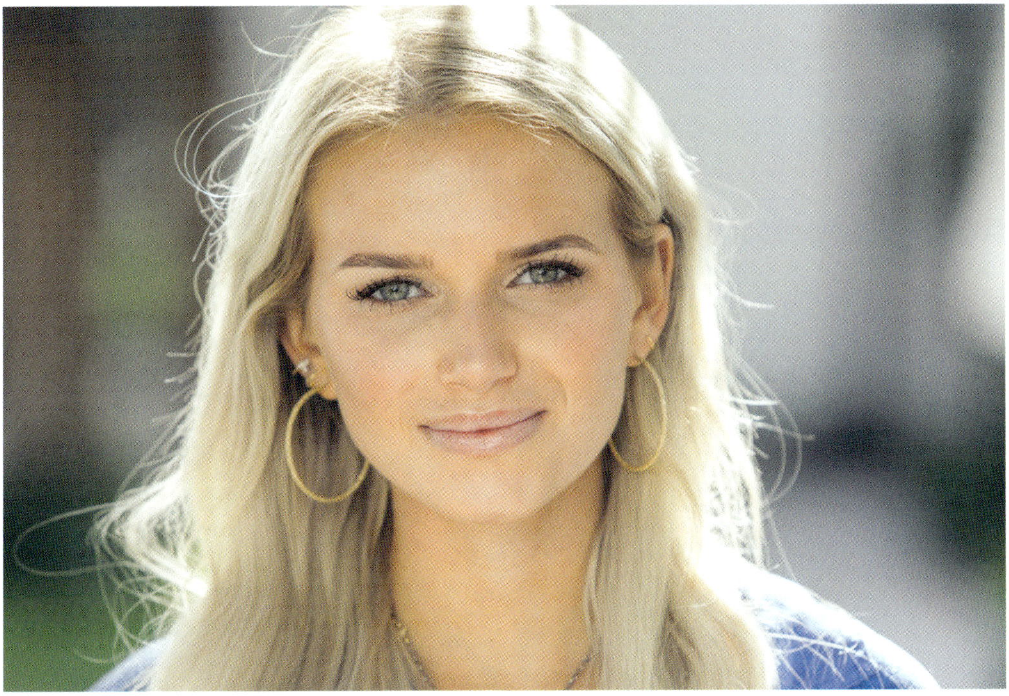

The lens choice and the focal length of the lens changes the shape of your subjects and the amount of separation between them and the background. Simply put, the focal length is measured in millimeters (mm), and the lower the mm number, the more zoomed-out the lens is, which creates a wider angle. Many starter cameras come with a cheap, low-quality lens with an 18–55 mm zoom that is often referred to as a "kit lens." When you zoom out your lens to 18 mm, it's going to offer the widest angle, show the most extra space in the sides of the background, and distort and stretch out your subject in potentially unflattering angles. Zooming all the way in to 55 mm compresses the image much more, showing less stretching and less of the background.

WIDE-ANGLE KIT LENS (18 MM)

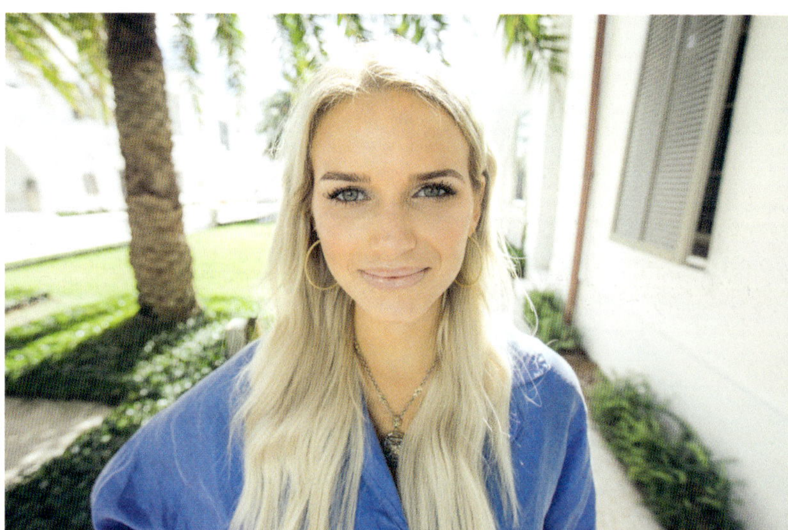

As you can see from these examples, the 18 mm lens at focal length creates a wider angle and shows much more of the background, stretching out everything in our images, including the human. As you zoom in to a higher mm (focal length number), you see less of the background, and more of the human's face fills the frame. You can choose what your viewer sees simply by adjusting the focal length.

Let's take a look at how lenses can stretch or compress your subject. Here are some photos of my friend Riley.

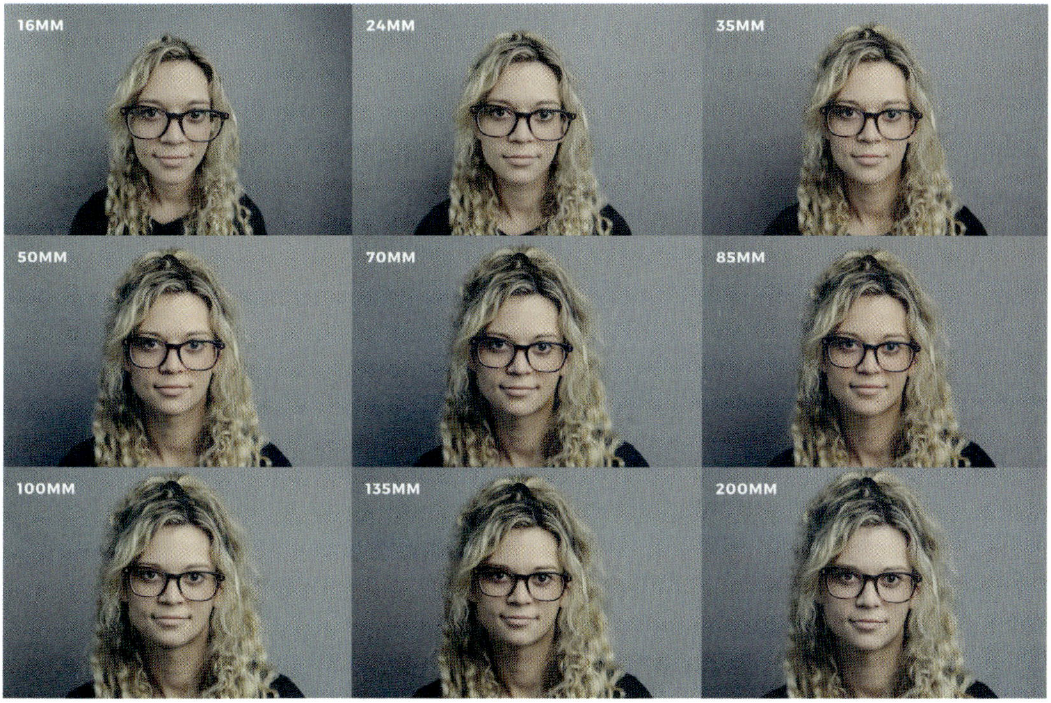

My goal was for her face to be approximately the same height in each of these images as I zoomed in and out. I had to physically step farther away from or closer to her while shooting the different focal lengths to ensure the same amount of her face took up each frame. The benefit of shooting like this is that the background remains the same and the difference in the subject is obvious. See how the lens focal length changes just the shape of her face?

Notice how the lenses with the smaller millimeter numbers stretch out her face more. This effect is especially noticeable when you're physically close to your subject. The higher the millimeter number, the more compression the lens is creating. Compression tends to flatten your subjects and can actually make them appear a bit thicker than is natural when you are zoomed in this much. Notice how much thicker and fuller Riley's hair looks in the 200 mm shot than in the 16 mm shot.

Your lens focal length matters immensely. When shooting portraits of an individual, I recommend shooting focal lengths between 50 and 85 mm for the most natural look.

PERSPECTIVE

Take a look at these shots of my kids and notice how perspective can change a story.

The focal length is the same, but only one image looks like kids playing on the beach. The other perspective shows my younger son, Christian, as a giant crushing his older brother, Judah—which, of course, is the funny story I'm trying to tell. The difference is my physical position and angle, or, in summary, the photographer's perspective.

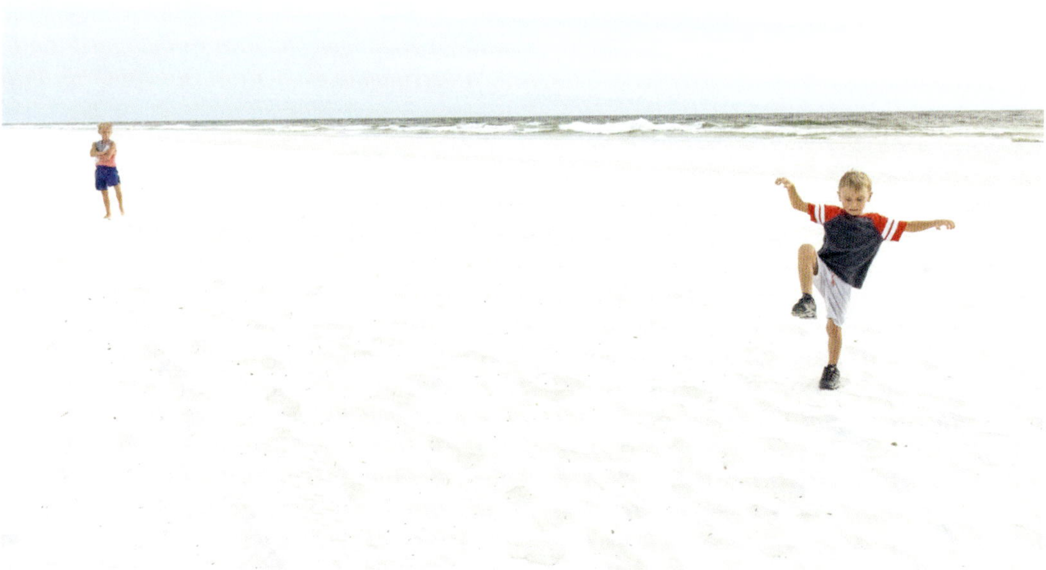

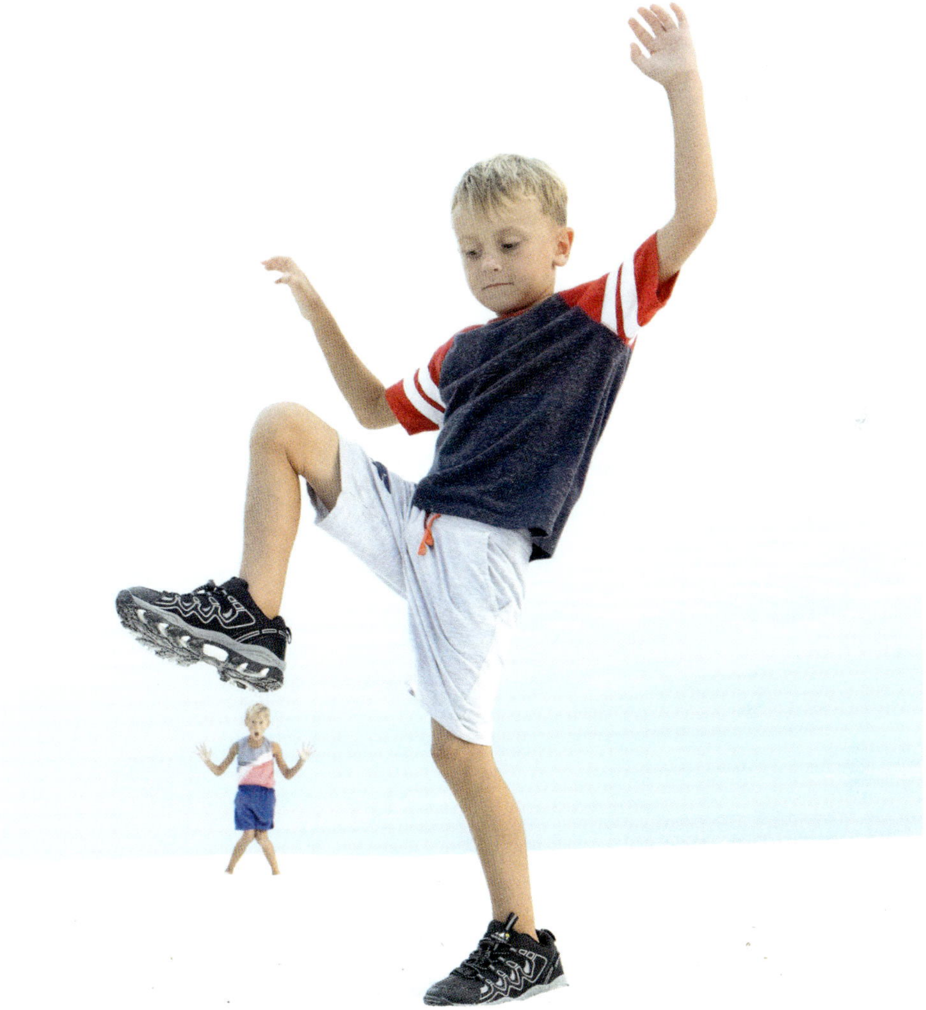

THE RULE OF THIRDS

There is a popular rule about composition that you may have heard of already. (Like I said, I typically like to call these *guidelines* rather than *rules*, because if someone gives me a rule, well, I just want to break it. But in this case, we'll stick with the word *rule* because what I mean is a timeless principle in photography.) Again, you don't always have to abide by this rule. But be warned that breaking it can sometimes have an awkward result. I'm talking about the rule of thirds, which has been scientifically proven to be aesthetically pleasing by creating more energy, interest, and tension in the composition. How is it proven exactly? Well, I dunno. But it's science, guys; trust me on this. In all seriousness, here's how it works: Imagine your shot broken down into nine equal parts, three vertically and three horizontally.

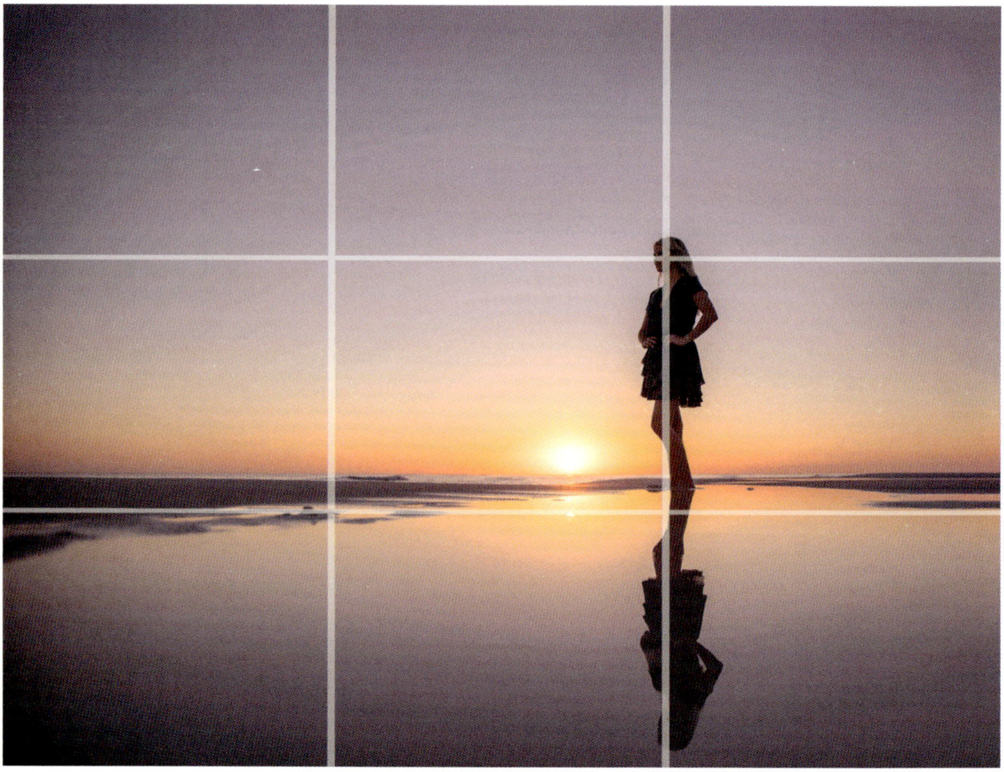

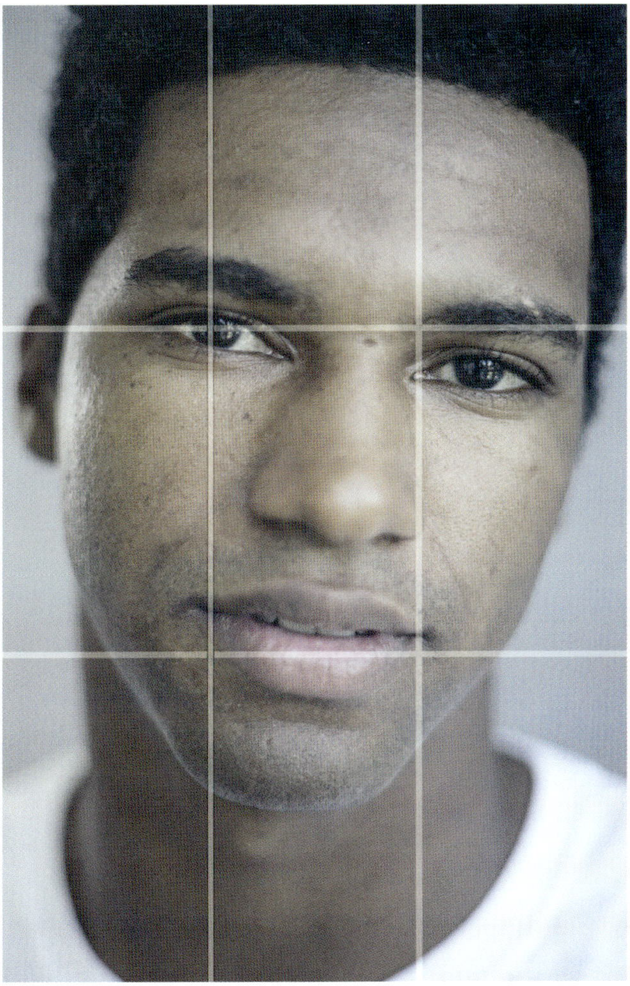

On this grid the lines cross each other at four points. The rule says that if you place points of interest on one of these four points or along any of the lines, your photo will look more balanced and natural to the viewer. I'm no scientist, so I can't prove it, but I can tell you that if you put the subject's eyes on one of the lines, it creates a pleasing image. Most phones even have a setting in the camera app where you can make this grid appear as you're taking a photograph to help you practice.

Look at the difference.

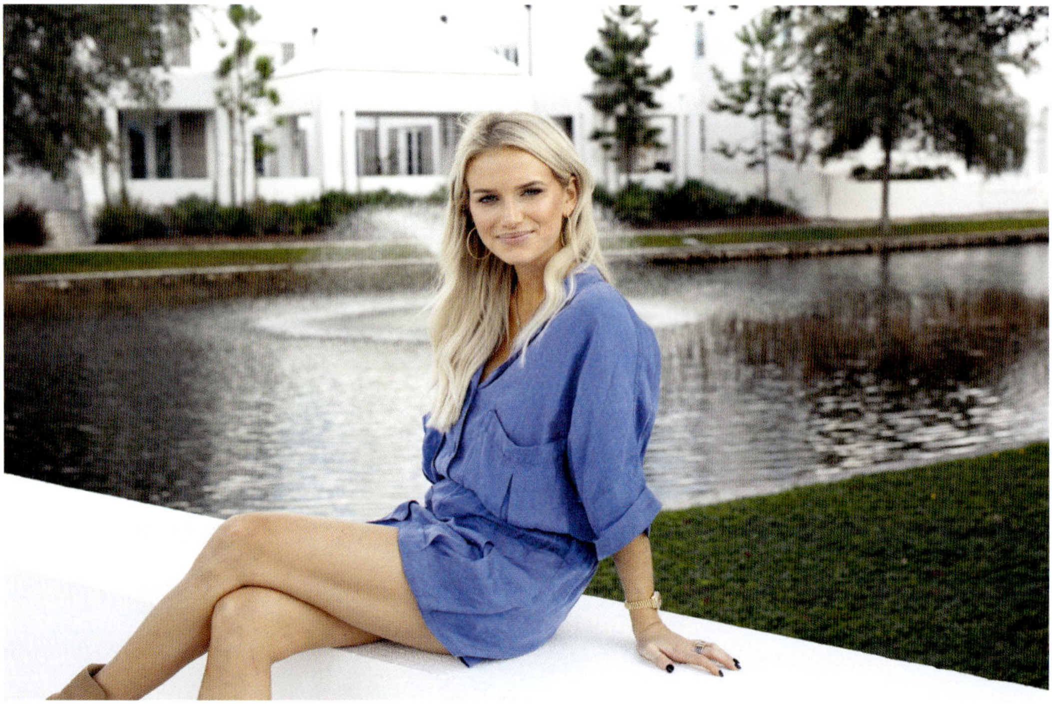

Here, we have Ashley sitting by a fountain. It looks like the fountain is growing out of Ashley's head. We definitely don't want that. Also, I'd like to see both her and the fountain balanced in the image. So to fix that, I placed her face on the intersecting thirds line in the top right corner.

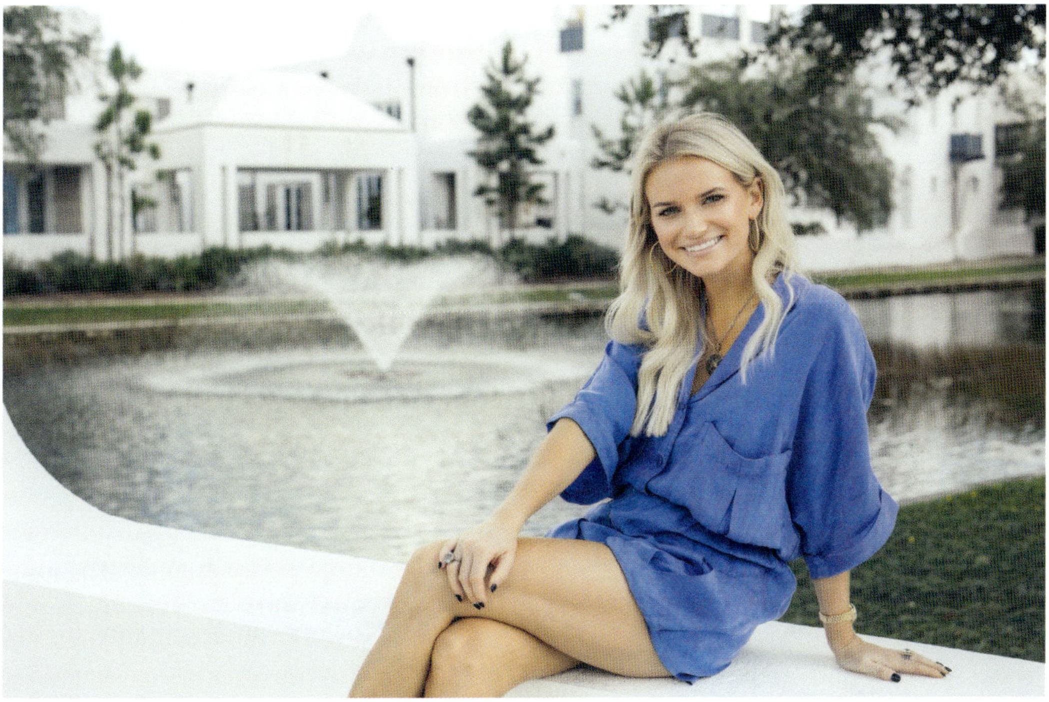

Look at the difference in the second image. Now you have a pretty balance of her face, the fountain, and the beautiful buildings in the background. The rule of thirds helped create that.

Frame your shot with the rule of thirds in mind. My rebellious nature aside, the rule of thirds is an incredibly helpful tool for creating expertly composed photos.

BLOCK OUT DISTRACTIONS

Next, consider body-blocking when setting up your shot. Use your subject to block the distractions in the background and compose the shot you want.

This first picture is a lovely shot, but the people in the background are a bit distracting and detract from the story I want to tell, which is about Ashley alone on the beach.

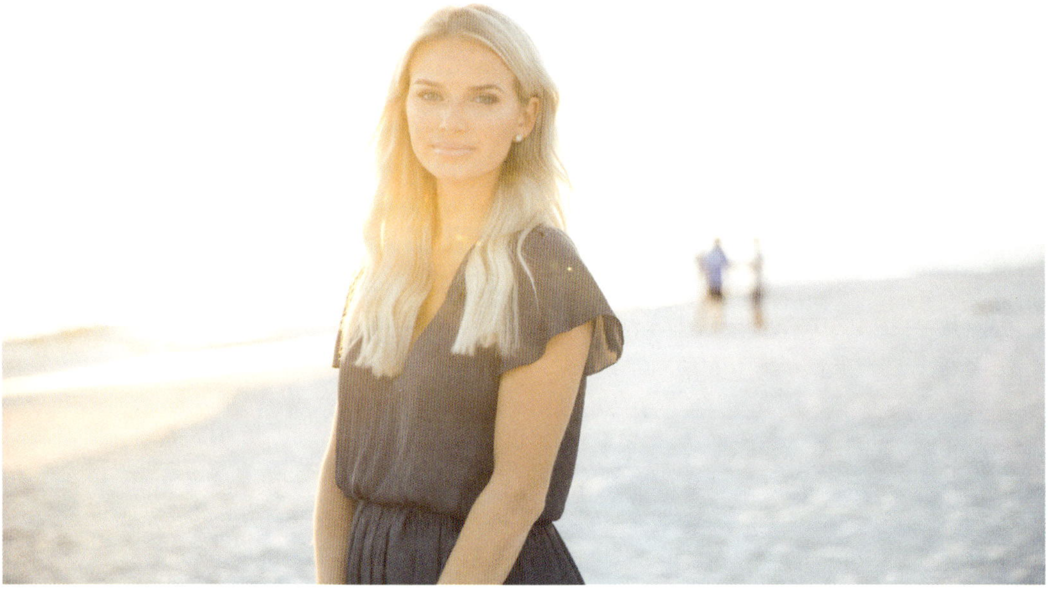

As the photographer, you can sidestep slightly and reposition your frame so your subject is in front of the distractions. In this case, I used her body to block the people in the background.

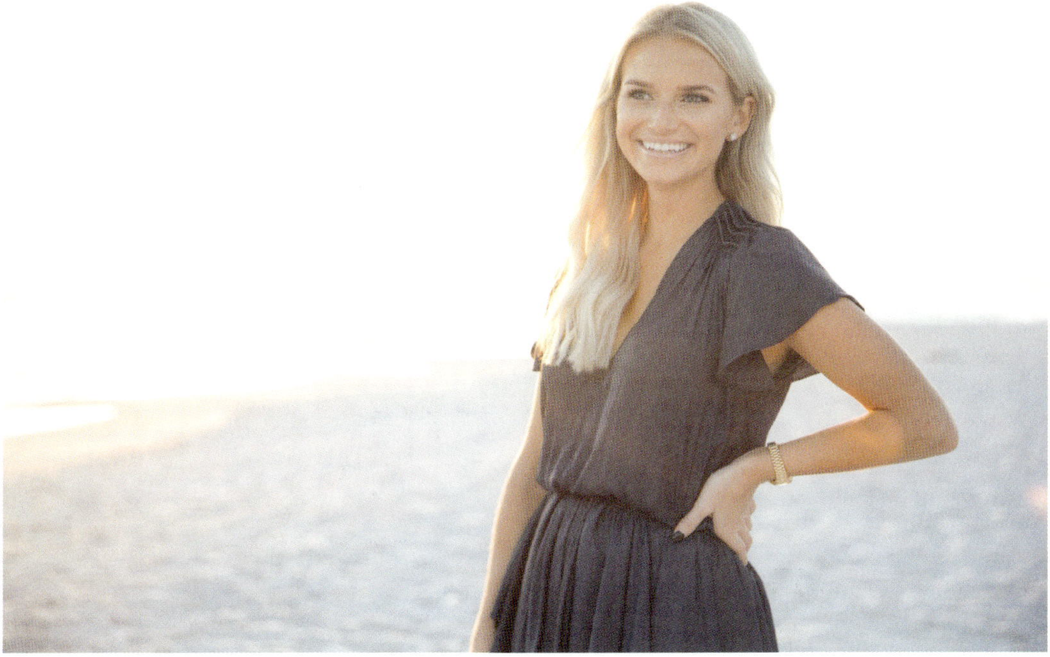

LIGHT

You can do everything "right" in composing your story and follow all the tricks I teach you in this chapter, but if your lighting looks bad, your shot will be ruined. The idea is to find the right type of light to tell the story.

There are a few techniques for this, including both using the light you already have and creating light that wasn't there before. If you're shooting a portrait of a beautiful model, you want to find flattering light to illuminate her face. If you're shooting a landscape, you might want to find the warm, soft light during the mornings or evenings. It's amazing how waiting a few minutes for the light to change, or even repositioning your angle the slightest bit, can completely change the way light hits your subject and make the image one hundred times better.

Let's take a look at three practical ways to use lighting better in your photos. In these examples, I'm talking about portraits, but the same concept can be applied to still lifes and landscapes, as well.

1. Reposition to find better light.

So many snapshots are taken in bad light without any thought that there might be better light close by if the photographer just knew where to look.

Here is a shot of Ashley in the bright sunlight. You can see the bright spots and harsh shadows on her face. Her face and hair are blown out (too bright) as well. It looks bad. Now look at what happened when Ashley and I backed up ten feet.

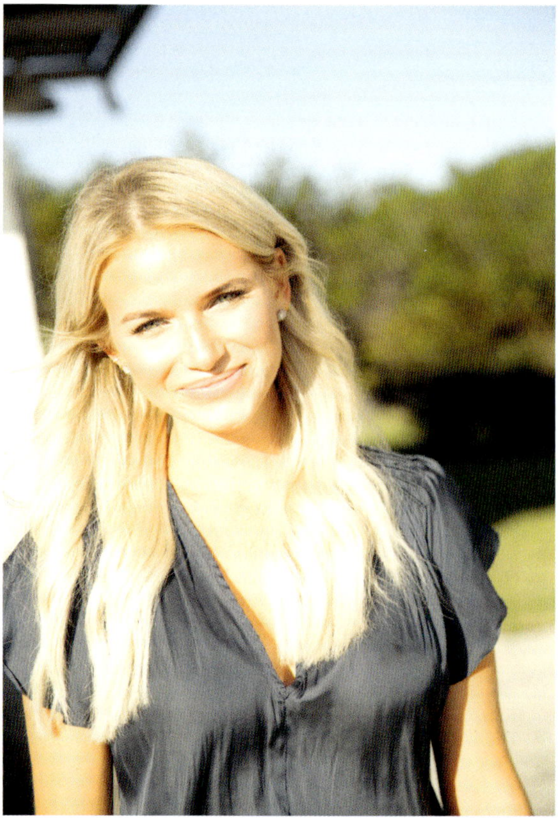

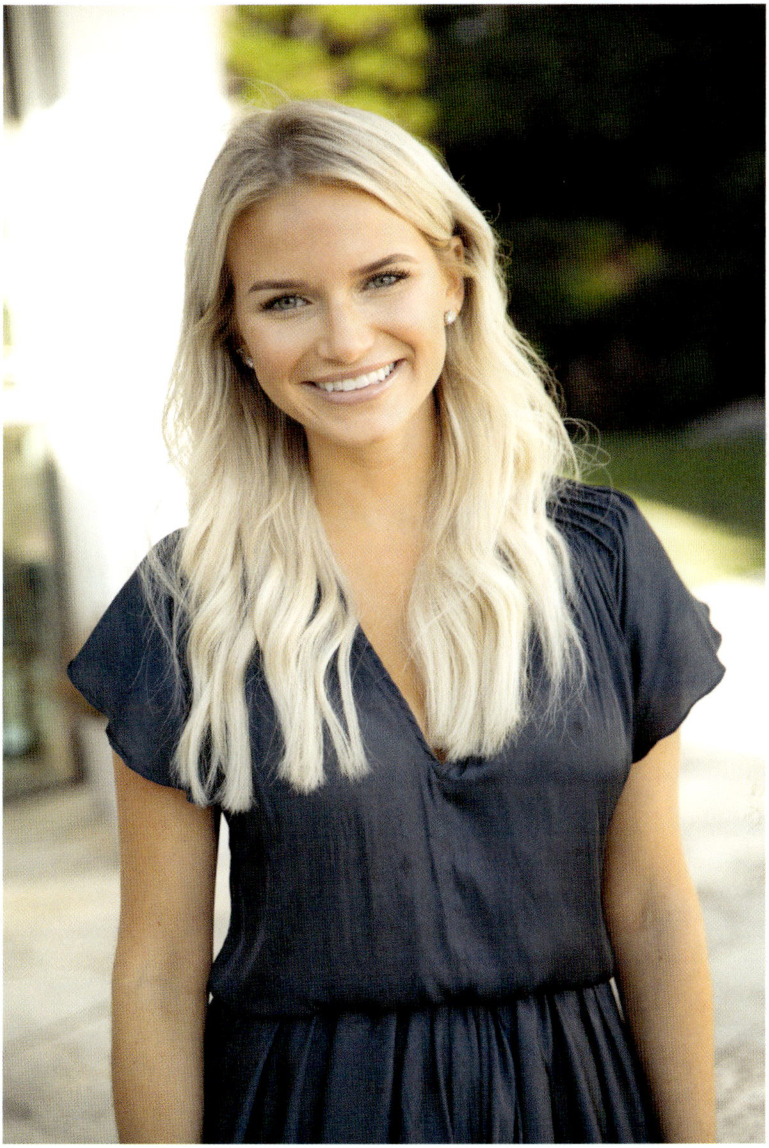

Now she's in the shade of the building. I'm shooting at the same angle and with the same background, but the softer light from the shade made for a more pleasant portrait. You can see the light is still harsh in the background, but now she isn't squinting. There are no harsh shadows or bright spots on her face.

Another example is of my second-born son, Christian, half-lit from direct sunlight. We were standing on the steps leading to the beach, and I snapped this shot of him while testing the lighting. The uneven light looked harsh. With the dark shadows and bright spots, it didn't convey his soft, friendly personality. That's not the story I wanted to tell.

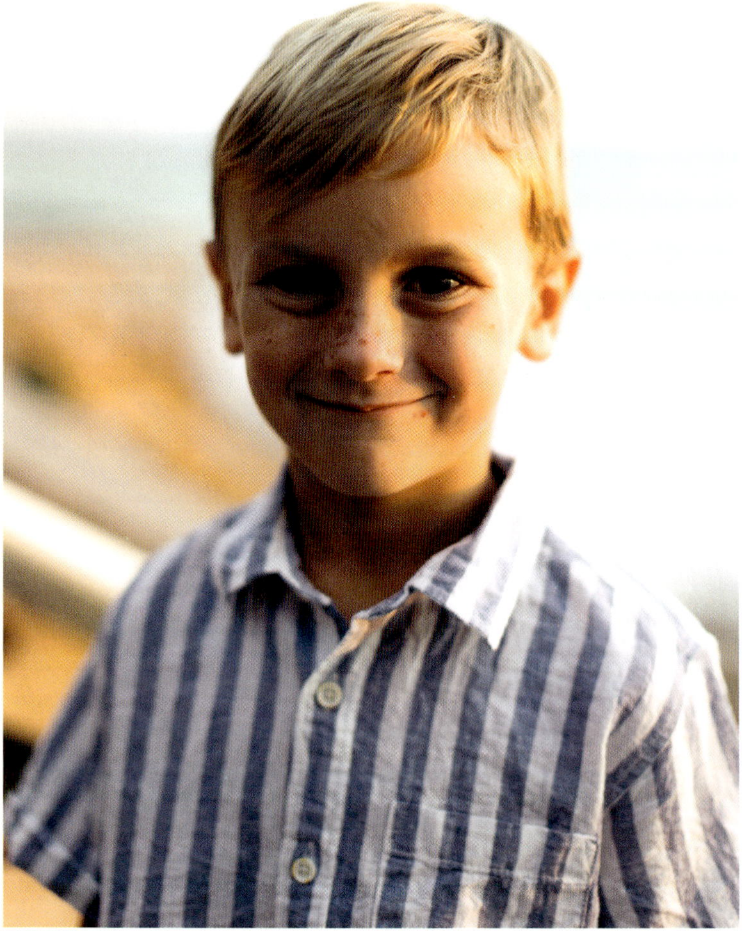

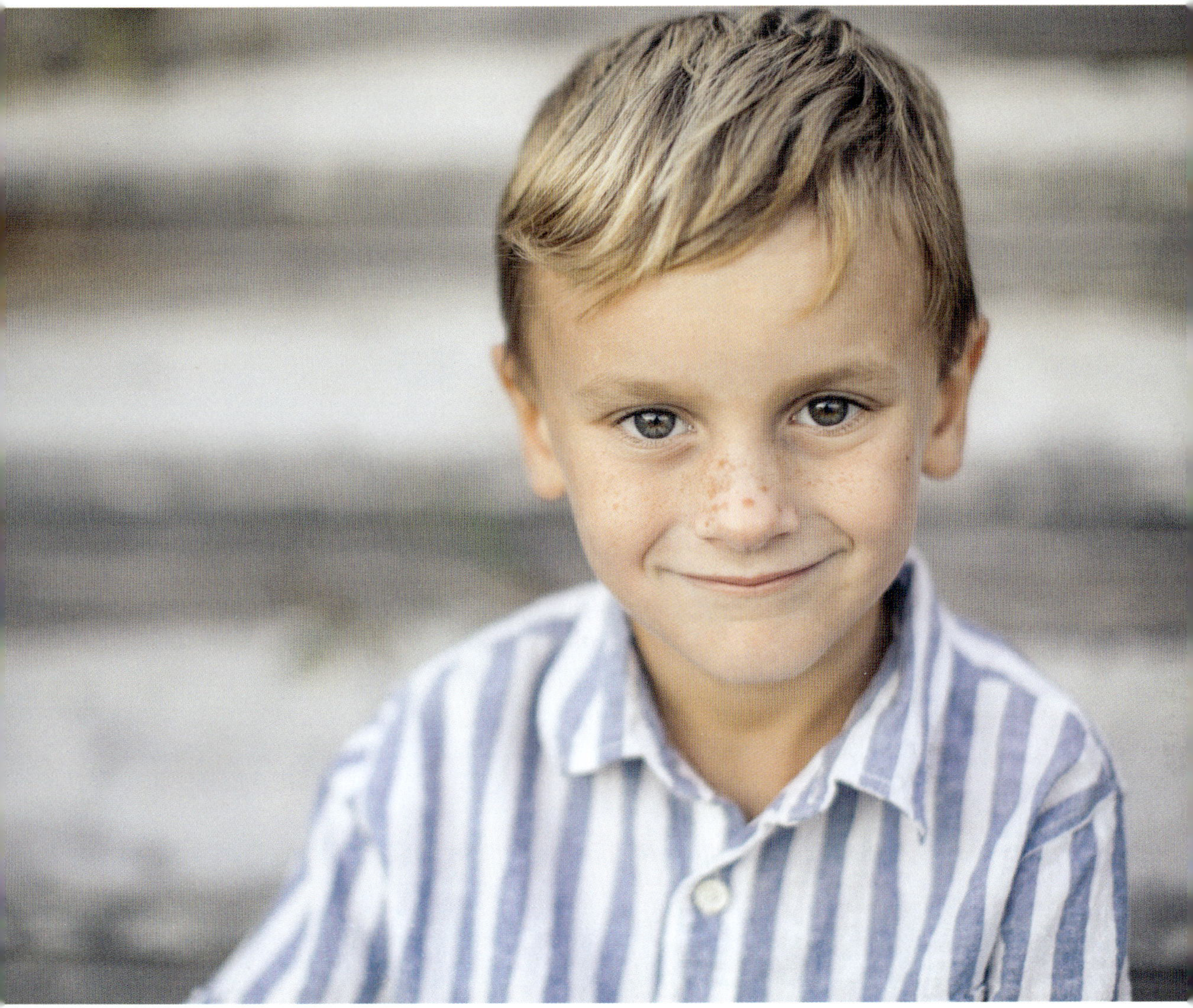

So I had him sit down on the steps below where he was standing before. The low sunlight was blocked by the sand dunes and he was now positioned in full shade. We altered the direction of our shot by 45 degrees, and I let the soft light from the blue sky illuminate his face in the shade.

What a difference repositioning a few steps and finding soft light can make.

2. Wait for the light to change.

Sometimes we're moments away from the sunlight completely changing, especially at dusk. The sun could sneak behind a cloud or even set for the day. Take a look at these photos taken just a few minutes apart, one right before the sunset and the other right after.

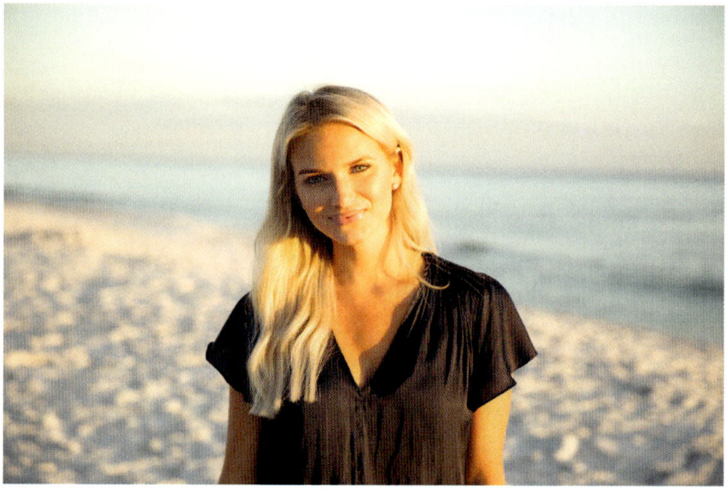

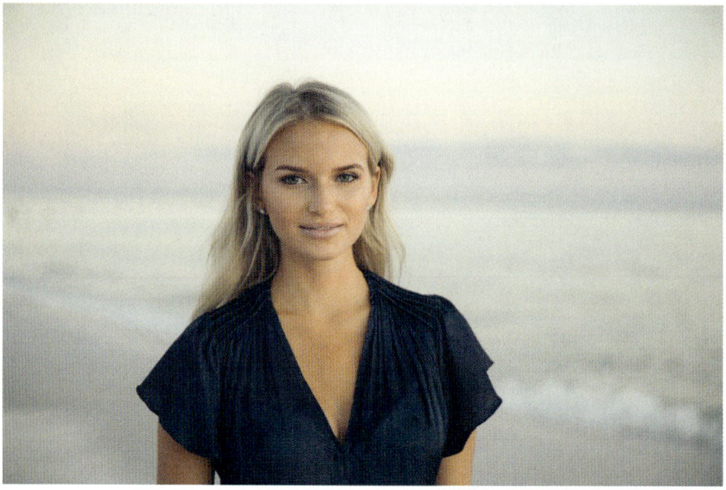

We are often moments away from a world-class photo if we're willing to be patient. But be careful here, because if you wait another minute or two, it may be too dark. Learning to see is also about understanding how fleeting every moment is. When you get a good shot, take it.

To be honest, sometimes the lighting can be a dud. If you love landscape photography, you've probably noticed not all evenings are the same. There's a spot I love in Grayton Beach, but on this particular night, the light wasn't anything special.

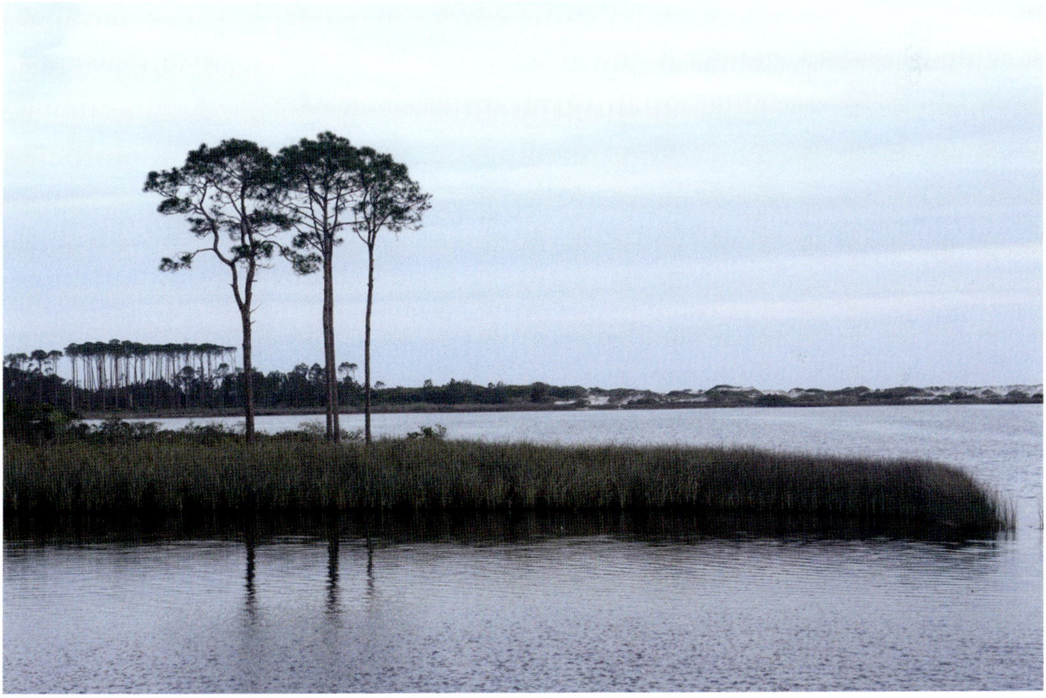

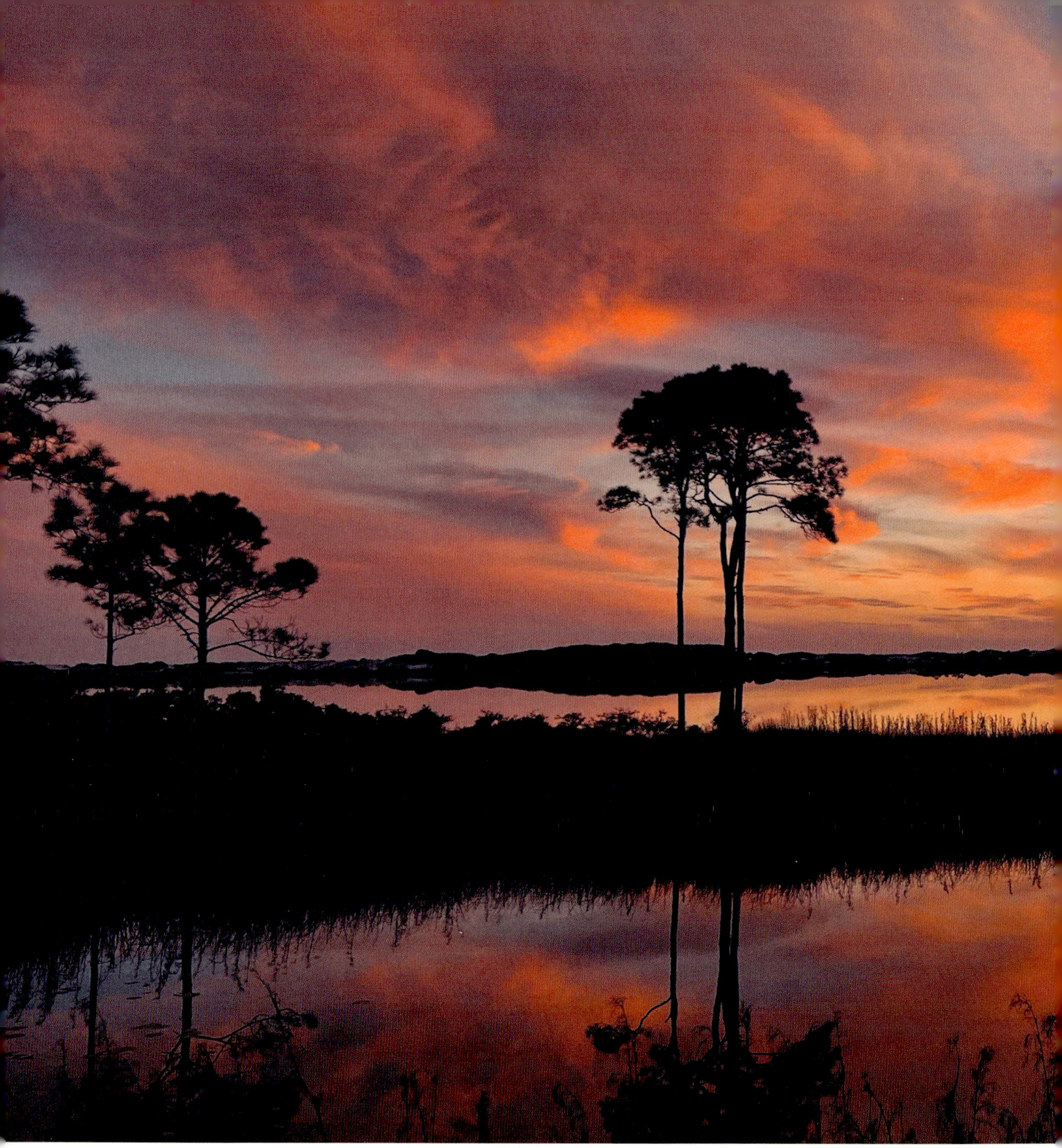

Contrast that with a different evening where the same location was on fire.

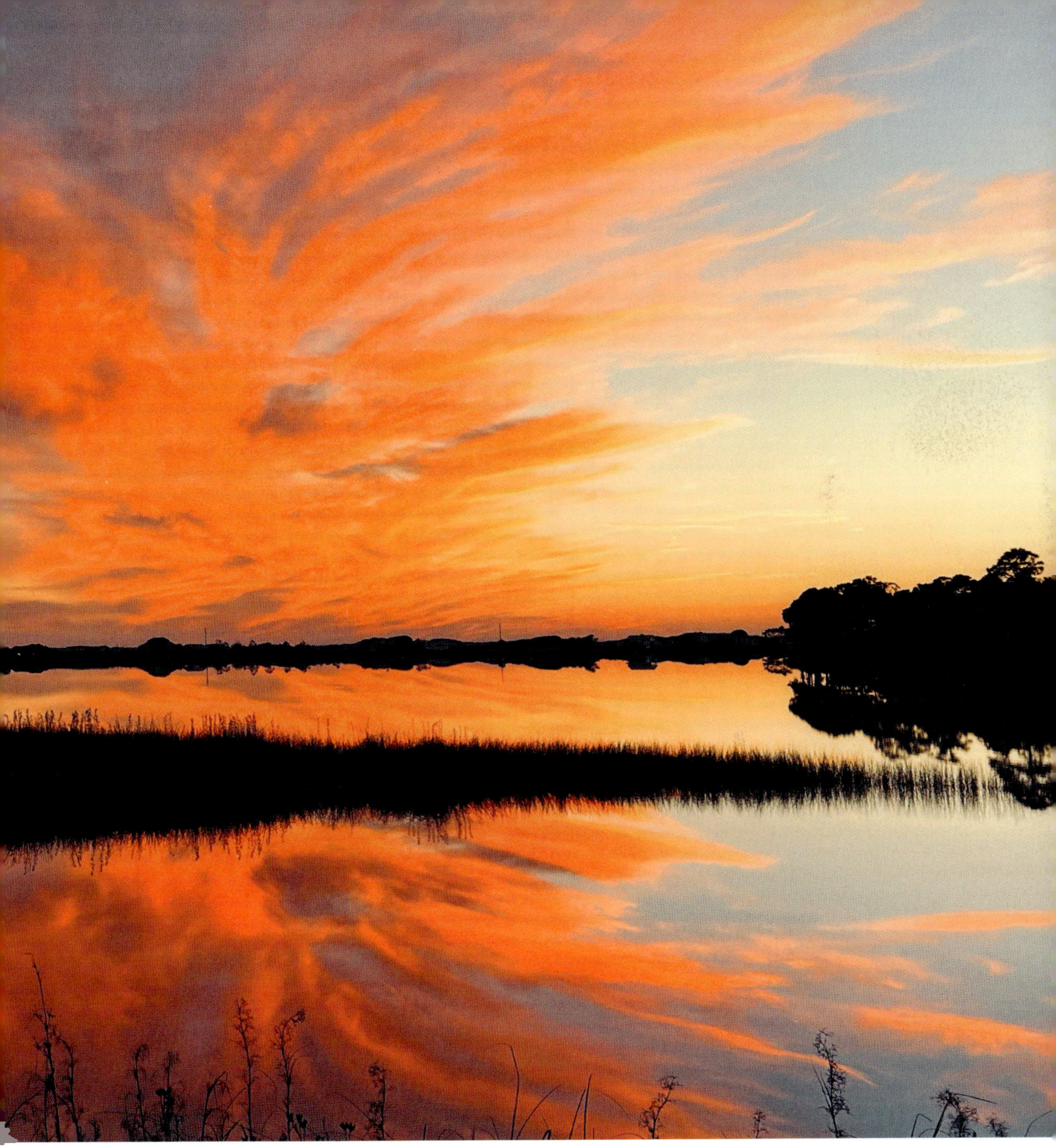

Sometimes patience and persistence will pay off. Especially for landscape photography.

3. Add supplemental light from strobes to make your subjects pop.

Many times the light is just a little flat or boring, but you have to get the shot that day, maybe even that moment. Here is a natural-light shot during the middle of the day. The light is "meh" in my opinion. See how the image is a little washed out? Some of the details are missing in the walls and the sky. To fix this, we can add a strobe. A strobe is an off-camera flash that is much more powerful than the flash that comes on a camera. Strobes are either powered by a powerful battery or directly plugged into an outlet.

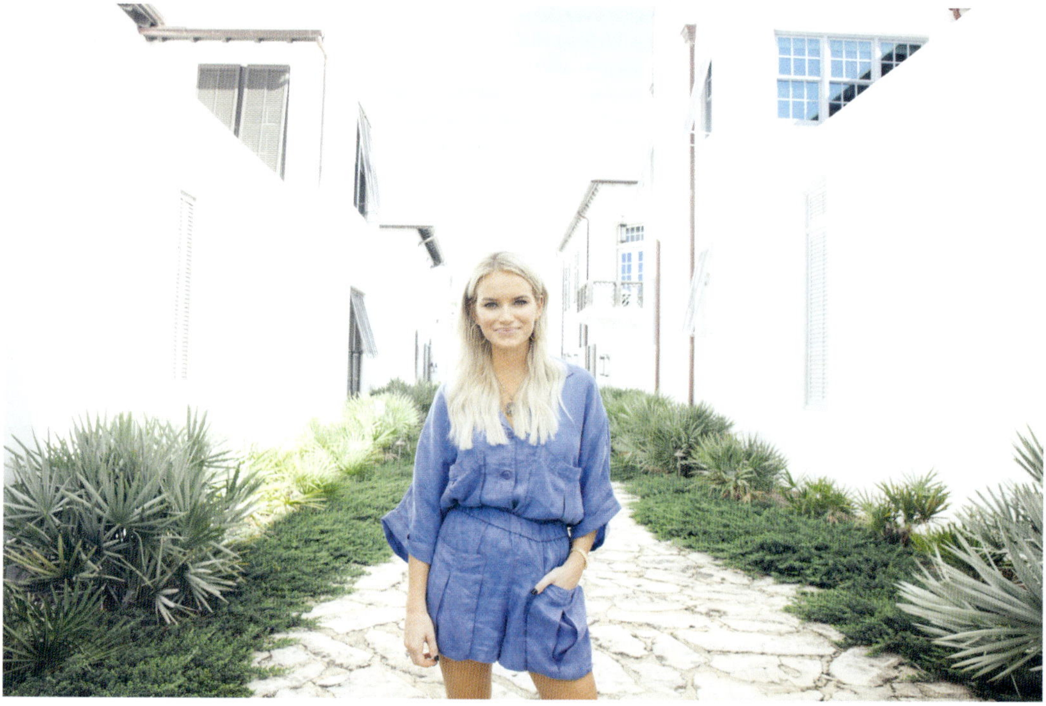

Look at what happened when I introduced a portable strobe light to make my subject pop and bring more drama to the scene.

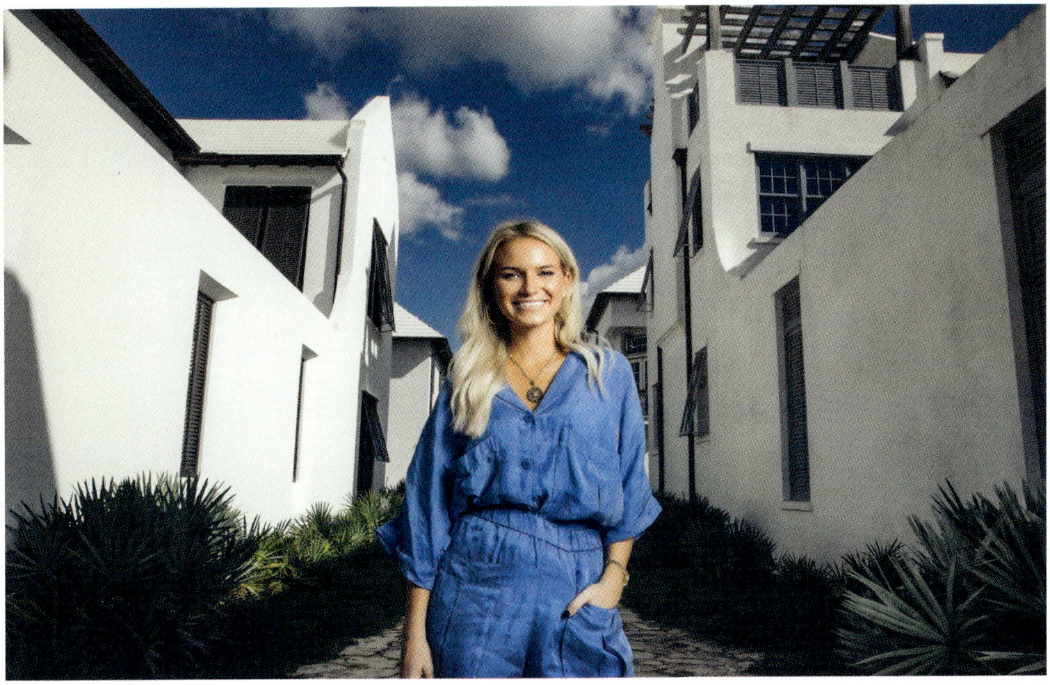

A bonus to adding supplemental light from strobes is that you can get both a vibrant sky and great light on the subject's face, which can be difficult to achieve in certain natural-light scenarios. In this case, I went a little more dramatic and used my strobe to overpower the available light. This made the sky darker than it appeared in person. This requires additional advanced equipment. Using flashes and strobes are advanced concepts that I teach step-by-step in my courses in The Photo Mentorship.

▶ The Photo Mentorship is an online community of photographers growing and learning together with step-by-step video tutorials and mentoring that is engineered to get results no matter where your photography interests may lie. To get a free sneak peek of it just for buying this book, visit PhotoMentorship.com/free.

LEADING LINES

There are some tricks you can use to draw your viewer's eyes directly to your subject, literally. Leading lines—when two or more lines collide with your subject—guide your viewer's eyes to go exactly where you want them to. For example, if there is a long, skinny walkway in your shot, put your subject in the middle of the lines the walkway creates.

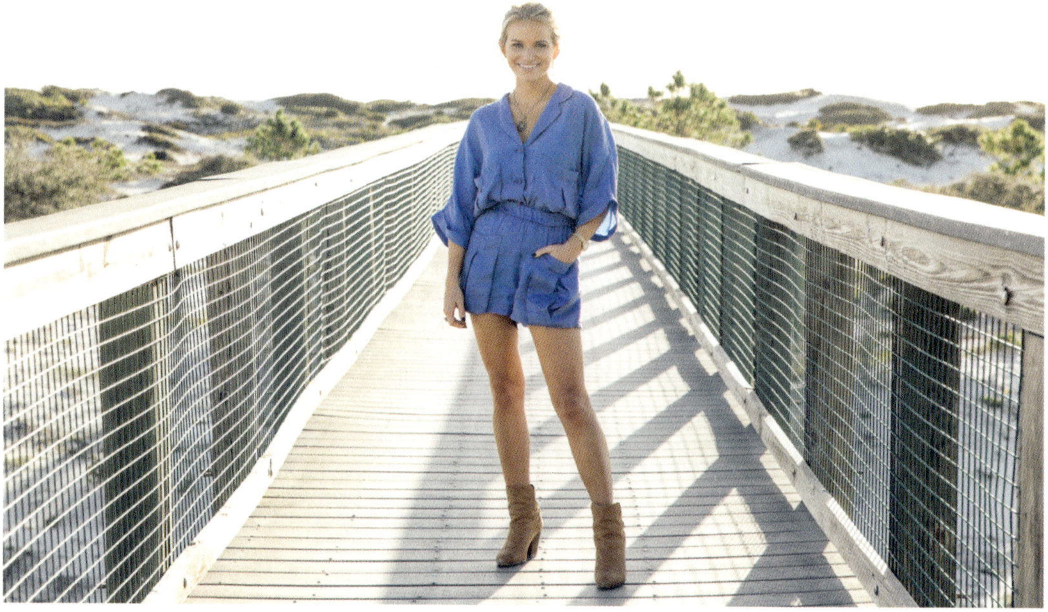

Find a way to position your subject so the lines will lead right to them. That will draw the viewer's attention where you want it to be. There are all sorts of ways to use leading lines to direct attention to the subject of your photograph. Experiment and have fun with it.

BLURRING THE BACKGROUND

If there's too much busyness in the background of the shot, you can play with a little blurring to help clarify the story. Again, think of snapshot versus story. A snapshot can show too much, making the focus of the photo hard to find. But a story emphasizes the subject in a way that is undeniable. It blurs the background so that the subject stands out.

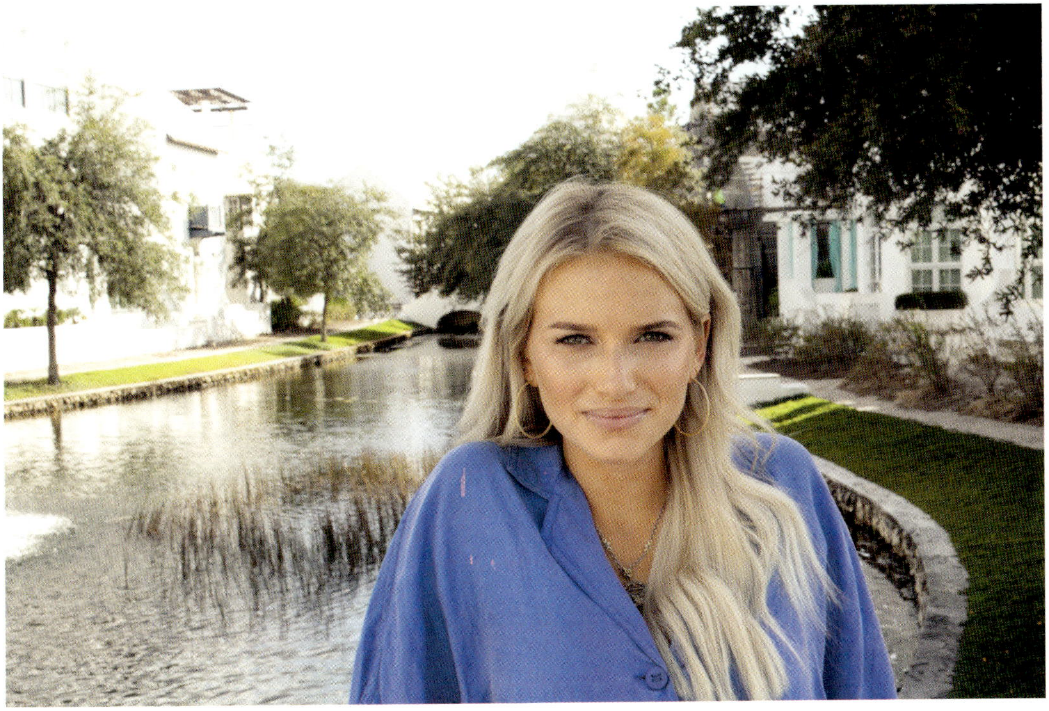

Take a look at this shot. Ashley looks awesome, but you can see I didn't put much thought into it. There's a lot going on in the background, and because everything in the photo is in focus, it's actually taking away the focus from her face, which is what I was trying to document.

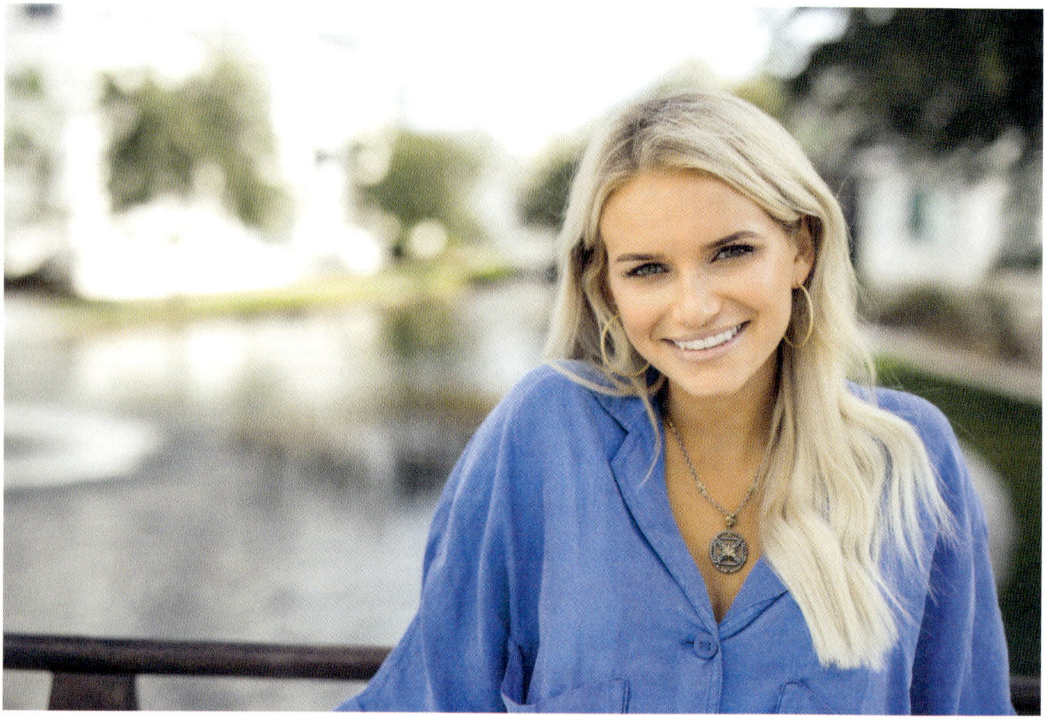

Blurring the background created some separation between my subject and what's behind her. I did this by adjusting my aperture to create a shallower depth of field, which is a concept I'll cover in the next chapter.

You don't always want to blur the background, of course; it's just another tool in your tool belt. But in this case, it's going to make everything pop, and that's going to tell a much better story. All the focus—literally—will go right to Ashley. What's behind her doesn't matter; in fact, in some ways the beauty behind her distracts from the beauty of her face. Blurring the background in this photo puts the viewer's attention on the primary subject, which is where you want it.

CROPPING

You can crop your photo at different points in the photography process. You could crop on the front end as you're taking the picture by zooming in with your lens or walking closer or farther from your subject. Or you could crop on the back end when you're editing the photo. Either way, the crop is determined by what is actually in the frame in your picture. Believe it or not, cropping can make a big difference in your story. If you have an image that is cropped too far out, you might see a lot of distracting elements in the shot.

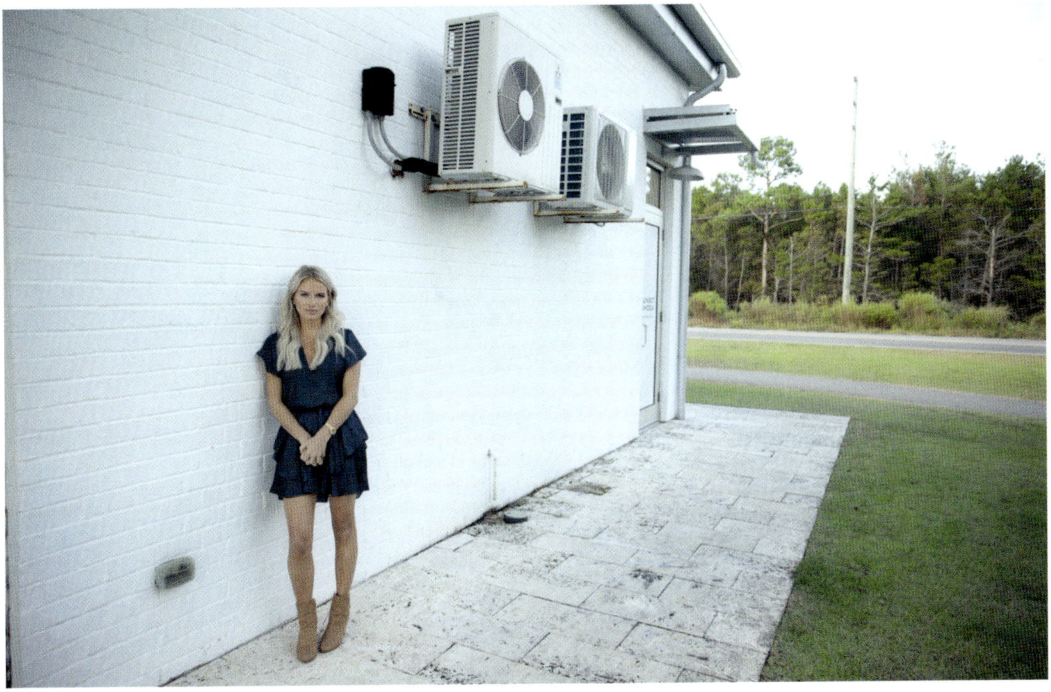

By cropping in just a little bit and removing the excess clutter, you're telling a better story. A good crop can completely alter the perspective and point of your story. In this example I cropped in the camera by walking closer to the subject and zoomed in to get rid of the distractions in the first shot.

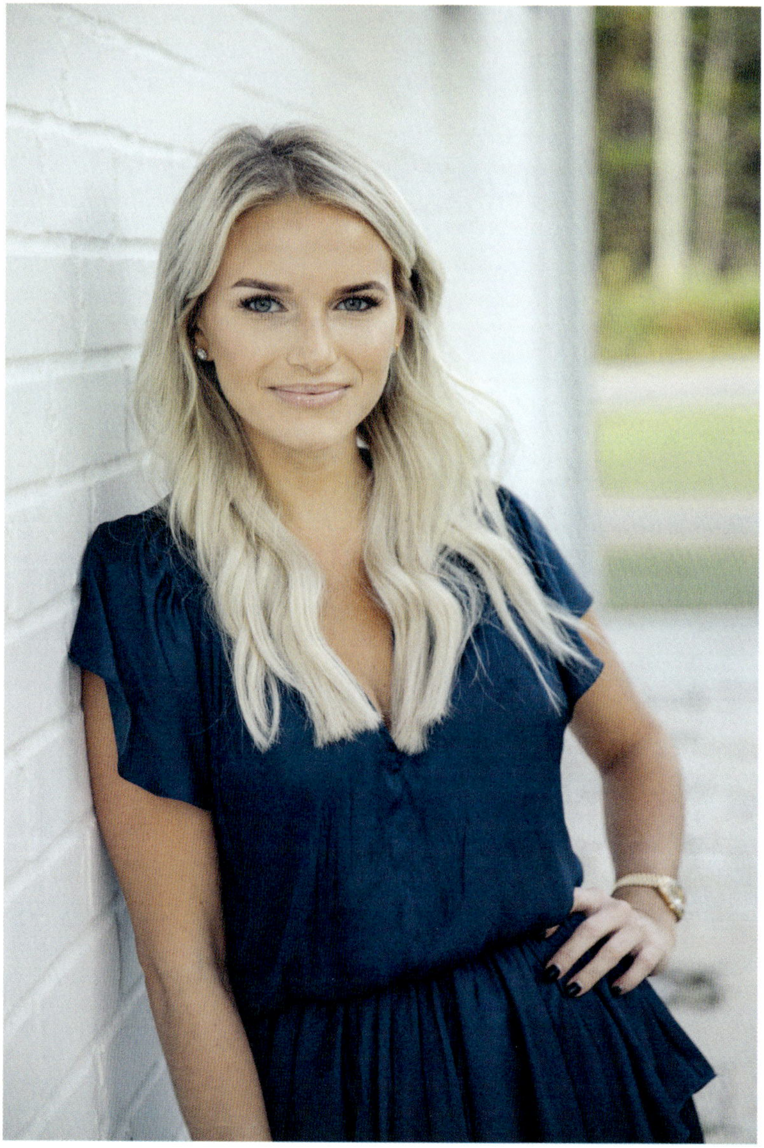

TIMING

When you're documenting an event, you need to be able to anticipate what's coming. To tell the story you want to tell, you have to be able to see the future, to visualize what's about to happen. When done well, getting the timing just right feels and looks like magic.

Put yourself in the moment when the bride is about to throw her bouquet. What do you need to visualize? Where is she going to throw it? How high is it going to go? Which reactions will be important? Who else do you need to capture? All this determines how you'll shoot.

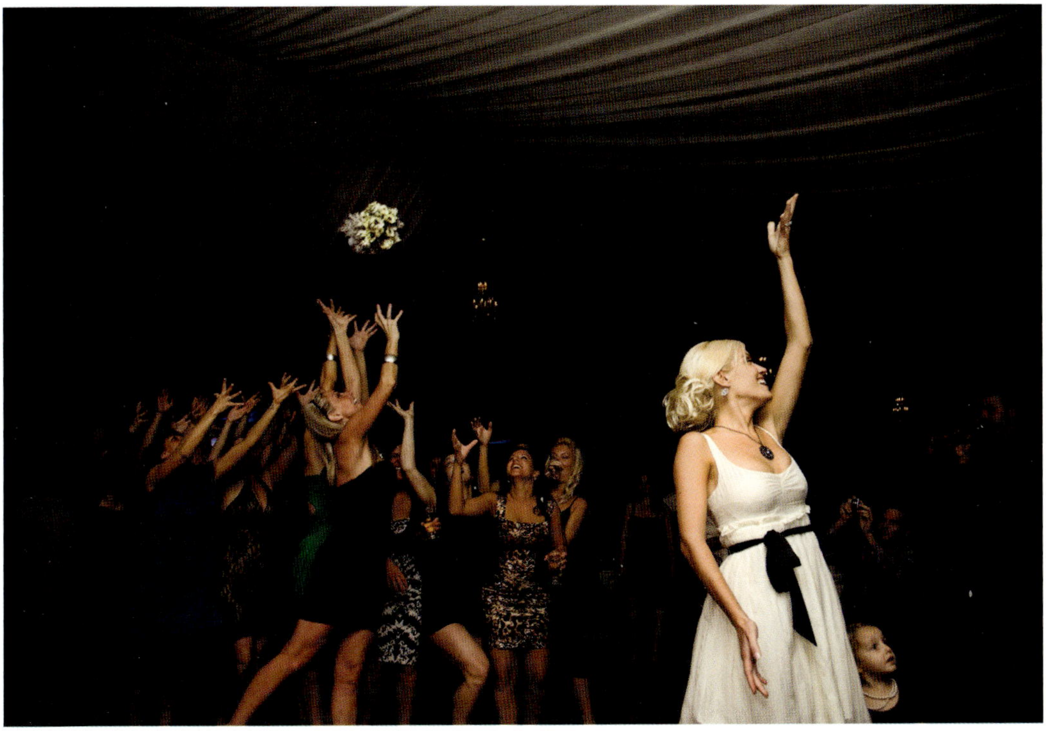

You could shoot the bride from the front angle, where you're actually seeing her face as she throws the bouquet backward. You'll capture her emotions and all her girlfriends in the background as they fight for the catch. For this image, I'm glad she didn't turn much more or I would have missed her expression. I had to visualize which angle would best tell the story, and I didn't realize she would throw the bouquet with her left hand. I got lucky here to still capture the whole story.

This is often why weddings have "second shooters," or secondary photographers, because obviously this moment cannot be captured from multiple angles at the same time without two cameras. The point is, you're trying to figure out where you want to click your shutter to freeze that moment in time. And to do that, you have to anticipate the timing of the events in the story and where to best capture it.

Think through what will compel your viewers. What will draw your audience in? Recognize the significant players in your story, like the father of the bride during the first dance or the grandmother burying her late husband. Sometimes you want to convey an emotion to the masses, and sometimes what you're capturing is deeply personal for just one person. Either way, timing your shots plays a part.

Once, somewhere outside of Atlanta, I saw a beautiful statue of an old man and woman sitting on a bench. So like any good photographer, I started taking pictures of it. And then, out of nowhere, a special moment happened. A man started walking past, and I thought, *This guy is walking by, looking all somber. He looks remarkably like the man in the statue, but without his wife.* It felt like a moment from the Pixar movie *Up* where the old man is reminiscing on happier days. I instantly knew the story I wanted to tell. Whether it was true or not, it felt poignant and important. So I quickly got into position to capture him as he walked by.

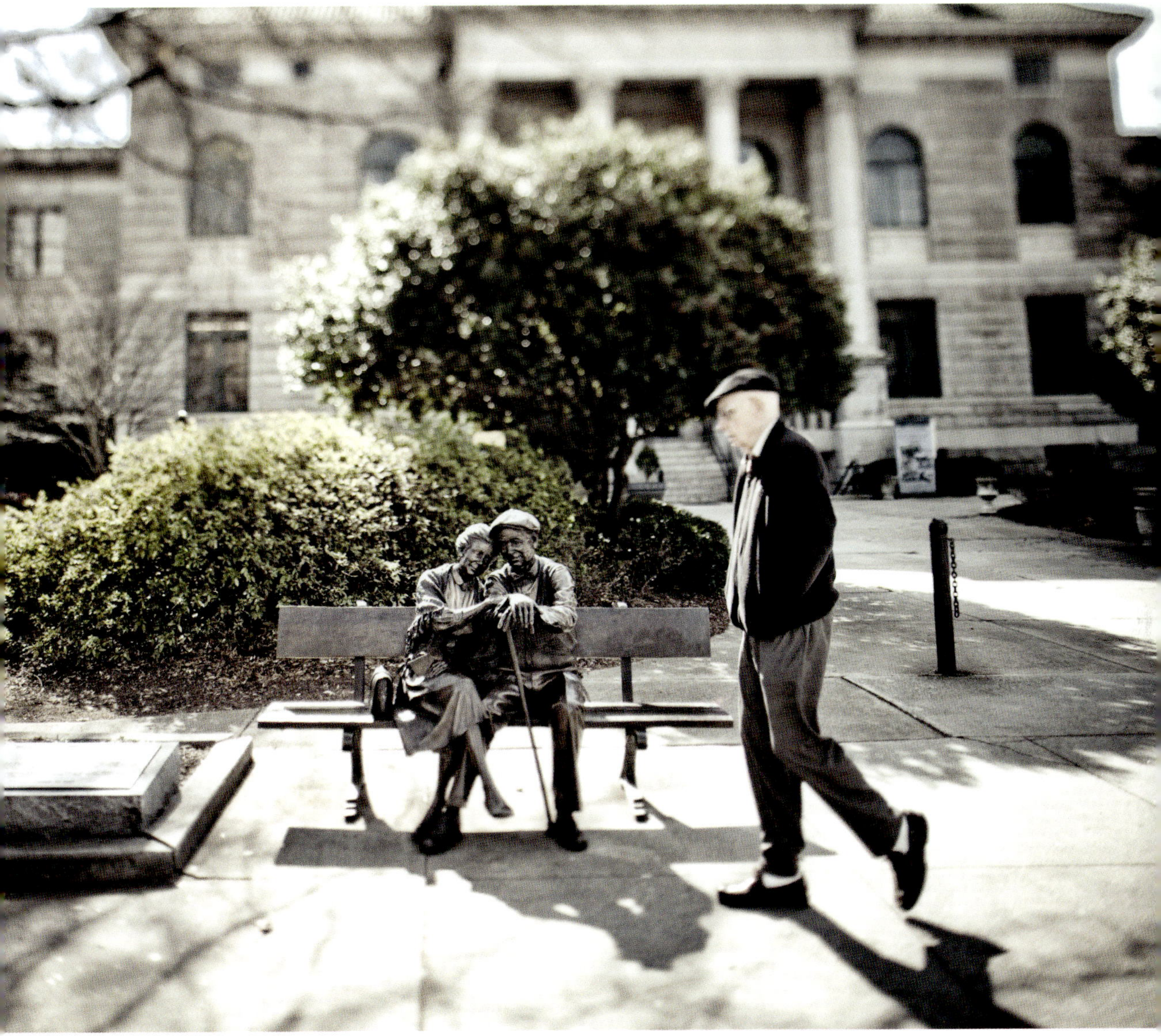

You can see the statues in the background of the shot. What made the moment magical was the timing. I anticipated the shot to convey the story I wanted to tell. Being late, early, or right on time makes a difference in crafting the story in your shot.

REFLECTIONS

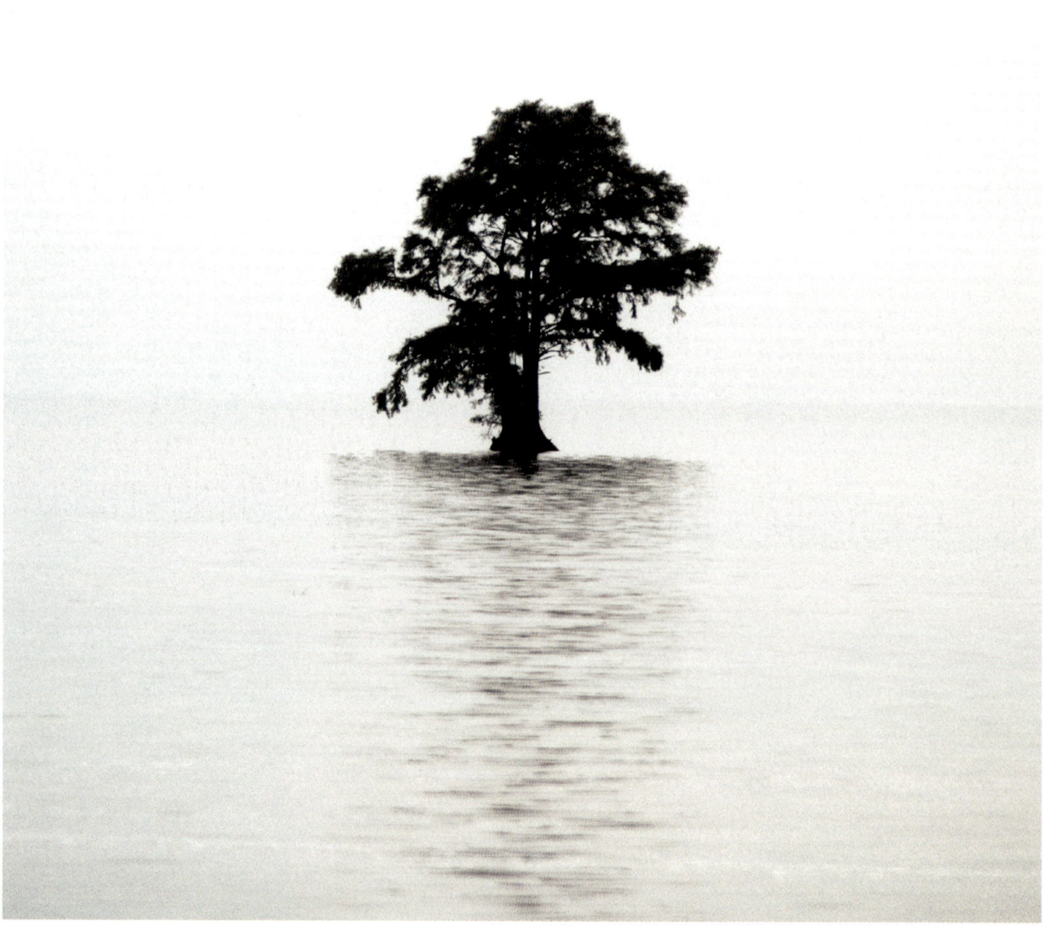

Reflections can enhance your photo immensely. They add layers and layers of beauty, typically below your subject. For example, my favorite thing to photograph with reflections is a sunset.

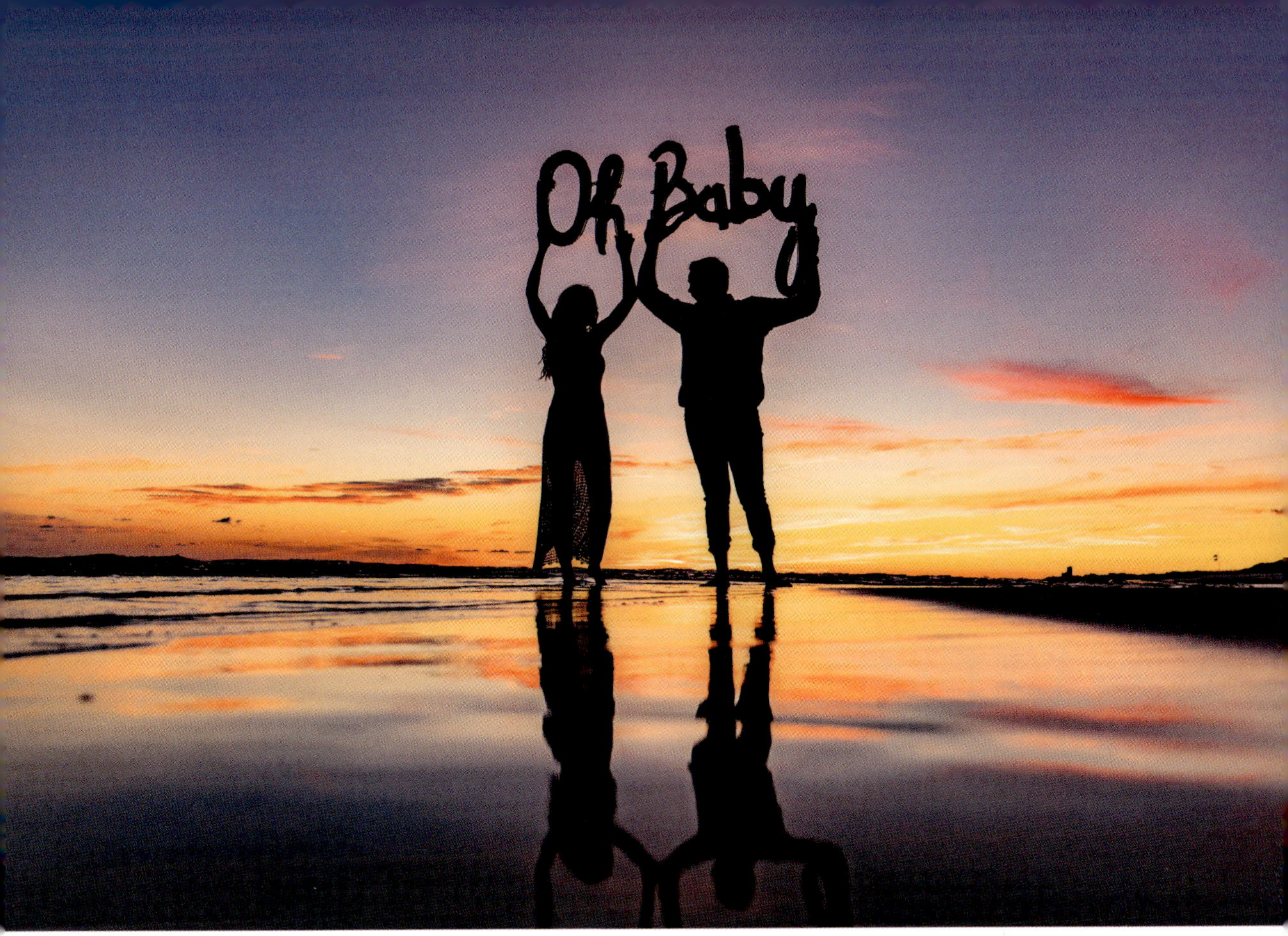

I love to find a smooth, glassy layer of water to reflect the sunset. I typically lower my position and shoot from a low angle to get the camera close to the water to put the reflection in the forefront. Reflections have a way of making the image come alive and enhancing the story by adding depth and beauty.

Composition Is Key

It is not enough to simply find beautiful things in the world and shoot them with your camera. Being a great photographer is about seeing what others might miss and then figuring out how to frame it. What goes in the shot? What do you leave out? What deserves our attention and therefore should be in focus, whereas what should be blurry? All these choices in composition matter. Knowing what to do and when takes practice, but these are the basic building blocks for telling a compelling story with an image. In the next chapter we'll get a little more practical and share some dos and don'ts so you can use these techniques and tools well.

CHAPTER 5

Magic Tricks and Rookie Mistakes

WE'VE TALKED ABOUT ELEMENTS OF COMPOSITION YOU CAN PLAY WITH TO craft your story. But what happens when something you try just doesn't work out?

Early in my career, I loved shooting from a low angle at my subjects. I thought it was a cool trick that led to showing some interesting leading lines in my compositions. It can do that sometimes. But one unintended mistake is that it can also really accentuate unflattering angles on humans. I made the mistake of shooting an album cover photo from a low angle. All the photos had this unfortunate perspective, and some of the band members didn't love the way they looked in the images. The angle stretched them out, showed unnecessary double chins, and made them look wider than they actually were. My wide-angle lens from a low position was what caused this unflattering angle and distortion. Unfortunately for them, we didn't have time for a reshoot and we had to use the only photos that we had. So they have photos floating around in the world that lots of people have seen of them where they look distorted. Guess what happened? I didn't get hired to do their next album cover shoot. And I never did another photo shoot for that record label again. If there is one surefire way to never get hired again, it's to make a celebrity look terrible in a picture.

Please do not make the same mistake I did. I beat myself up for a long time about this. I learned my lesson and never shot promo pictures from that angle again. It doesn't matter if tens of millions of people will see the photo or not; you want your subjects to look their best, regardless of whether you're shooting food photography or human subjects. As a storyteller, your job is to find the right angles. If you don't, not only will you be unhappy with your images, but so will your subjects. I mean, we all know this from the world of selfies, right? You never want to take a photo of yourself from an unflattering angle. Make sure your camera is a little bit above the head to capture a flattering angle for yourself for that perfect Instagram post. Shout-out to all my readers taking selfies from an overhead angle with duck lips! Come on, I know some of you are guilty! The truth is, you're just trying to look your best. You want the same when shooting others. Nobody wants to look worse in pictures than they really do. Especially if that person is paying you. The goal is to make them comfortable in the shot so that they look and feel as great as possible on camera. And a lot of this can be done by simply avoiding unflattering angles.

Imagine shooting the most beautiful person in the world. If you put them at the wrong angle, nothing can help. You can make any beautiful thing or person look terrible from the wrong angle. You could make Audrey Hepburn look like the Hunchback of Notre Dame with a bad enough angle. The goal isn't to alter what's there but rather to find the angle that enhances and accentuates the beauty in your subject and your story. Selfishly, you don't want to look like an amateur to your clients; altruistically, you want your subjects to feel good about themselves. When that beautiful family photo is ruined because the tree in the background now looks like it's growing out of someone's head, when a seemingly small light pole takes up the entire frame, when it looks like a baby is growing out of her mother's shoulder instead of resting on it. These are the kinds of situations new photographers don't realize they have on their hands until they sit down at their desks to edit. Some can be undone with a lot of editing work; many cannot. The good news is they can all be avoided. You can save yourself the frustration if you know what to look for early on and can think ahead. Let's dive into the most common rookie mistakes and the corresponding photography magic tricks to help you avoid them.

Rookie Mistake: Don't Use Spotty Light

One of the most common mistakes I see my students making is shooting their portraits in spotty light. Maybe they are trying to get their subjects out of the bright sunlight, so they explore and find a place where the light seems softer. They place their subjects under some trees. That seems like a better idea, right? But actually, the light is really just patchy. There are patches of sunlight and dark coming in, and it just looks weird.

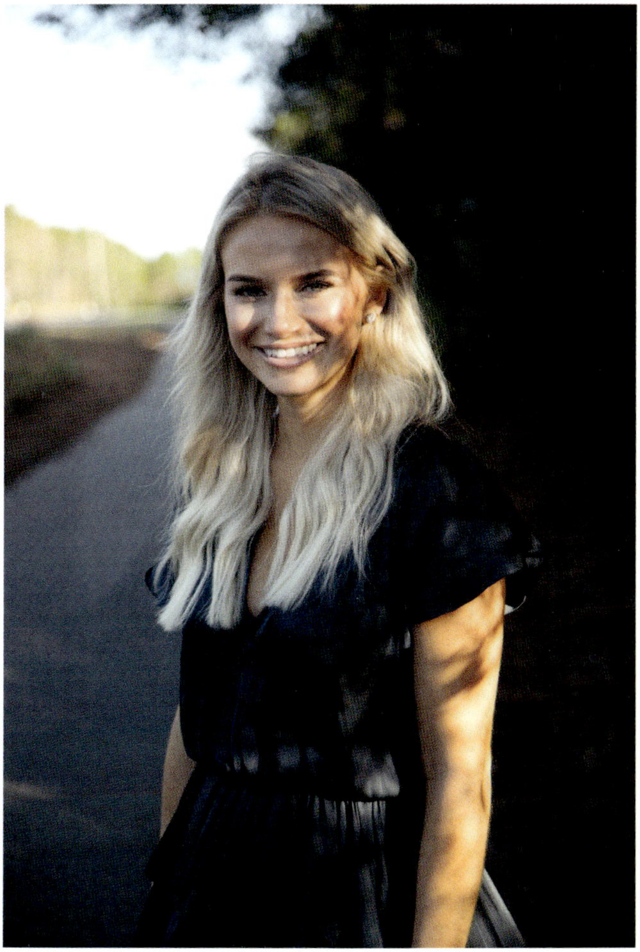

Magic Trick: Find Soft, Even Shade

It's astounding how much of a difference a few feet can make. Our model Ashley was repositioned to where there was solid shade on her face and the photos are ridiculously better. If you are in spotty light, you may just need to reposition your subject slightly to where they are in total shade. If the sun is getting low, you might have to change the direction you are shooting and place the sun behind your subject. But in this example, we were able to find a solid area of shade and still shoot in the same direction.

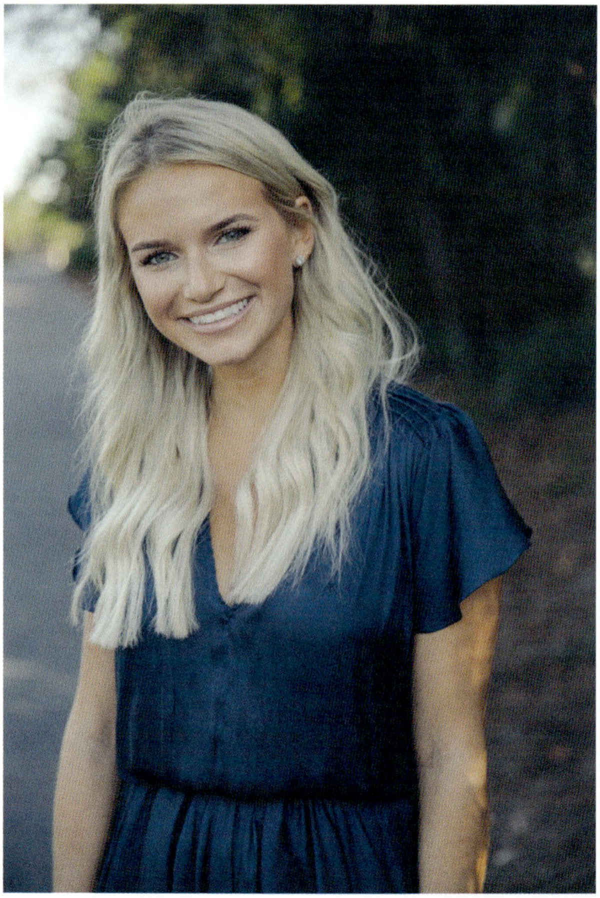

Rookie Mistake: Poles Growing Out of People's Heads

Here's an example of Ashley sitting right in front of a tree, and the tree looks like it's growing out of her head, making an awkward composition. If she had brown hair, it would be even worse.

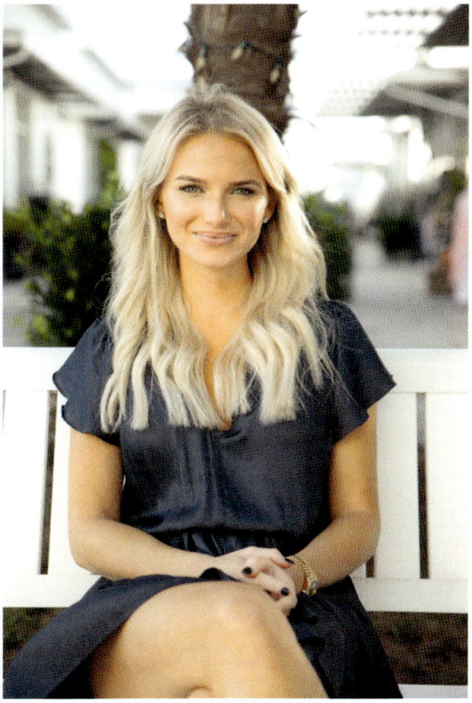

This is more common than you might realize. Poles, trees, sticks, and all kinds of pointy objects have a way of showing up in the background of our pictures, often without us realizing it. Swipe through some old photos on your phone and I bet you'll find a few. Let's say you're at a historical monument and there is a flagpole in the background; be careful you don't line your subject up with that pole. I took a *poll* and ten out of ten moms said they don't like *poles* growing out of their kids' heads in family portraits.

Magic Trick: Pivot Your Angle So Background Objects Have Negative Space Around Them

Be aware of what's going on in the background, and try not to position obnoxious background objects so they merge with your subjects. If you can't completely block out the distraction, at least give it some space so it looks separate from your subject. Empty space in a photograph is often referred to as "negative space." Consider placing your subject in a less busy part of the frame so the background doesn't distract, or it doesn't look as if an object is unnaturally protruding from your subject. Notice how Ashley is off to the side in this example. The palm tree is no longer growing straight out of her head and is not distracting anymore. The image looks intentional.

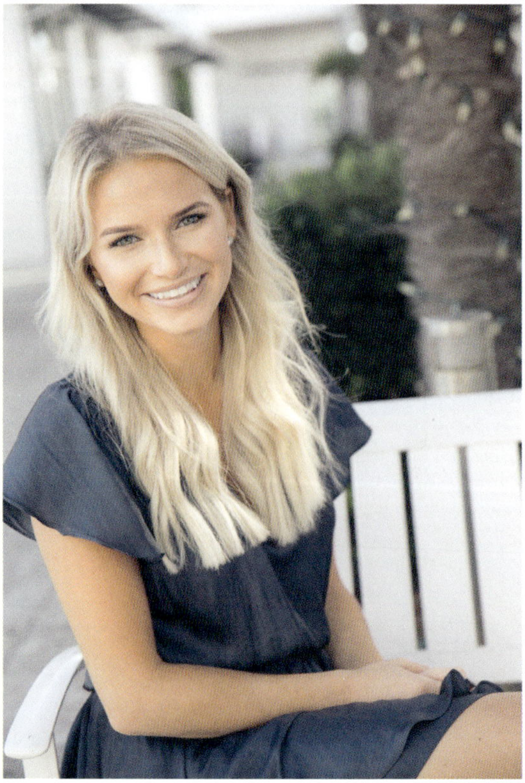

Rookie Mistake: Don't Shoot From Unflattering Angles

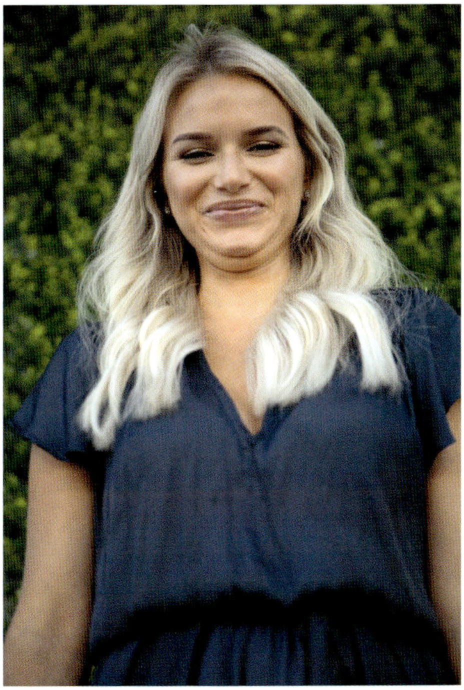

Remember the band I mentioned earlier? The band who never hired me again? Well, this is an exaggerated example of what I did wrong: I shot from a very low angle, and it made our slender model look like she had a double chin, which, in a way, was impressive to achieve because she certainly didn't. No one wants additional chins or to appear stretched out, but that's what happens when you shoot from below. I personally can be made to look like I have four chins when shot from below, so when my wife asks a stranger to take a photo of us on an iPhone, I give them strict orders not to shoot from below. Because you and I both know that the least flattering photo of yourself is the one that somehow always manages to get posted on the internet.

Magic Trick: Find Flattering Angles

For humans, a low angle is hard to make flattering and 99 percent of the time looks just plain bad. An easy trick is to shoot portraits from eye level or slightly above for the most natural and flattering angles. Often, images shot from slightly above can create a slimming effect. Keep in mind, whatever is closest to the camera will appear larger. So if you shoot from below, it will make people look like they have bigger hips, potentially thicker legs, and a tiny chest. I don't know about you, but my observation is that most humans, regardless of gender, would prefer to have a larger chest than look like they have a huge bum.

This after shot is much better. I shot it where the camera was a little higher than the height of her eyes. How much better does this look compared to the other shot? Notice you see a shadow below her chin, and it feels pleasant and natural. Nothing looks abnormally large, nothing stretched out or unnatural.

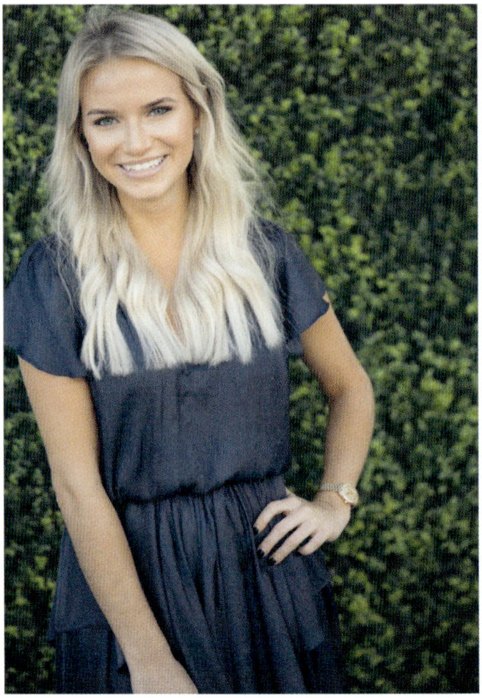

How do we learn to see these flattering angles? Here's some advice from my fellow photography mentor Rich Coleman: "Remember this three-step process: shoot, pivot, improve. Take a picture, look at the picture, pivot to change the angle, and improve the next shot. It's a simple idea. You just need to remember to do it every time, in every new location. This extra ten seconds will change your photography life."

When you follow Rich's advice, you'll start to notice the difference in angles and how they affect the feeling of your images. When you keep on pivoting and noticing the changes your pivots make, you'll see patterns. You'll start developing your style and figuring out what angles work best for you and your subjects.

Rookie Mistake: Distracting, Busy, or Unflattering Backgrounds

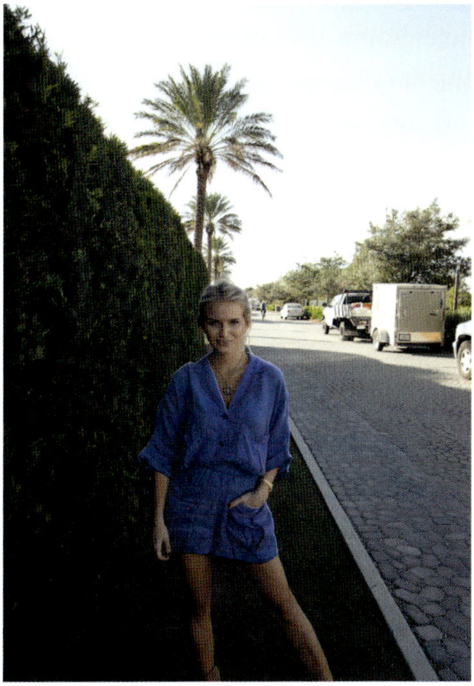

So many photos have too much going on in the background. Pretend we are on a senior portrait photo shoot. Take a look at the example shot on the previous page. There is a large trailer attached to a worker's truck, a biker, and several other parked cars. None of these background objects are crucial to the story of our graduate.

Oftentimes what is in focus will show people what's important in the image. If you leave a bunch of unimportant distractions in sharp focus, it can often take away from the subject. The truck and trailer have nothing to do with the story you're trying to tell of a senior portrait, right? Paying attention to *what* is in focus and *how much* is in focus is so important to visual storytelling. Once again, I want to be clear here: you don't always have to have a blurry background. There are no rules, remember? It's just a trick that you have available to you. Depending on the subject and the audience, you may choose to employ this tool or another one. No specific tool does the trick every time; that's why we're exploring each of these. I just want you to understand how they work and when they work. In the case of this image, it feels busy and I'm not quite sure where I should be looking. There are also a few details—the trucks in the background, the trees behind her, even the street—that don't necessarily contribute to what I want to say visually.

Magic Trick: Blur the Background and Crop

This second image has the background blurred. I also cropped so the bright truck and trailer weren't in the shot. Now the focus is only on our subject, and the background elements that were previously distracting are no longer a problem. You might be wondering, *How do you actually blur the background?* We're going to get more into that when we talk about depth of field in the next few chapters. But here's a hint: a shallow depth of field will create the blurry background.

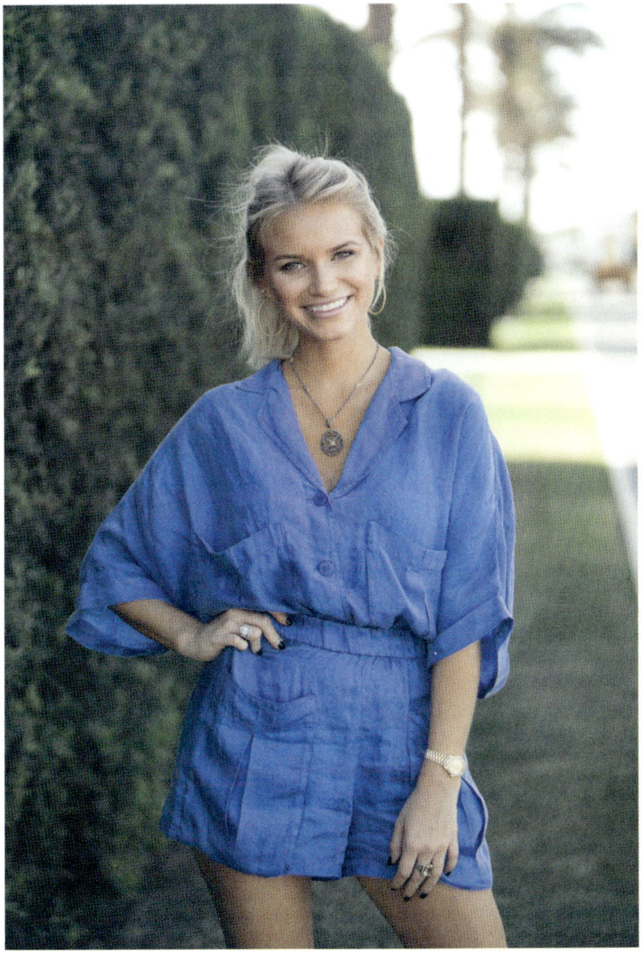

Rookie Mistake: Shooting with Sunlight Directly in Your Subject's Face

If you shoot with your subject's face in bright sunlight, we can't be friends. I'm kidding—but seriously. Direct sunlight in people's faces looks horrible 99.9 percent of the time. I know I've said there are no absolutes in photography—that's why I left room for the 0.1 percent—but this principle is pretty dang close to absolute. It's not good for two reasons: (1) the light will look horrible, and (2) your subject will be fighting to keep their eyes open and won't be able to relax their face. So just don't do it. You won't like fighting the harsh light, and your subjects will be temporarily blind and will probably try to kick you in the shin at the next opportunity.

I placed my friend Abbey in the bright sunlight and she couldn't even open her eyes. We have bright spots and dark shadows and just an awful-looking image. Friends don't let friends do drugs . . . or shoot people's faces in bright sunlight.

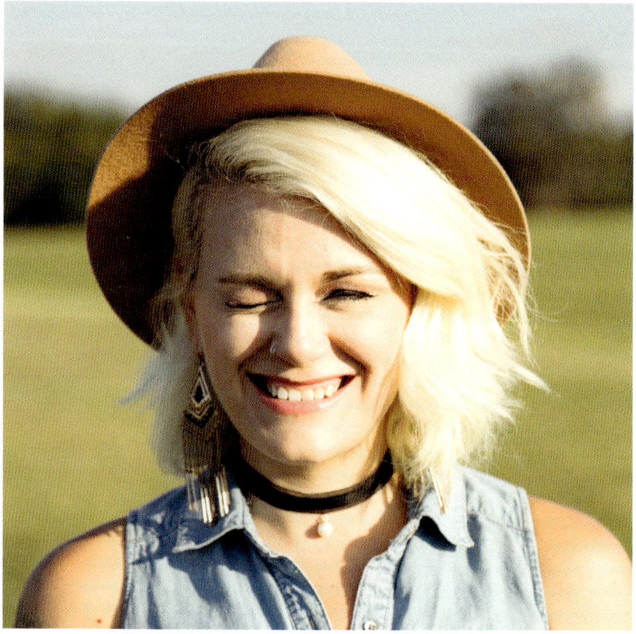

Magic Trick: Shoot Backlit or Find Soft, Even Light

So how do you shoot in bright sunlight, then? The first thing is, don't shoot outdoor portraits while the sun is at high noon. Ideally you want to wait until the last few hours of the day or the first few hours of the morning. Once the sun is no longer straight overhead, shoot your subjects backlit. Position your subjects between you and the sun, then make the brightness on their faces look correct to you. This could be tricky to do when shooting in an automatic mode because, well, auto mode is lame. In fact, I like to refer to it as the devil. But this trick is easy to do when you're shooting in manual exposure mode. Don't freak out now, because I'm going to break down manual exposure step-by-step in the next chapter.

Check out how natural and pleasant this image feels. We have a correct exposure on our subject's face, and we have the sun hitting the back of her head instead of the front. This causes a nice rim of light on her head and shoulders, and nice, soft light filling in on the front of her face and body. If it's sunny out, shoot people in the face, backlit. Just do it.

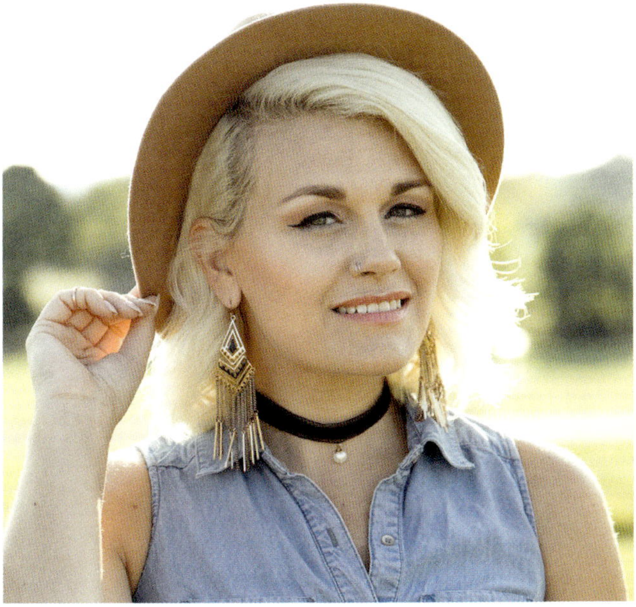

Rookie Mistake: Overexposing the Highlights of Your Landscape Images

Overexposing the highlights of an image—or a bright spot in a photograph, like the sky or light skin tones—is another common mistake I've made many times and see my students make often. Be careful not to shoot the image too bright so the highlights don't get recorded in your shot as completely white. I'll teach you how to take manual control of your camera in the following chapters. If you take a picture and the highlights of your image are recorded as completely white, that area is overexposed. Once the bright parts of the image have been overexposed, the information in the details of those bright spots is gone. Take a look at this landscape image of my favorite vineyard, Arrington Vineyards. The sky is completely blown out. It's overexposed, and all the details in the sky are gone forever. There is no way to bring those details back with editing—unless you Photoshop a fake sky, of course.

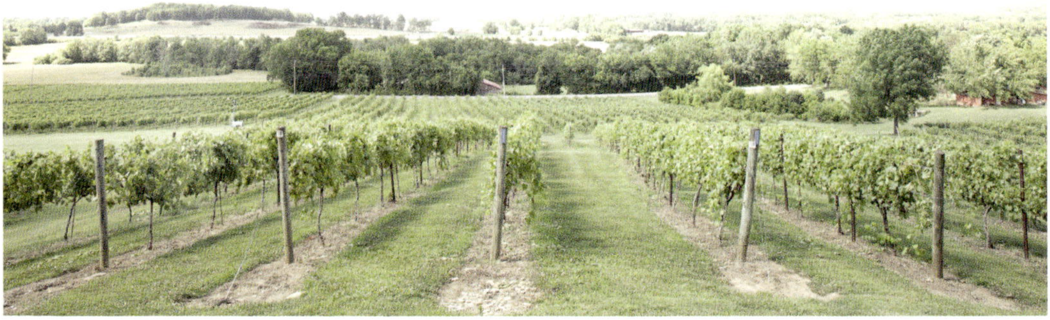

When you view the image on the screen, edit it, or even try to print the picture, the overexposed areas just look like plain old white because there's simply no information there. You have to be careful not to overexpose the highlights, especially when you are shooting fair-skinned people and bright skies. You will lose those details and essentially ruin the photo. More often than not, our cameras can't capture all the details the way we see them with our God-given eyes. We can see all the details in the highlights and the shadows at the same time. Our cameras, by default, can't see what we can see. But this is why we edit (which we are going to learn about in a later chapter). Editing, of course, has its limitations. You can't successfully darken an image that is too bright, but you can brighten an image that is a little too dark, which brings me to our next magic trick.

Magic Trick: Expose Your Images for the Sky in Landscape Images

Often when you are shooting you have to choose between whether the bright or dark part of your image looks correct. This means whether the highlights in the sky look great or the shadows beneath the horizon do. Here's the thing: you have to choose what to expose for. Because when you are shooting, you can't pick two brightnesses. You can only choose one, so here's the trick: expose your images for the bright part. Make the brightness look correct for the brightest part of your image, or in this case the sky.

Here's why: within reason, you can brighten the dark parts of an image. But if an image gets too bright, you *cannot* darken, or bring back the details of the bright parts of your image that have been recorded as all white (overexposed highlights).

Here's a little rhyme I came up with just for you:

Image too bright? Editing fright!
Image a little dark? A walk in the park!

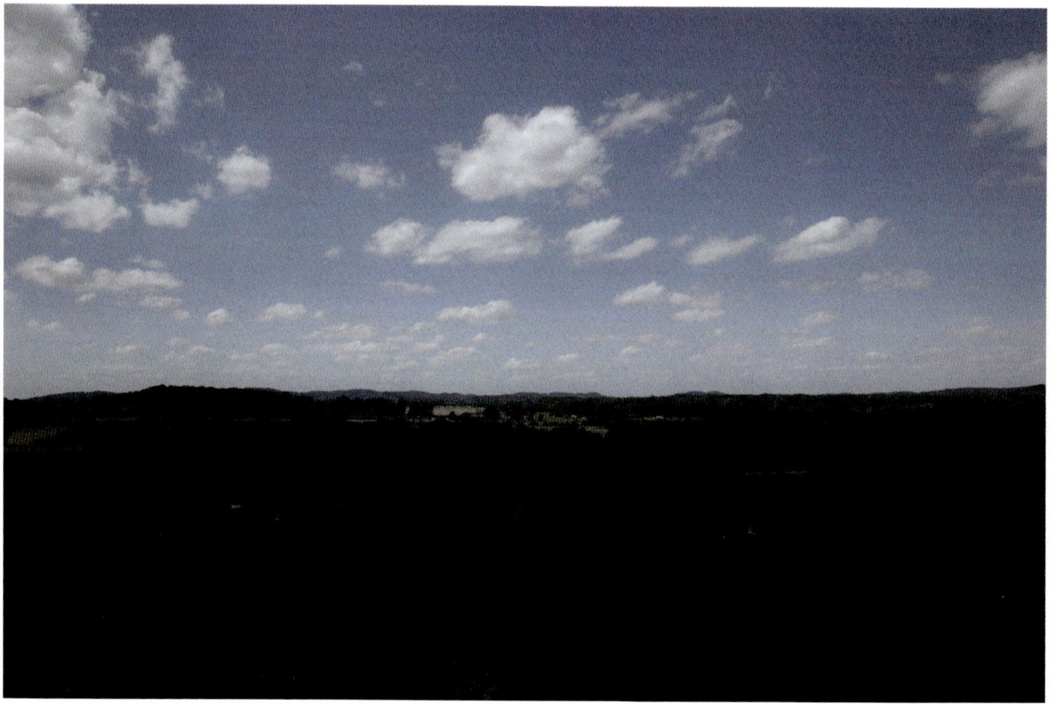

Take a look at this final edit of the image where the sky looks correct but the vines look too dark. In the editing process you can easily brighten up the areas of the image that are a little too dark and make the entire image pop. In a later chapter I'll share more on this, including how to use editing to re-create the emotion you are trying to capture with a photo.

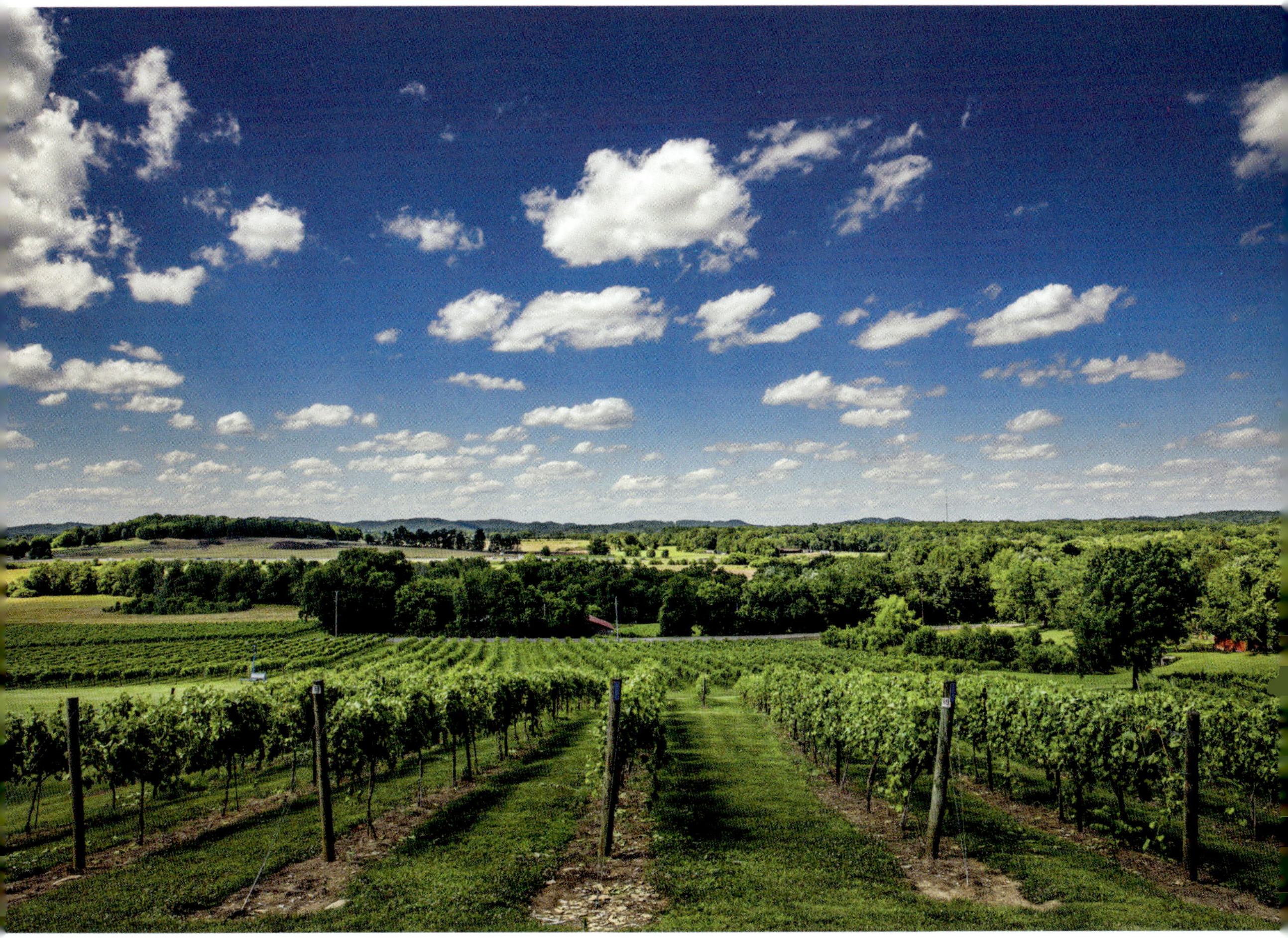

In summary, it's better to shoot your image slightly too dark than too bright. Dark is (mostly) fixable. Bright is not.

Rookie Mistake: No Separation Between Subject and Background Objects

I cannot tell you the number of times I see a photo of a girl next to the trunk of a tree and I have to wonder why. What's the point? "Here's a girl and some bark." Why? It's boring, distracting. There is no story here. If you like trees, show the tree in the background. Often you can't even tell what kind of tree it is in the picture. I have no idea what is supposed to be happening in the picture below. Separate the girl and the tree, and let them each be free. If you love trees (I mean, who doesn't?) it can seem counterintuitive to separate the girl from the tree, but believe me, that's exactly what needs to happen.

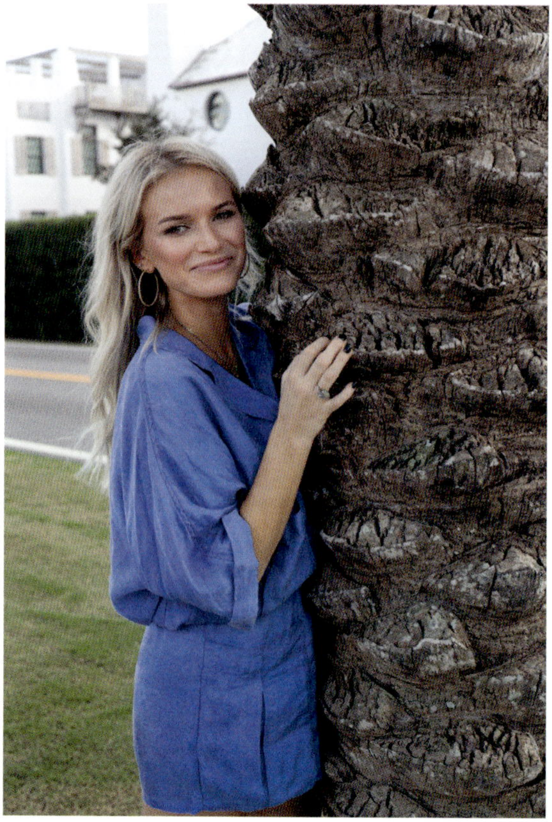

Magic Trick: Create Separation Between Your Subject and the Background Objects

Creating distance and separation between our subjects and the details of the environment gives context to the location. After we separate the model from the tree, we have the context that she is in a warm environment with palm trees. Now we are showing more of what makes a palm tree beautiful—the top of the tree—not just an ugly part of the trunk. To be a good storyteller, help your viewer understand the setting. Sometimes all you need is a little separation from your crazy kids, er . . . I mean from the background (sorry, was in the middle of potty training a toddler when writing this book).

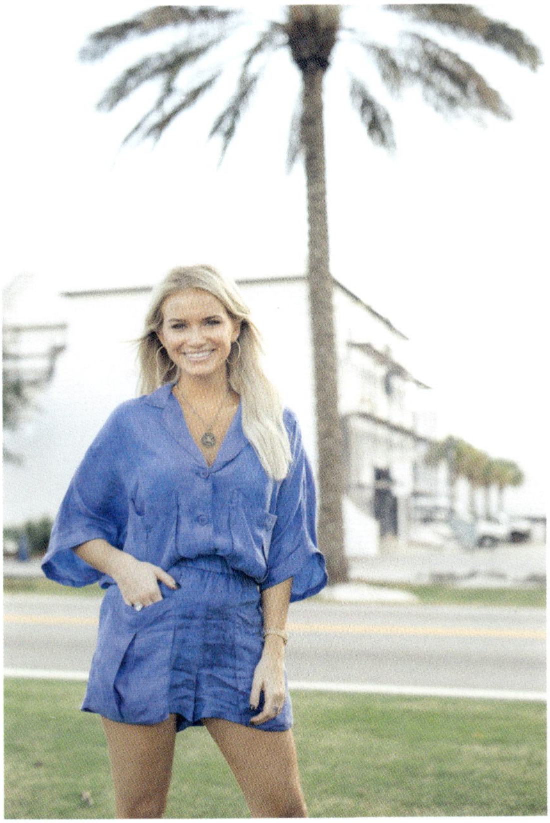

Rookie Mistake: No Catchlight from Raccoon Eyes (and Harsh Indoor Lighting)

What is a catchlight? It's where you can see someone's eyes lit clearly and see the twinkle in them. Typically this is a reflection or bright spot in the pupil. If a portrait does not have a catchlight, it generally is not as appealing.

I see so many of my rookie students shooting their photos right below a harsh spotlight indoors. Their subjects' faces are in just plain old bad lighting indoors. This harsh lighting takes away the catchlight in your subject's eyes, which is crucial to making your portraits look professional.

Take a look at this image of my daughter Rose. We're indoors and the light is mostly behind her. There isn't enough light hitting her face. You can't really see her eyes that well, either. Shooting your photos like this screams amateur hour.

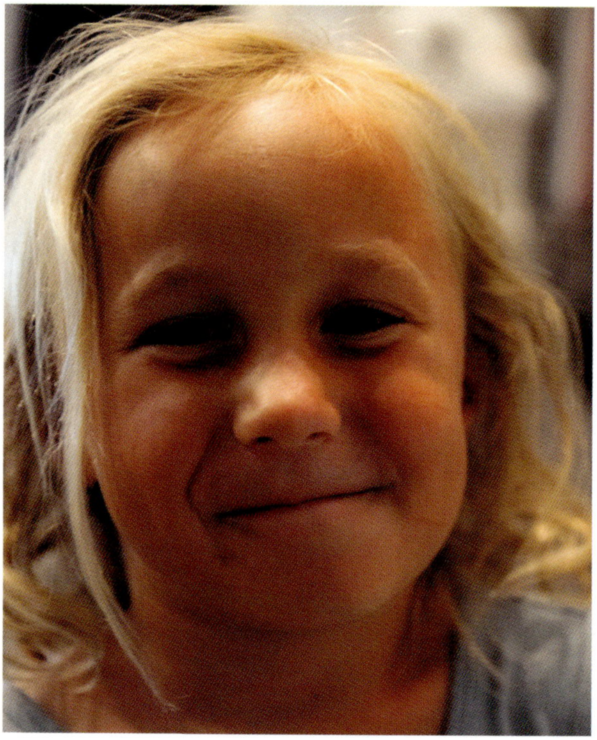

Magic Trick: Find Good Catchlight from Soft Window Light

Here is Rose, ten feet away from the previous location, but facing the incoming soft light from a window.

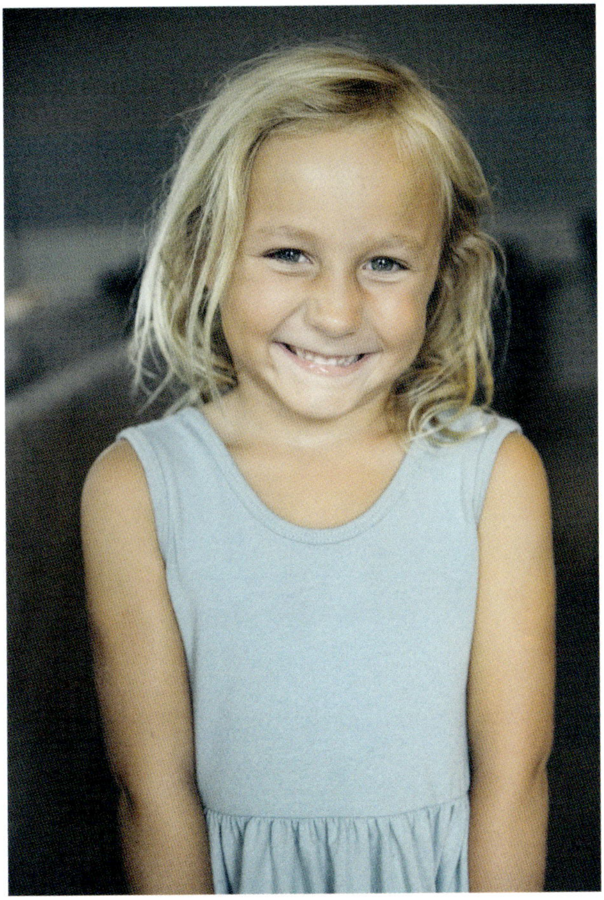

There is beautiful soft light from the window hitting her face and providing a nice catchlight. Notice the twinkle in her eyes? It grabs your attention, doesn't it? Always look for the catchlight or your portraits will look amateurish and feel dull.

Rookie Mistake: Motion Blur (You Don't Need a New Camera, Karen!)

"I need a new camera because mine takes bad photos." *False!* Your camera isn't taking bad photos. I hate to break it to you, but the photographer is the problem. We're going to learn about controlling your camera in manual mode in the next chapter, but what I want you to understand is that often, blurry images like this happen because the photographer is not taking proper manual control. When you learn how to control your camera manually, you'll learn about shutter speed. A fast shutter speed is what freezes motion. And if you let your camera shoot in automatic mode, you'll find a couple of major mistakes caused by shutter speed. The motion can get blurred in your photos, and you'll often get what's called "camera shake."

If you don't shoot at a fast enough shutter speed, then you will have a blurry photo simply because humans can't hold the camera steady enough to capture a crisp photo.

This image of my daughter Juliet on her scooter has both issues at the same time. I was shooting at a slow shutter speed (1/25 of a second), so you are seeing her motion blurred. And if you notice the rest of the image, it's shaky as well. The entire image would be crisp if shot at a fast enough shutter speed to freeze the motion of her scooting and prevent my hands from physically shaking the camera.

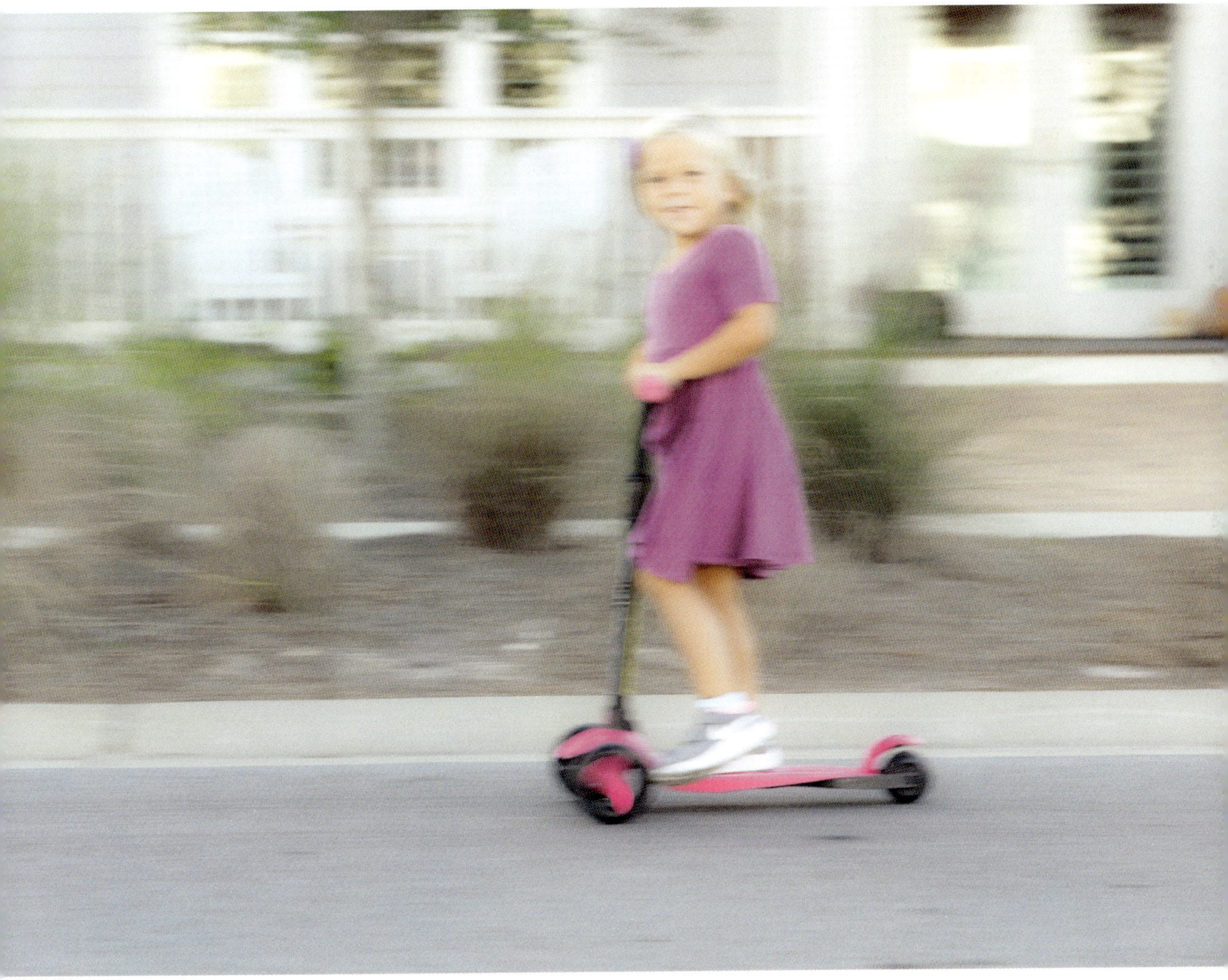

Magic Trick: Freeze Motion with a Fast Shutter Speed

A lot of newbie photographer problems can be solved by simply shooting at a faster shutter speed. As I said, we're going to dive deep into controlling your camera manually later, and I'll teach you all about shutter speed. But when you shoot the exact same shot with a fast shutter speed, you'll freeze the action and prevent any motion blur from your subjects and camera shake from the photographer. Take a look at this image of Juliet shot at the fast shutter speed of 1/1250 of a second. Now that's a lot better, right?

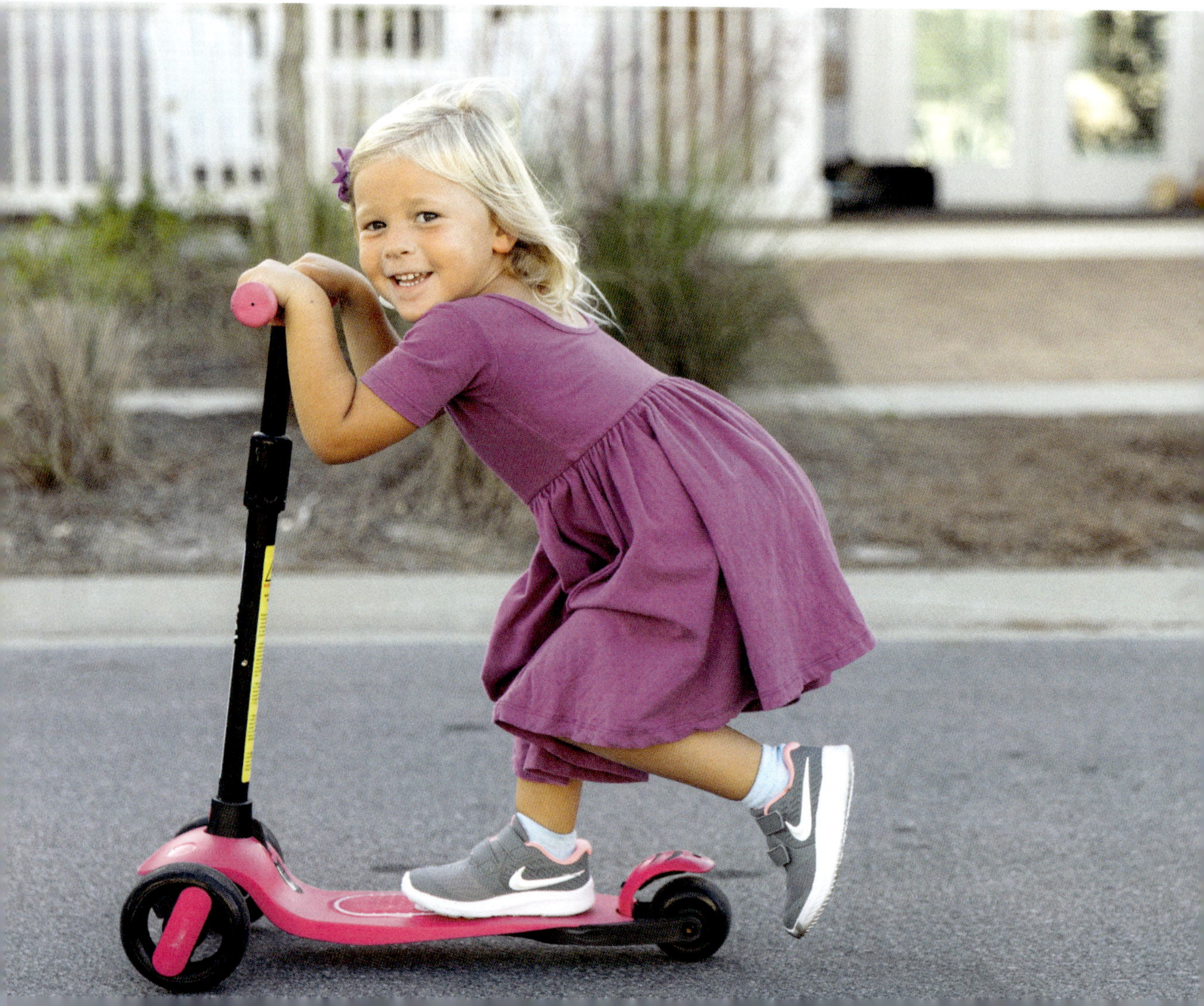

Shoot Like a Pro

Now that we've covered the basics in terms of what it takes to see like a photographer, it's time to pick up your camera and start shooting like one. Are you ready to dive in, learn how to master your camera in manual mode, and start capturing the images you see in your head? It takes work and commitment, but if you've come this far, well, by golly, keep reading. The next section is going to rock your socks off.

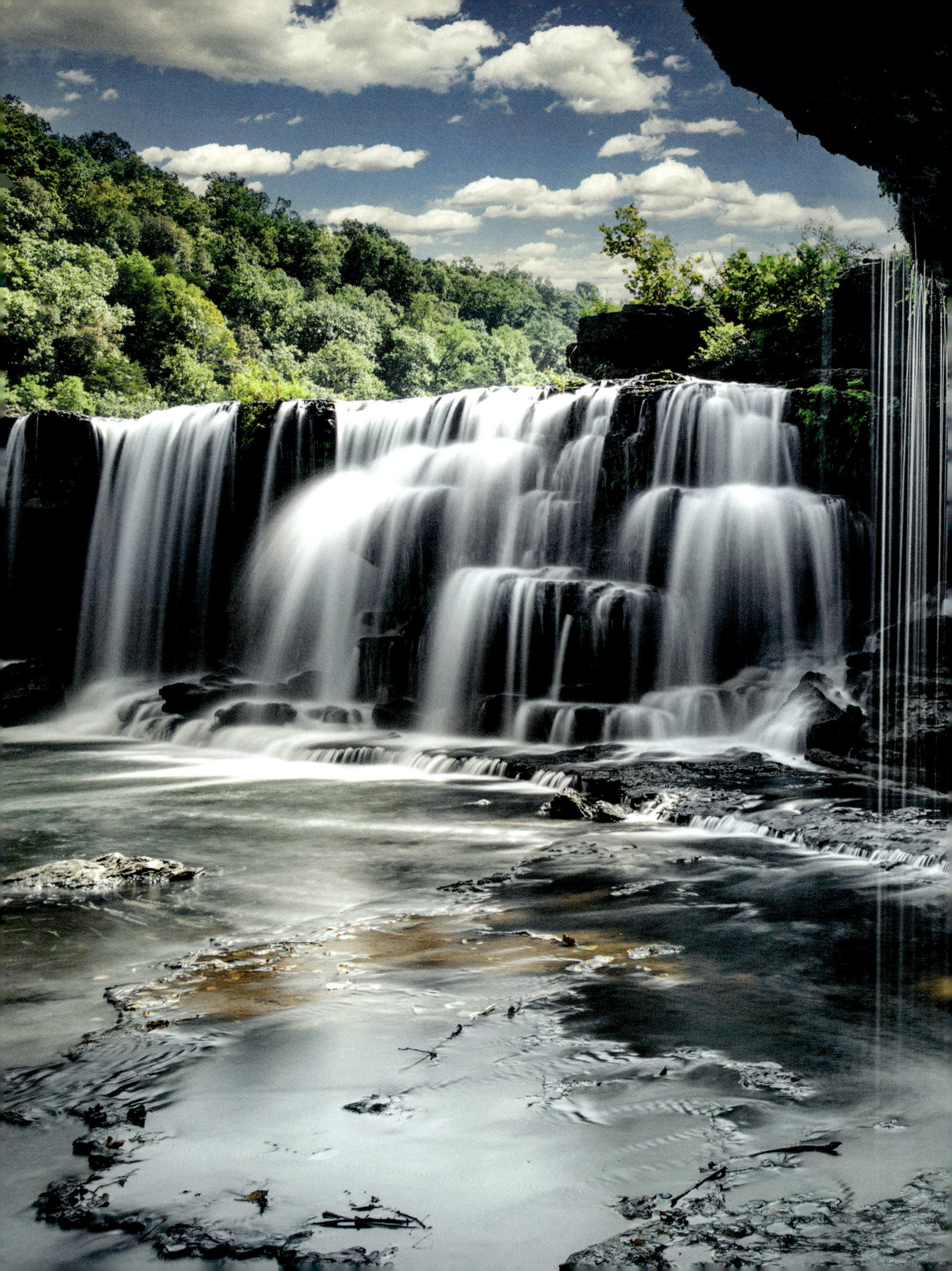

PART 2

SHOOT

This part is all about understanding your camera. If you picked up this book to learn how to control your camera, this is the content you were hoping for. But without learning to see first, without understanding the storytelling elements that make up a photograph, the rest won't get you where you want to go. Here, we will dive into shooting in manual mode and how to properly use aperture, shutter speed, and ISO. Don't be intimidated if these terms are new or mysterious to you. With a few simple explanations and illustrations, along with a little practice, all this seemingly technical jargon can become second nature.

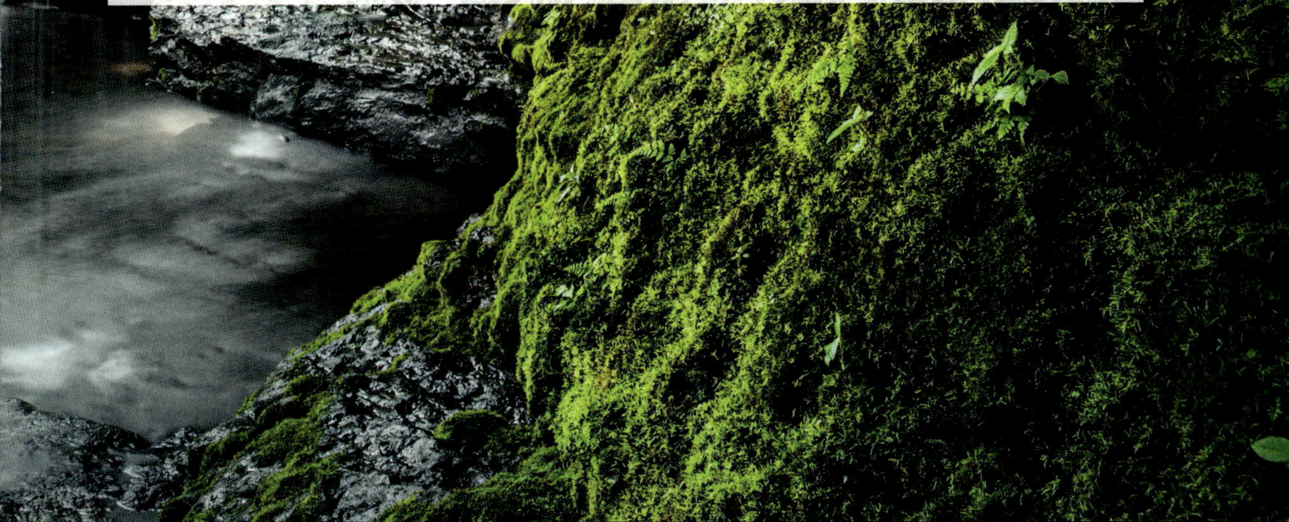

CHAPTER 6

Master Your Camera: Shooting in Manual Mode

AFTER WE LEARN TO SEE LIKE A PRO, NEXT WE NEED TO LEARN TO SHOOT like a pro. But you might be saying, "Whoa, whoa. Wait a second, Davey Boy. I don't know if I want to be a pro photographer yet. I just want to have fun with my camera." That's fine. Keep reading anyway. Because if you want to capture powerful stories using the magic tricks from the previous chapter and shooting the images you see in your head, you need to control your camera and shoot as a professional would. Which means shooting in manual mode. So forget about earning money with photos for a minute; this chapter is about quality of work. Of course, when we do great work, the money will follow, but more on that later. This is about excellence.

You may be thinking, *Why can't I shoot in automatic mode?*

Because in auto mode, your camera is guessing! As amazing as cameras are these days, they still can't read your mind. Your camera is not hard-wired into your brain (yet), and it has no idea what you want your photo to look like. Auto mode is like bowling with bumpers up. Not only is it for toddlers (cheater!), but you never know what you're going to get. You don't know how many pins you're going to knock down. You might get at least one pin knocked down, but your results are going to vary widely when your bowling ball is bouncing all around. There's hardly any strategy, just luck.

What, specifically, could get screwed up from shooting in auto mode? Well, there are three massively important factors that you do not want your camera guessing for you.

1. Your camera doesn't know what brightness you want.

You may think you want a darker silhouette, like this moment I captured of my pregnant wife and my sons at sunset.

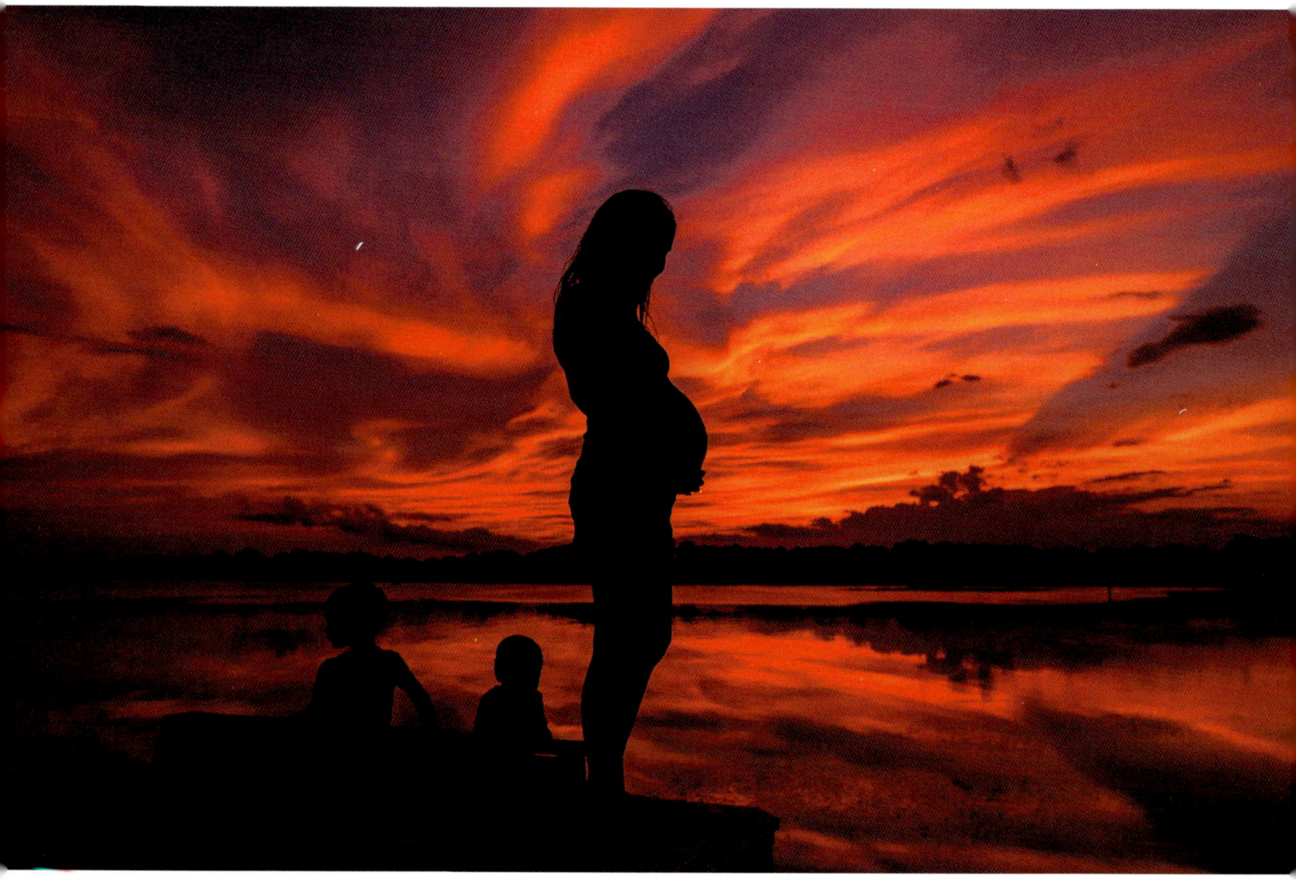

Or you may want to create a bright and airy image like this shot my wife took of me and my firstborn son.

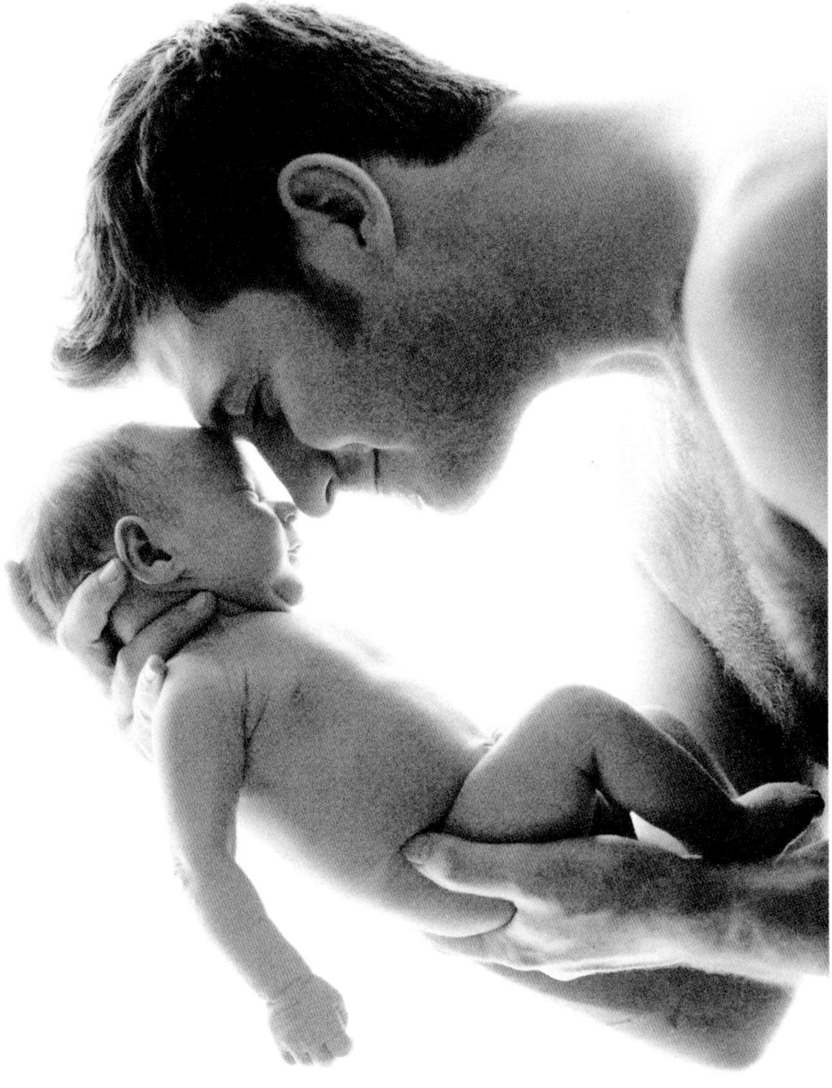

Your camera has no idea what you want. And the frustrating thing is, your camera wouldn't choose either of these options. It would create an average of the light in between and make for potentially very blah images. It would have caused us to totally miss out on the opportunity to capture the feeling in these two important moments in our family's story. You have to decide what kind of story you want as the photographer and communicate those choices to the camera by making selections in manual mode. In other words, you've got to show this machine who's the boss.

2. Your camera doesn't know how much distance you want in focus.

You may want to have everything in focus, like this landscape photo I shot in the Swiss Alps.

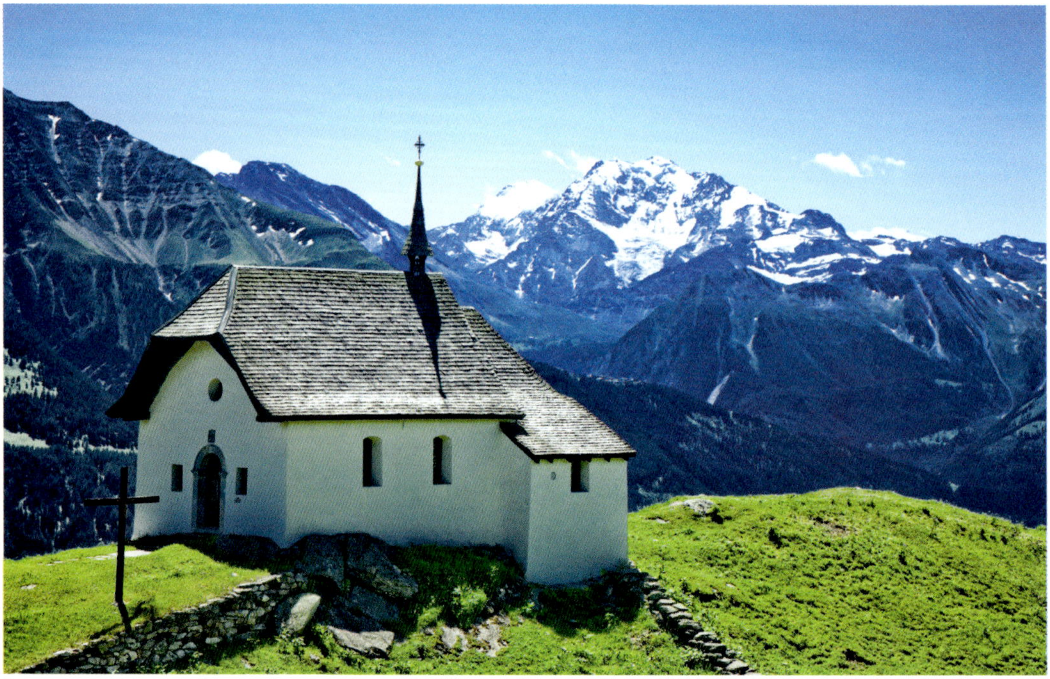

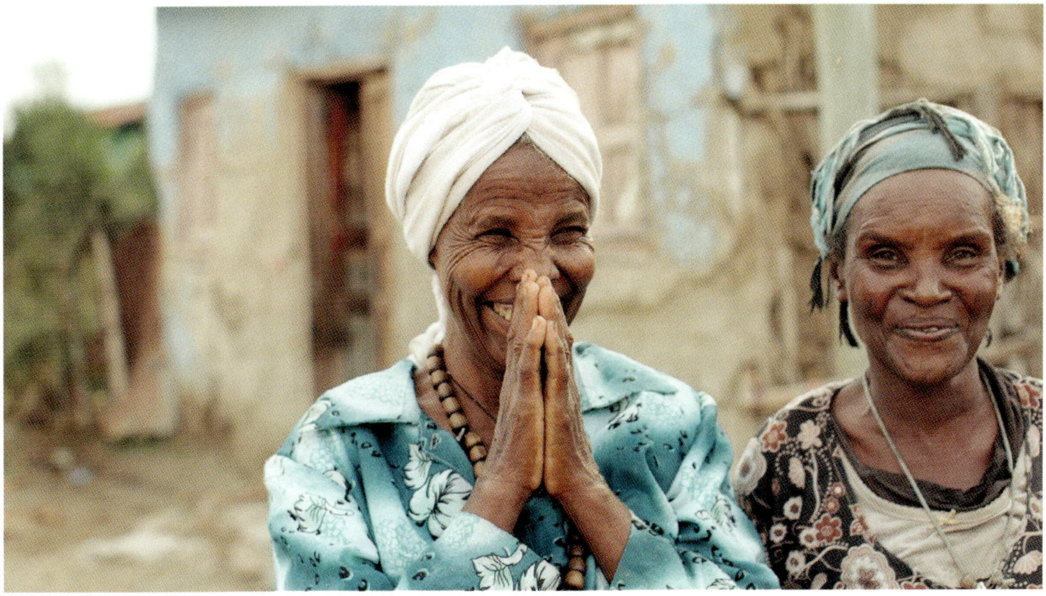

Or you may want to focus only on the smiling face of the matriarch of an Ethiopian family but have the background beautifully blurred to remove any distractions.

3. Your camera doesn't know if you want to freeze motion or show it.

You may want to shoot a fast shutter speed and freeze the motion of individual water droplets.

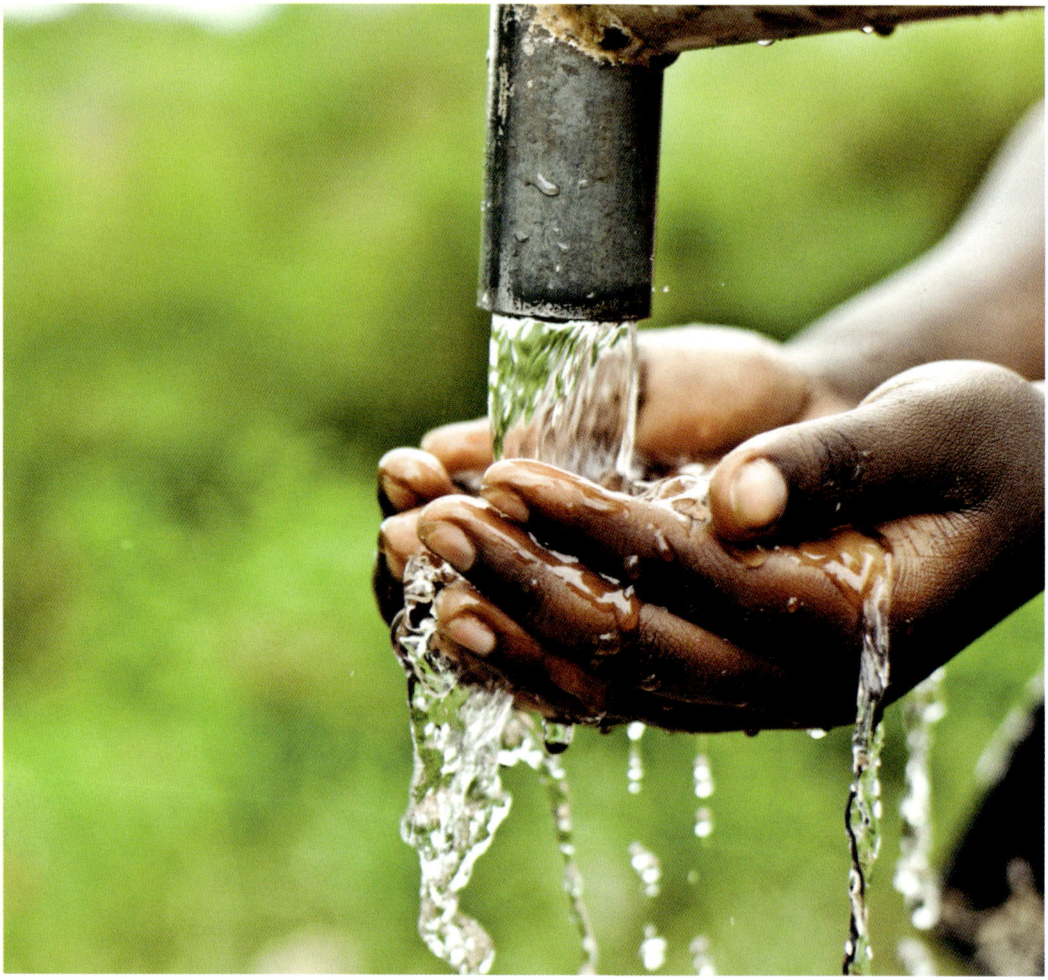

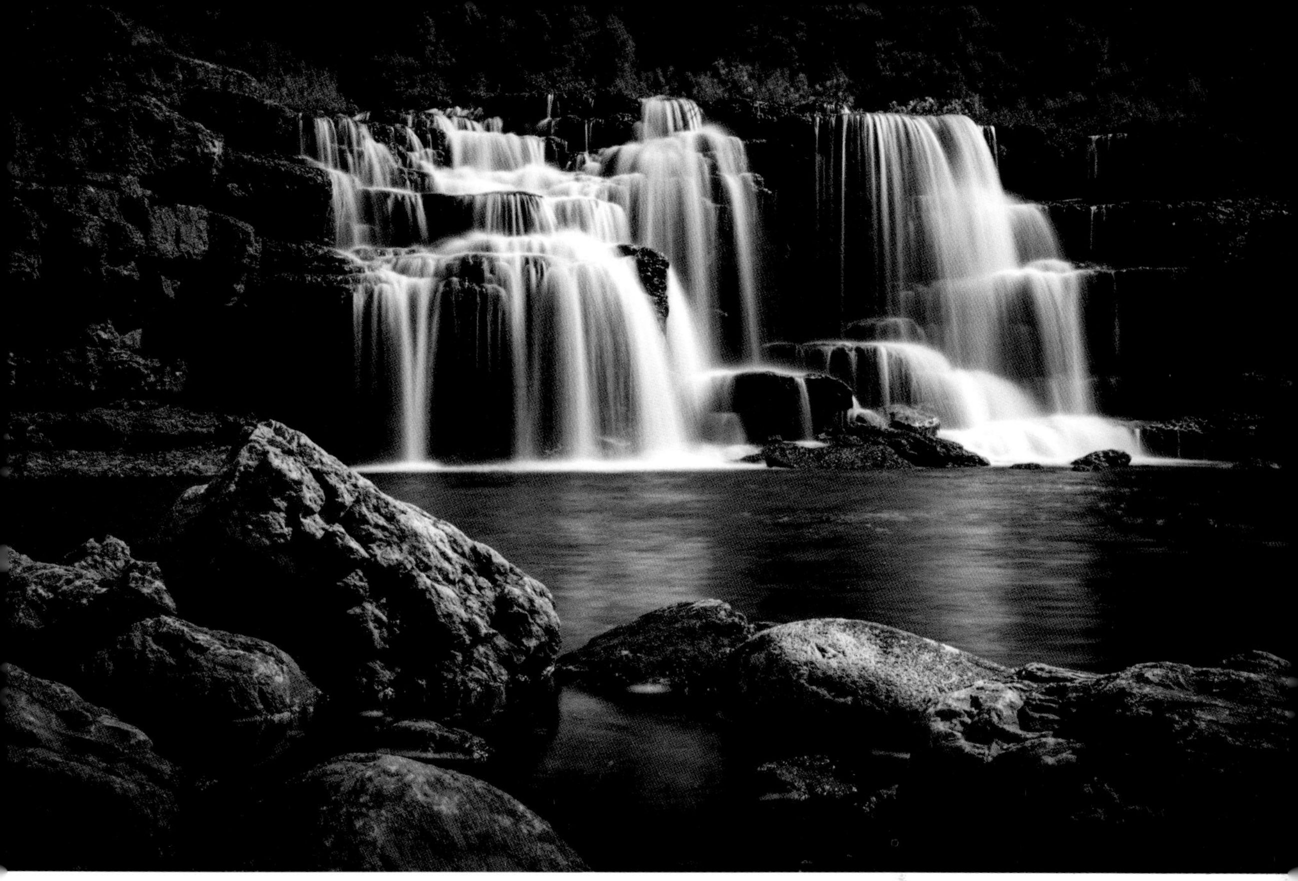

But then again, you may want to allow the motion of the waterfall to be flowing through your image.

Guess what? Your camera can't tap into the flow of your thoughts and it certainly can't guess this correctly for you. Simply put, again, auto mode is the devil. I already told you this was my motto. So say it out loud with me: "Auto mode is the devil." There. We said it! I hate auto mode, and you'll learn to hate it too.

What is the solution to all your camera problems? It's learning how to master your camera. It's learning to shoot like a pro photographer. It's learning to shoot in that "not as scary as you think" manual exposure mode.

You must learn to take manual control of your camera if you want to consistently take the world-class images you see in your mind.

You might be thinking, *Okay, I'm warming up to that idea now, David. So how do I shoot in manual exposure mode?* Great question. It all starts with learning about how to get a correct exposure.

What is a correct exposure?

What do we mean when we say "exposure"? That's a technical term we've tossed around already, but let's get very clear about it: a correct exposure is an image that's not too bright and not too dark based on what the photographer thinks it should be. Meaning, the correct exposure or brightness of an image is subjective to the individual photographer of a particular image. A "correct" exposure is completely subjective to you. All photographers will see images in their minds differently.

A correct exposure is when an image is

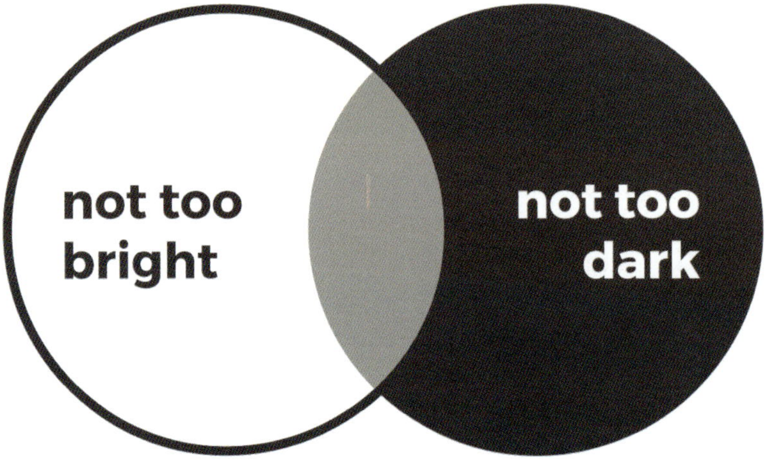

based on what the photographer thinks.

The next two images were lit similarly. Both are backlit, meaning the main source of light is coming from behind the subjects. In the first image, the subjects are silhouetted. Some people may say the image has a dark exposure or is underexposed, but as the photographer, it is exactly the way I wanted it to be.

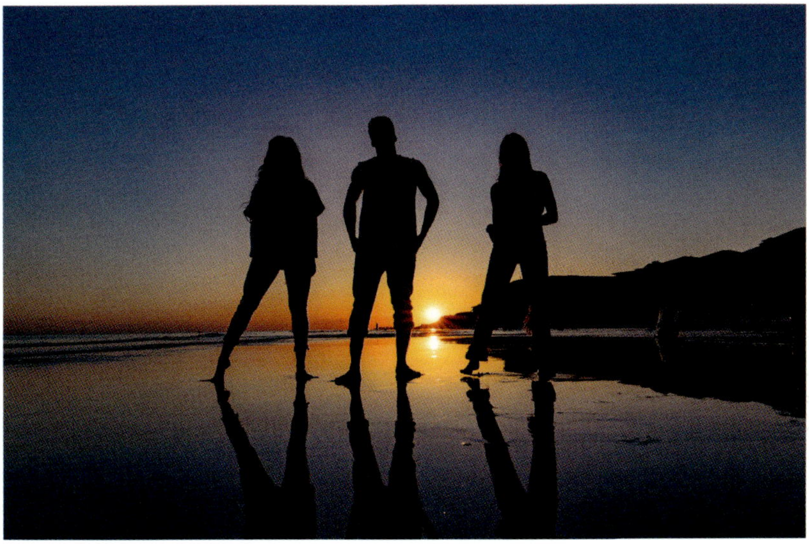

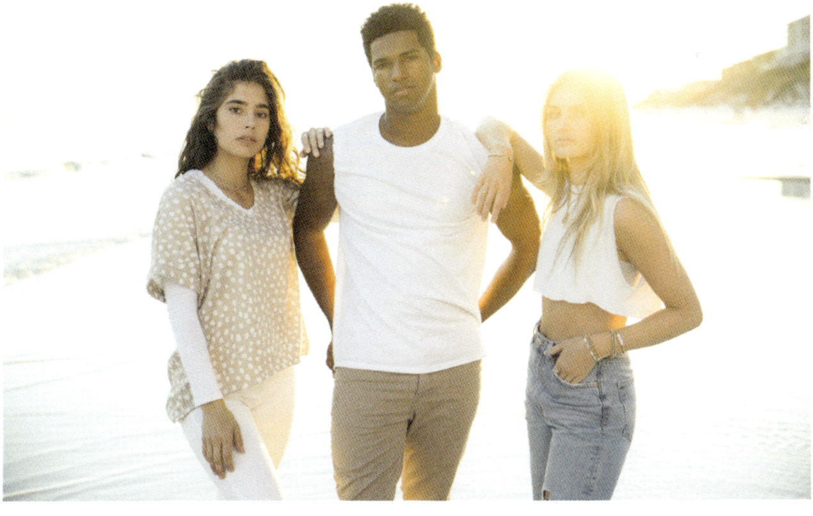

Take a look at this second backlit image. The exposure is super bright and the background is blown out, which means the details are gone in the highlights of the image. But this isn't a problem in this scenario because it's exactly how I intended it to be. And it turned out great.

A correct exposure is the correct brightness, but "correct" is subjective to the way the photographer intends it to be. You decide what correct means.

But how do I use manual mode to get a correct exposure? First, you need to understand how your camera works and how your camera records light.

How does your camera work, anyway?

Your camera works just like a water faucet. You can grab the handle or knob and manually control how much water flows out. You do this by controlling two factors: how long the water flows and the size of the hole the water flows through.

With a water faucet, you fill up a drinking glass with the water, but with a camera, you fill up a photograph with light. Think of your camera as a "light faucet" and a photograph as a container to catch the light.

Imagine you fill up glass A with a blast of water coming out of the faucet. The glass fills up with water super fast because you allow the faucet to flow wide open with the largest possible hole the water could flow through. The water fills the glass so quickly you have to be careful not to leave the faucet open for too long or the glass would overflow. But as long as you shut the faucet off at the perfect time, you'll have a sufficiently full glass of water.

Now, conversely, imagine you fill up glass B with a slow trickle of water. It might be painfully slow. But if you're patient enough, you would eventually fill up that glass with a slow drip. You're only opening a very small hole in the faucet for water to drip through, but you're allowing the faucet to stay open for a very long duration of time to compensate for the tiny opening.

You fill glass A with a blast of water | **You fill glass B with a slow trickle**

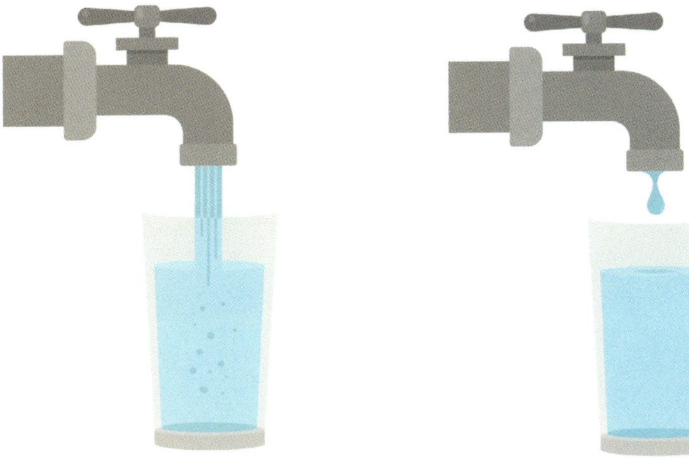

So now we have two identically full glasses of water: glass A and glass B.

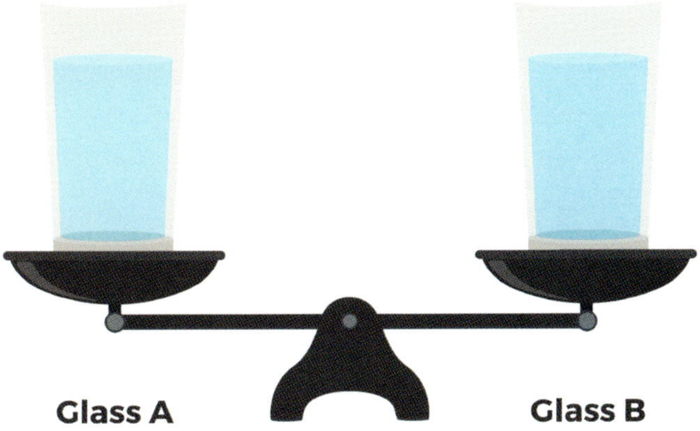

These glasses were filled up differently. One was filled quickly and the other was filled very slowly. But at the end of the day, there are two identically full glasses of water.

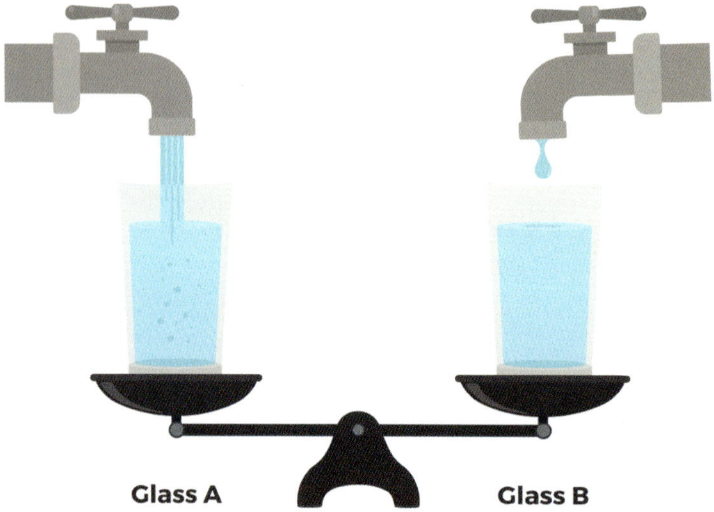

To expand on this idea, you could fill up your glasses of water with infinite combinations of the duration of time and the size variation of the hole the water is flowing through in your faucet. You could have a medium-sized opening in the faucet, which would require a medium amount of time to fill up the glass. The point is, as long as you stop the water faucet at the appropriate time and don't let it overflow or be under-filled, then it will be a sufficiently full glass of water.

Your camera works the exact same way as a water faucet.

You could fill up your photograph with a full blast of light, or fill it up with a slow trickle of light. The important thing is that you get the correct amount of light in your photograph. Not too much or too little.

If you let too much water fill your cup, it will overflow. The photography equivalent is if you let too much light fill your photograph, it will be overexposed, meaning too bright.

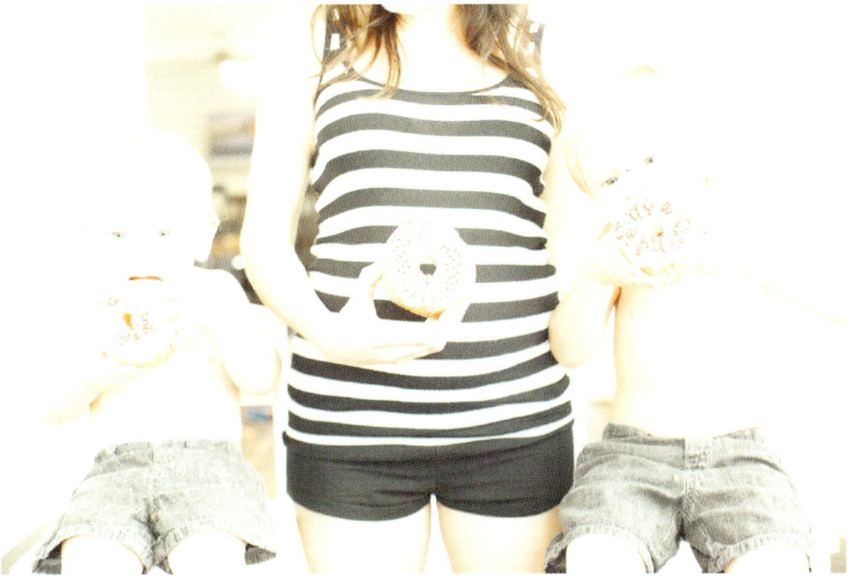

Likewise, if you don't let enough light fill your photograph, then your photo would be underexposed, which means your image would be too dark.

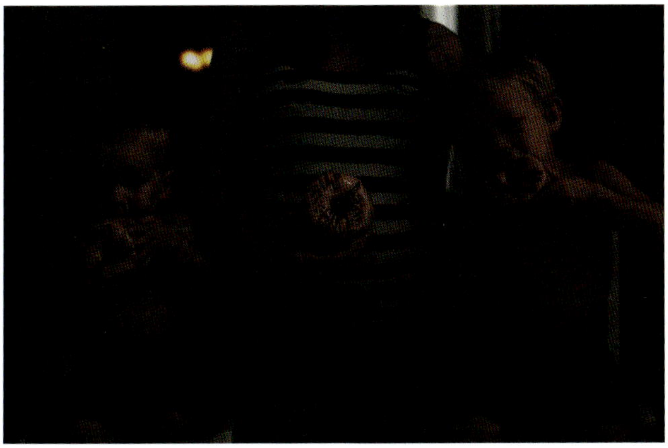

In my opinion, a correctly light-filled photograph would look like this:

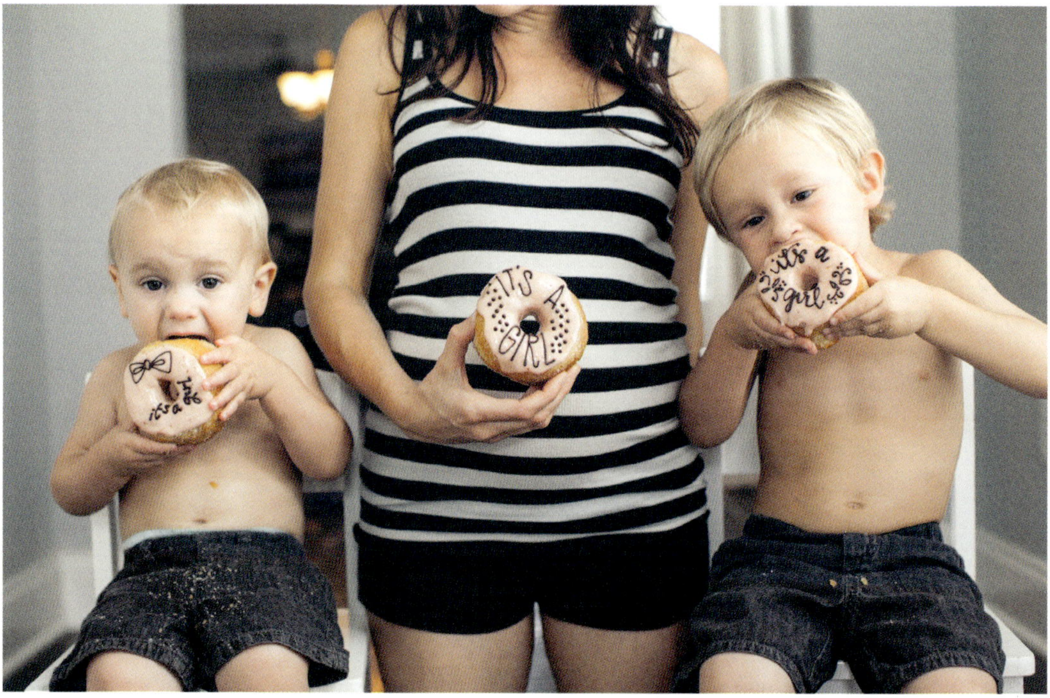

How does your camera record light?

All camera setups have three crucial parts in them to record light, regardless of which type of camera or camera brand they are. It doesn't matter if it's an old-school film camera, an iPhone, a DSLR (Digital Single Lens Reflex) camera, or a fancy new mirrorless camera, light is always recorded in a similar way.

1. FILM OR DIGITAL IMAGE SENSOR

The first component is the digital image sensor. The light is captured and recorded on the image sensor. This used to be film, but most photographers in the industry have stopped developing photos in a darkroom. Your image sensor is what is responsible for collecting the light. It is just like an empty water glass. Every time you click the button on your camera to take a picture, your image starts off completely empty. You want your camera's sensor to capture just the right amount of light to achieve the desired brightness in your photograph. The image sensor resets to empty in between each click of the button. It's your job as the photographer to fill it up correctly each time. And of course every lighting situation is different.

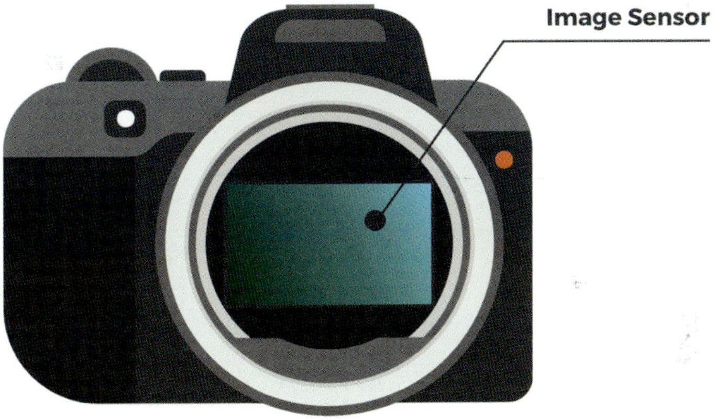

2. TIME

The second component is a shutter curtain. This is like a door or curtain immediately in front of your image sensor that protects it from any light while it's closed. You can control when the curtain opens and for how long it is open. No light will record on the sensor unless the shutter curtain is open. This means that your "water glass" stays empty until the shutter curtain is open. So while it is open, your image sensor is filling up with light. Just like controlling the timing of a water faucet, you can control the duration of time your shutter curtain is open. This is called the *shutter speed*.

Shutter speed is the amount of time you expose light to your image sensor.

Of course, you can control whether your shutter speed is fast or slow or somewhere in between. It's all up to you. And if you think about it, the longer you leave your shutter curtain open, the more light will seep into your image sensor.

Longer amount of time = more light
Shorter amount of time = less light

As a side note, while most cameras have a shutter curtain that physically goes up and down, some digital cameras do not. These cameras simply start and stop recording light for a set amount of time.

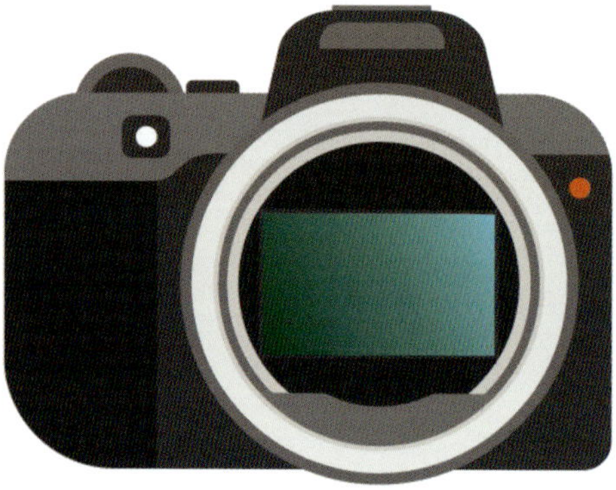

THE SHUTTER IS OPEN
The sensor is exposed to light.

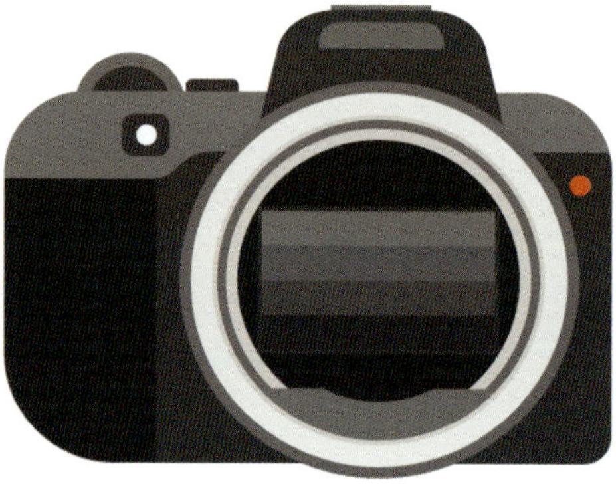

THE SHUTTER IS CLOSED
It's like a door; you can control how long it's open.

▶ Visit PhotoMentorship.com/LTS to view a list of exact gear I recommend.

3. HOLE

The third component in every camera setup is a hole in the lens that lets the light seep through. This is different from the shutter curtain. This hole is always in your lens and is right in front of the shutter curtain. It's the first thing the light has to get through on its journey to the image sensor. With most camera systems, you can control the size of the hole in your lens that the light is coming through. You could make it a tiny pinhole and barely let any light trickle through, or you could open the hole as wide as it goes and let light blast through. This hole inside your lens is called the *aperture*.

Aperture is a variable-sized hole in your lens that lets light into your camera.
Larger hole = more light
Smaller hole = less light

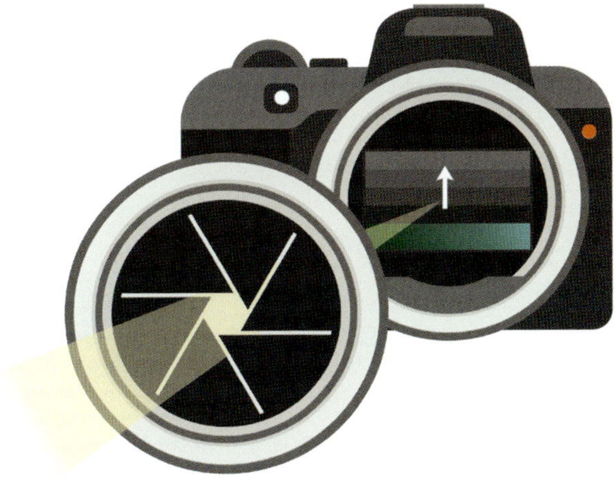

Light comes through the aperture in the lens and the shutter curtain opens to reveal the image sensor.

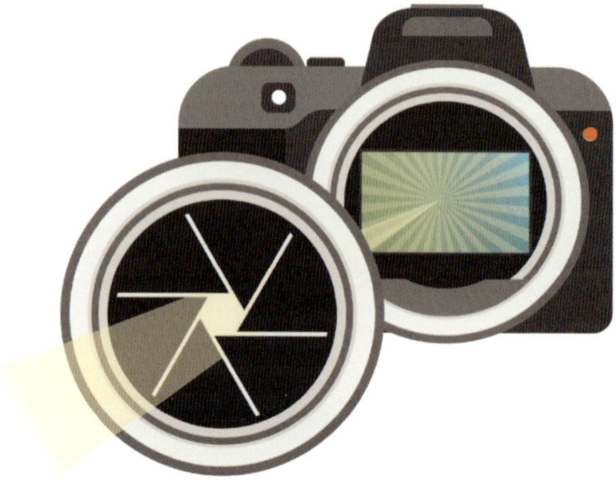

Light records to the image sensor while the shutter is open. The shutter curtain closes after the picture is taken.

In photography you can control how long you take the picture with shutter speed, and you can control the size of the physical hole that the light will travel through. The goal is that your glass of water is 100 percent full or that your photograph has 100 percent enough light. So in theory, aperture is responsible for producing 50 percent of the light, and shutter speed is responsible for producing the other 50 percent.

As you can imagine, there are lots of combinations of the amount of time you let light in with the shutter speed and the amount of light you let in with the size of the aperture. It's not always a fifty-fifty split. This is how the light/faucet metaphor we mentioned earlier works: If you reduce the hole size, you need to let more light in with a longer duration of time. If you increase the hole size, you need to let less light in with a shorter duration of time. That said, it would be nice if there were only two factors that make up the 100-percent light-filled photograph. But there is actually a third factor I didn't tell you about, which we will cover in the next chapter.

CHAPTER 7

Aperture, Shutter Speed, and ISO

WHY DO WE NEED DIFFERENT VARIATIONS OF APERTURE AND SHUTTER speed if they achieve the same result of a correctly exposed image? Seriously, if we can get the same brightness in an image that looks great to us in a bunch of different combinations, why do we care? Why do we want the variations? Well, we care because shutter speed and aperture control important factors other than just the brightness or exposure of an image. Let's dive deeper into what they actually do.

The Exposure Triangle

Three factors control how bright your image is, and it's a dance between those three factors to determine the results you intend as a photographer. These three factors together make up what's commonly called the *exposure triangle*. The factors are aperture, shutter speed, and ISO. Let's dive into those three right now.

Aperture

Not only is the aperture the size of the hole that is letting light into your camera to expose your camera's sensor, but it is also one of the main factors that control depth of field.

Depth of field is the amount of distance in focus in your photograph.

It's not where you focus. You can choose separately where you focus your camera. Depth of field is how much or how little of your image is in focus in front of and behind the subject you are focused on. When your subject is in focus, depth of field is what else is in focus. The most noticeable thing about depth of field is whether the background is blurry or crisp.

SHALLOW DEPTH = BLURRY BACKGROUND

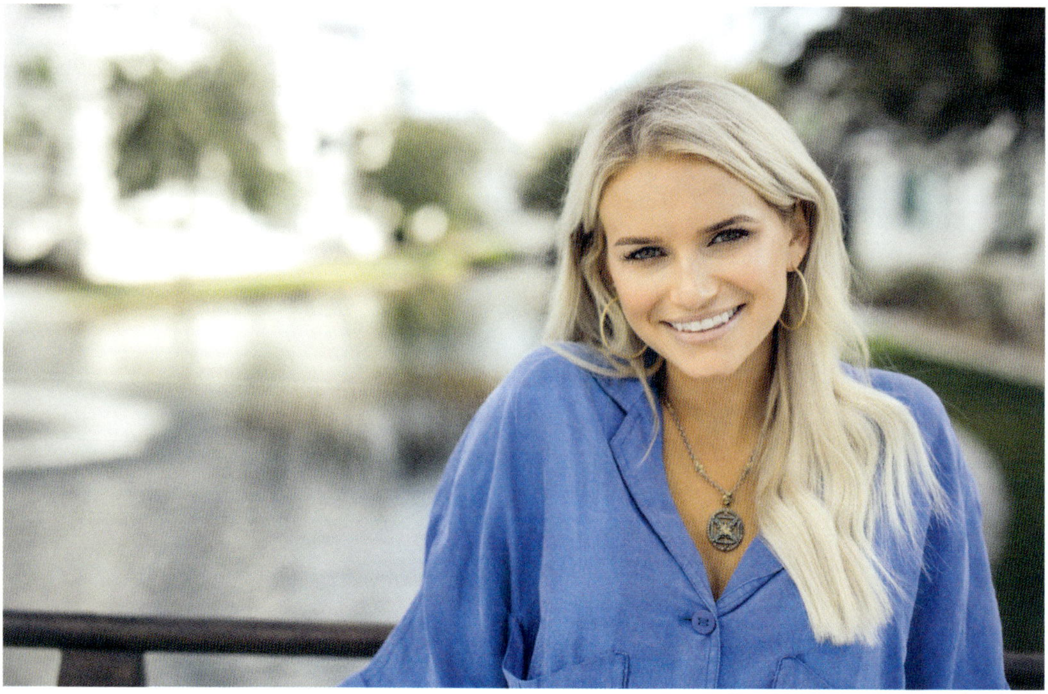

DEEP DEPTH = CRISP BACKGROUND

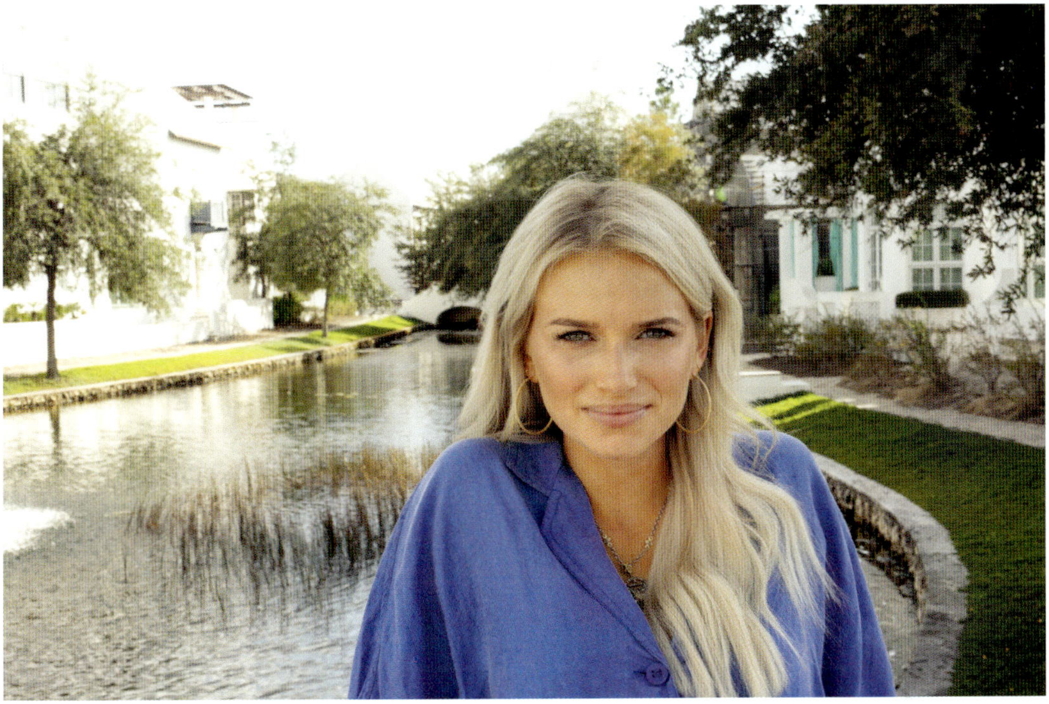

You can choose to have a shallow depth of field, a deep depth of field, or somewhere in between. And the main control mechanism of the depth of field is the size of the aperture hole itself.

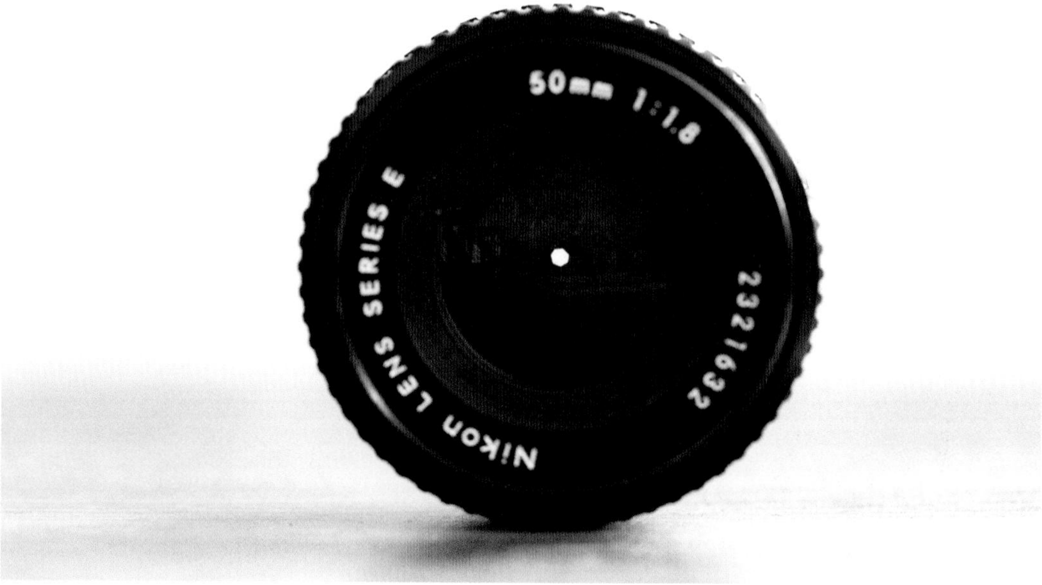

A small aperture hole creates a sharper background. This means that if the physical hole in your lens (aperture) is smaller, it will create a deeper depth of field with more distance in focus.

Smaller-sized aperture hole = deeper depth of field (less background blur or a crisper background)

A larger-sized aperture hole creates a blurrier background.

This means that if the physical hole in your lens (aperture) is large-sized, it will create a shallower depth of field with less distance in focus.

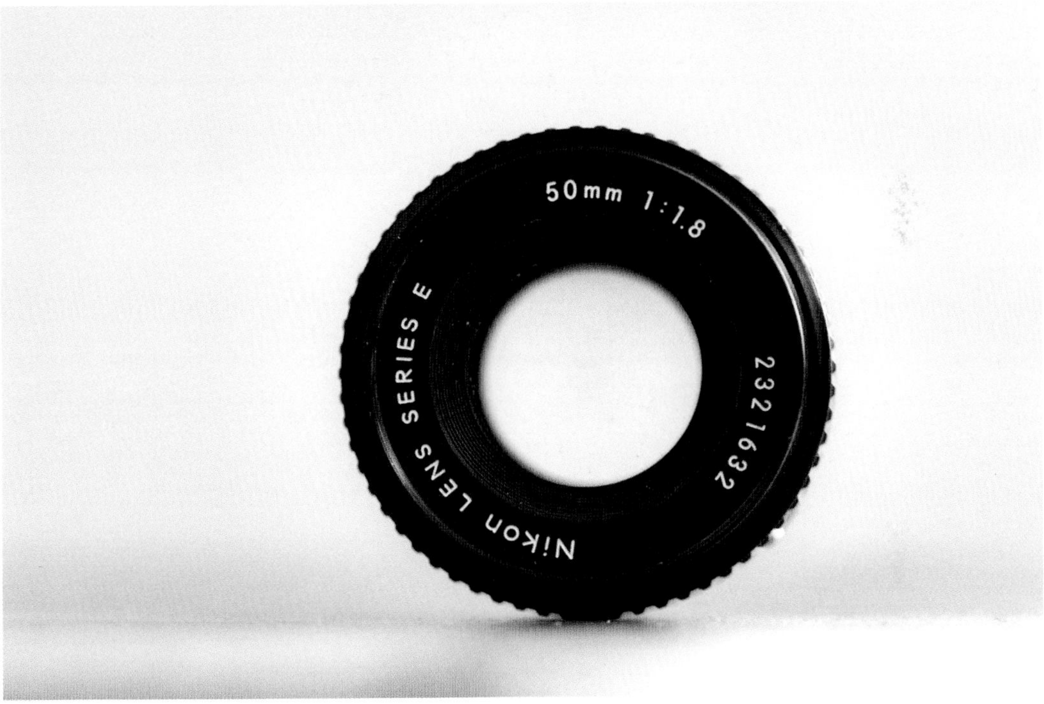

Larger-sized aperture hole = shallow depth of field (more background blur or a less crisp background)

Look at the example illustration on the next page. Notice how the largest hole is showing the mountains the blurriest? That's because it's the shallowest depth of field. And notice how the smallest-size aperture hole is producing the sharpest view of the background mountains? That's because it's the largest or deepest depth of field in the illustration.

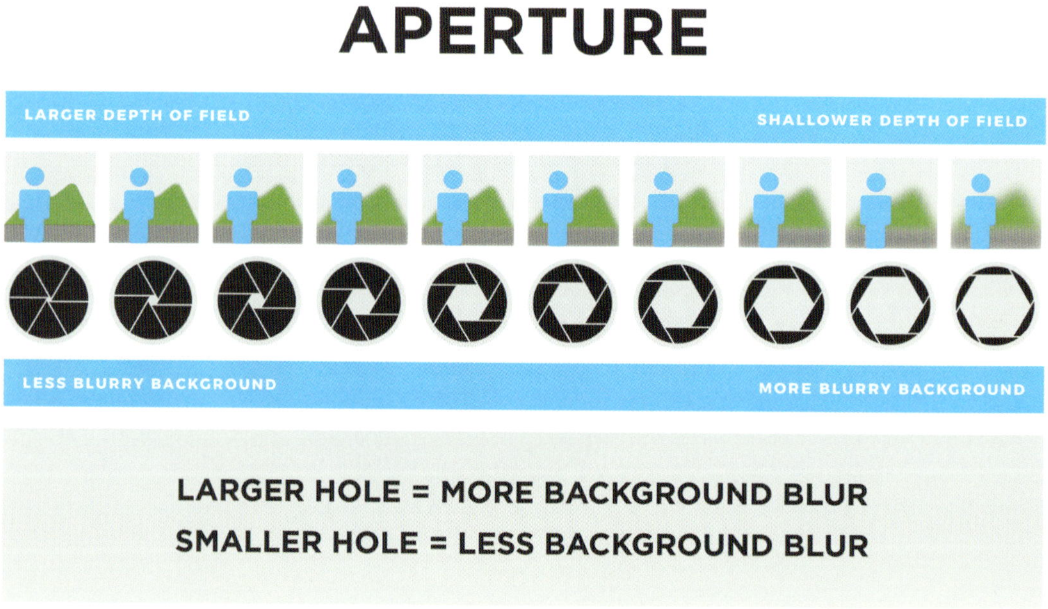

F-STOPS

F-stops are an increment to measure the size of the aperture opening and help you gauge how much light you're letting in. You might have heard numbers like f/22 or f/1.8. Here's the thing about aperture and f-stops: the numbers are the opposite of what you'd expect. A large number refers to a small hole. A small number refers to a large hole.

It can be confusing, I'll admit. But there is "science" behind it. And because nerds invented cameras, they like to confuse mere mortals like us (or the cool people who actually use them). So here's a cheat sheet to remember f-stop numbers.

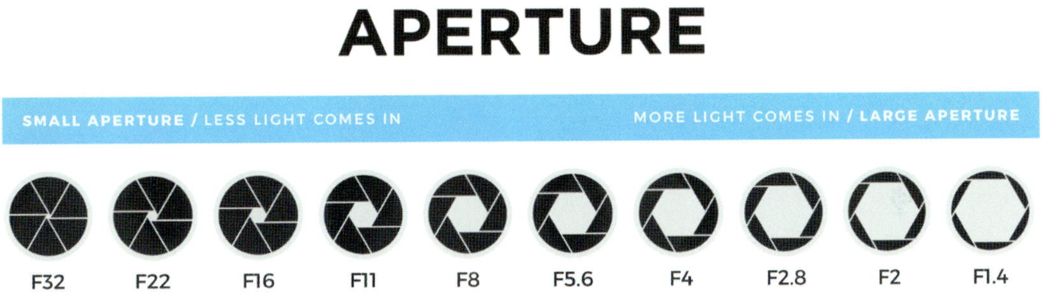

Notice how the largest hole is actually the smallest number? And vice versa? Just remember:

Larger hole = more light but smaller number

Smaller hole = less light but larger number

APERTURE PRIORITY MODE

The f-stop numbers and decimal points can be confusing to manually adjust, but don't fear. There is a mode built in to most cameras that makes it easy to learn and practice using aperture. This is where you set your f-stop number to reflect the size of the aperture that you want so that you can get the depth of field you want as well. And the awesome thing is the camera will automatically set everything else for you. It will set the shutter speed and the ISO (you'll learn about this in a bit). This mode is called *aperture priority*.

Since this is a book on how to work with professional-grade cameras and potentially turn professional yourself, we don't get too deep in to how to use smartphone cameras. But just so you know, these are features typically only on more complex devices. Some smartphones simulate them with software, but it's not the same. On a Canon camera, for example, you would set your mode to "AV." On Nikon and Sony cameras, you would want to simply set it to the "A" mode. This mode prioritizes setting the aperture, and your camera will set the rest.

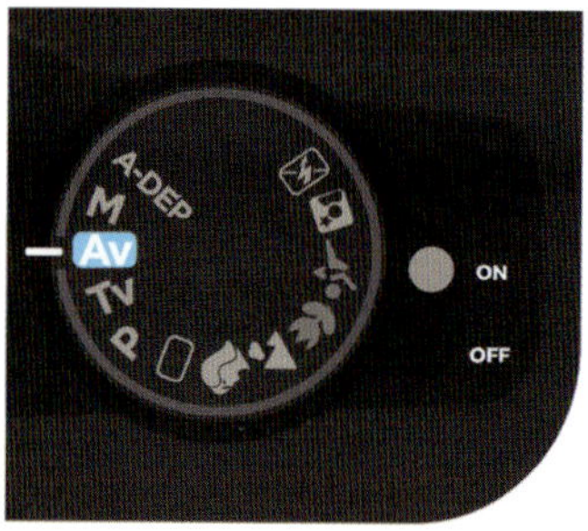

CANON

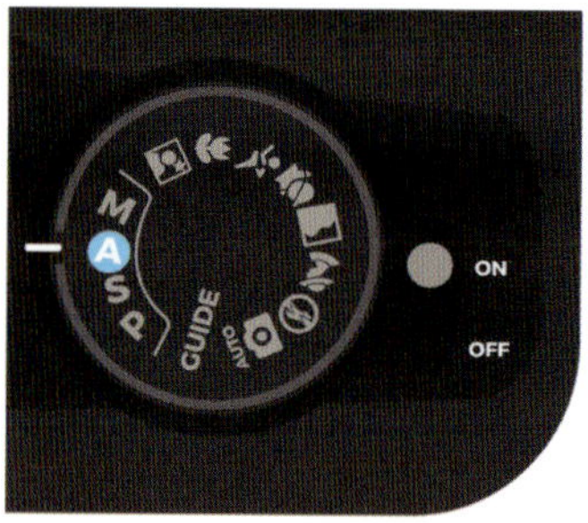

NIKON

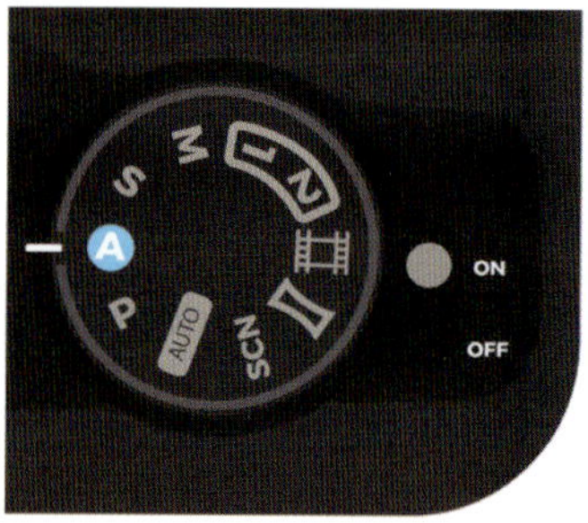

SONY

Let's say you want to shoot a beautiful senior portrait and you want a super blurred background. No problem. Set your aperture to the lowest f-stop number your lens will allow. If you have a lens like a "nifty fifty" (a 50 mm lens with a fast aperture), you can go down to f/1.8. This is a lens I always recommend newer photographers buy because of how inexpensive and awesome it is. This super small f-stop number will create a large-sized aperture (because the number is the opposite of the size) and will create a very shallow depth of field, which will create a substantially blurry background. All you have to do is make sure to focus on your subject's eyes and you will have a blurred background in your portrait. You won't have to worry about the other settings since your camera will set those for you.

This shot of my friend Akimie was shot with the 50 mm f/1.8 lens. Notice how it's a super shallow depth of field and just his face is in focus. The depth of field is so shallow that even his ears are getting out of focus, which can be a really cool way to make your subject's face pop out.

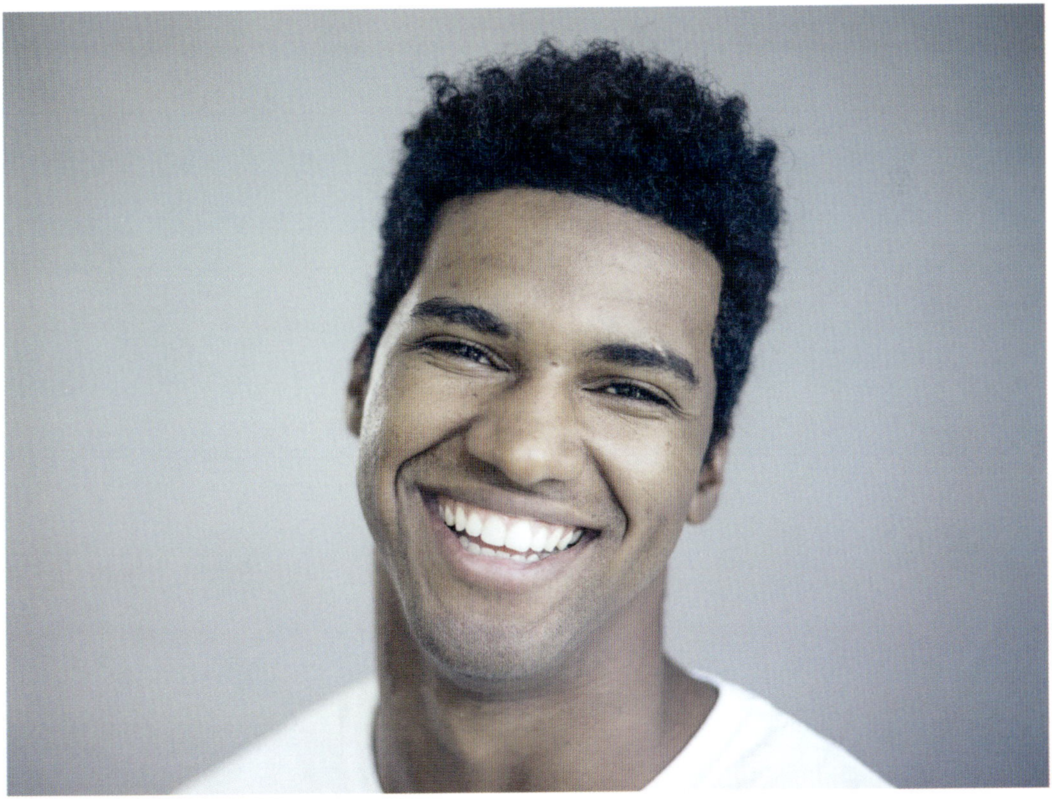

Here's my practice challenge to you. Go set your camera on aperture priority mode and try to get the blurriest background possible. If you are having trouble getting shallow depth of field, buy an inexpensive 50 mm f/1.8 lens for your camera brand. I promise you it will be a lot of fun for portraits and great for low-light situations.

Shutter Speed

Not only is shutter speed the amount of time you are exposing your image sensor to light, it is also what controls whether you freeze or show motion flowing in your photograph. Here's what I mean.

A fast shutter speed freezes the motion. Notice how you can see the individual specks of powder?

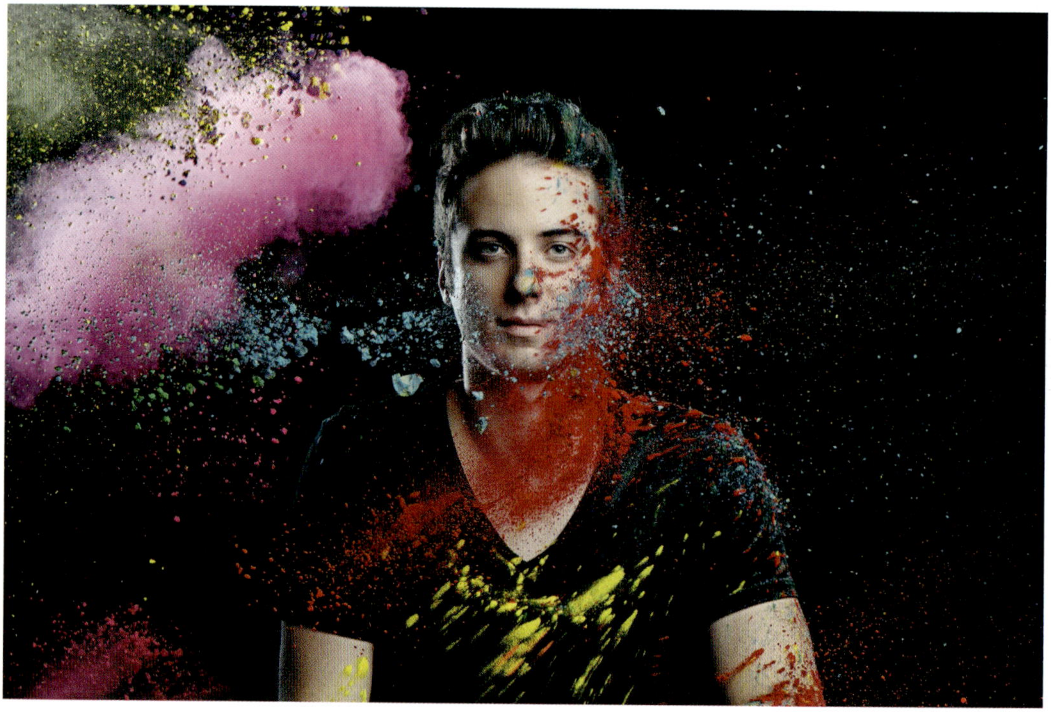

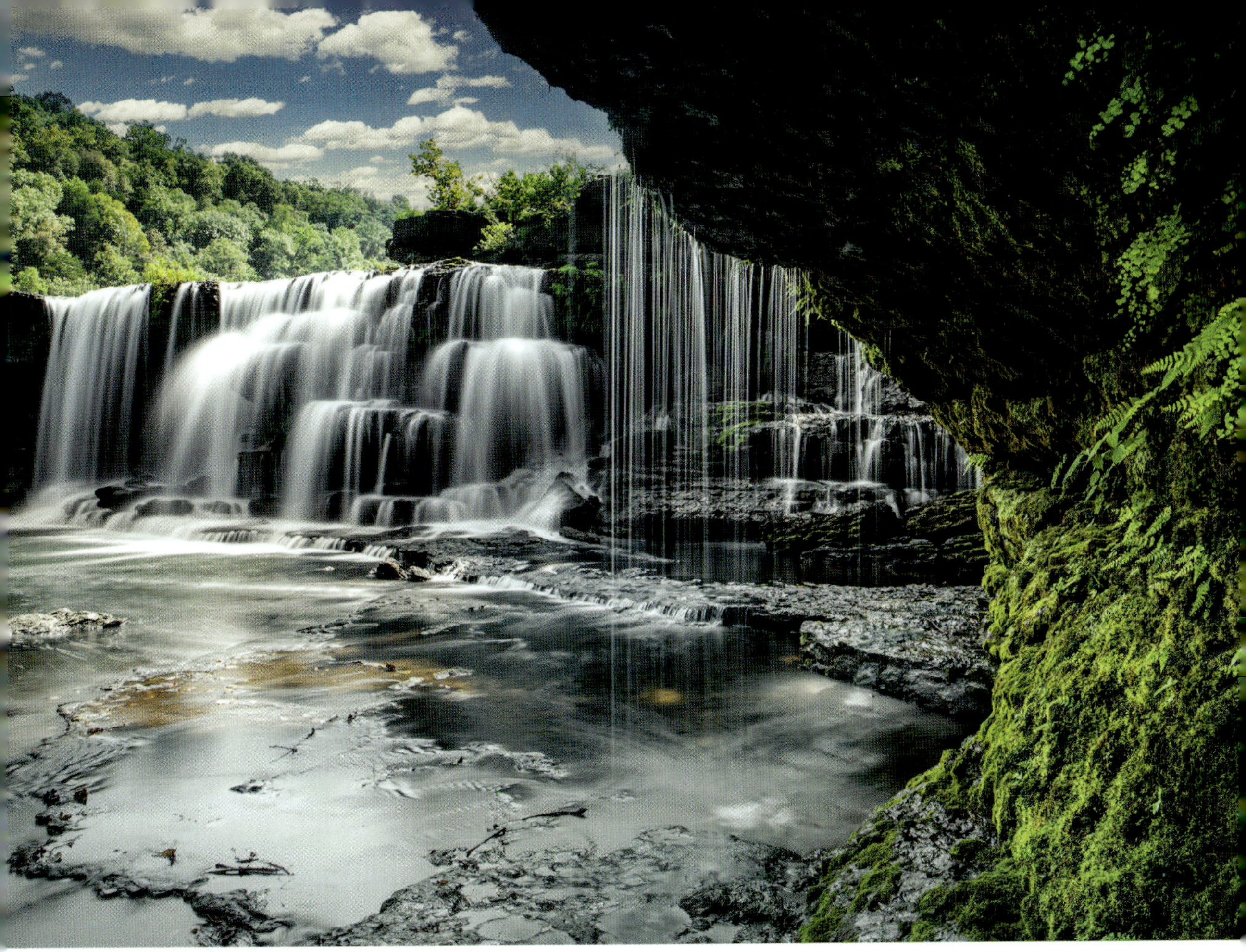

A slow shutter speed shows the movement and motion like this photograph of a flowing waterfall.

Here's how shutter speed works. Shutter speed is measured in fractions of a second. For example, 1/50 of a second or 1/125 of a second are shutter speeds. Some cameras display 1/125 as 125, but forget worrying about the fractions for a second. Let's keep it simple. What I want you to understand is that shutter speed is like miles per hour (or kilometers per hour for other parts of the world). The higher the number, the faster the speed. So for instance, 1/125 is like 125 miles per hour. It's faster than 1/50, which is like 50 miles per hour. Make sense? In other words: *the faster the shutter speed, the crisper and more frozen the motion will appear in your images*.

So for instance, 2000 miles per hour is really fast. And 1/2000 of a second is *really* fast. On the other hand, 30 miles per hour is kind of slow for a camera's shutter speed. At 1/30 of a second, you're shooting really slow and you're going to experience some motion blur.

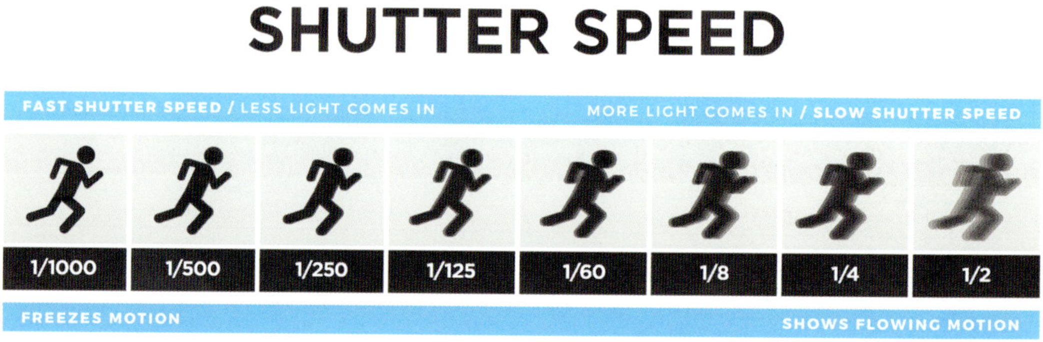

Take a look at this image of my son Judah sliding down the slide. It was shot super slow at 30 miles per hour, or 1/30 of a second:

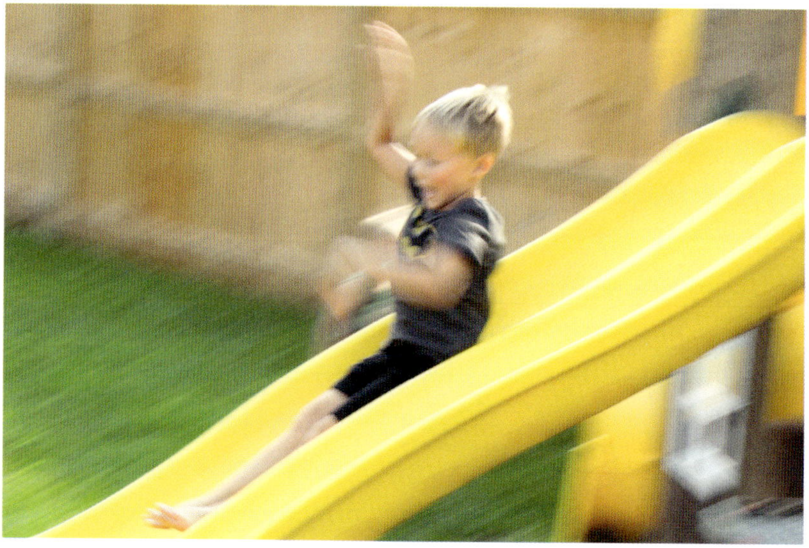

You're seeing lots of motion blur and camera shake too. Now let's look at a photo taken at 100 miles per hour:

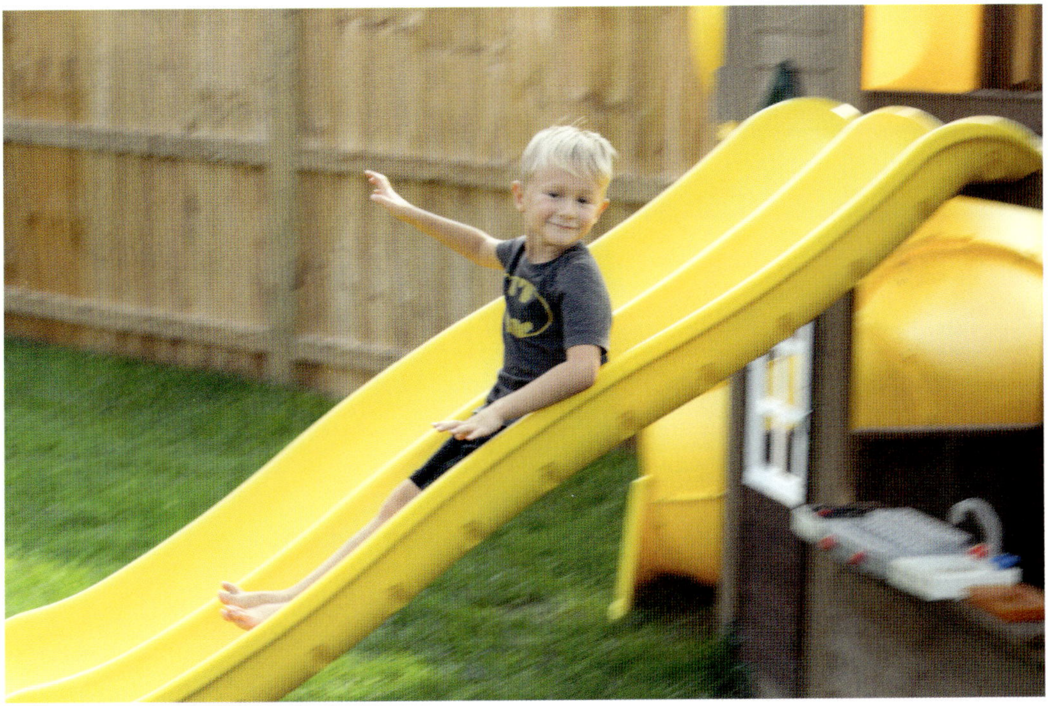

The 1/100 of a second shot is a little better and crisper, but not quite what we'd want. He still looks a little blurry. This brings me to the final shot that was at 1250 miles per hour, which is pretty darn fast.

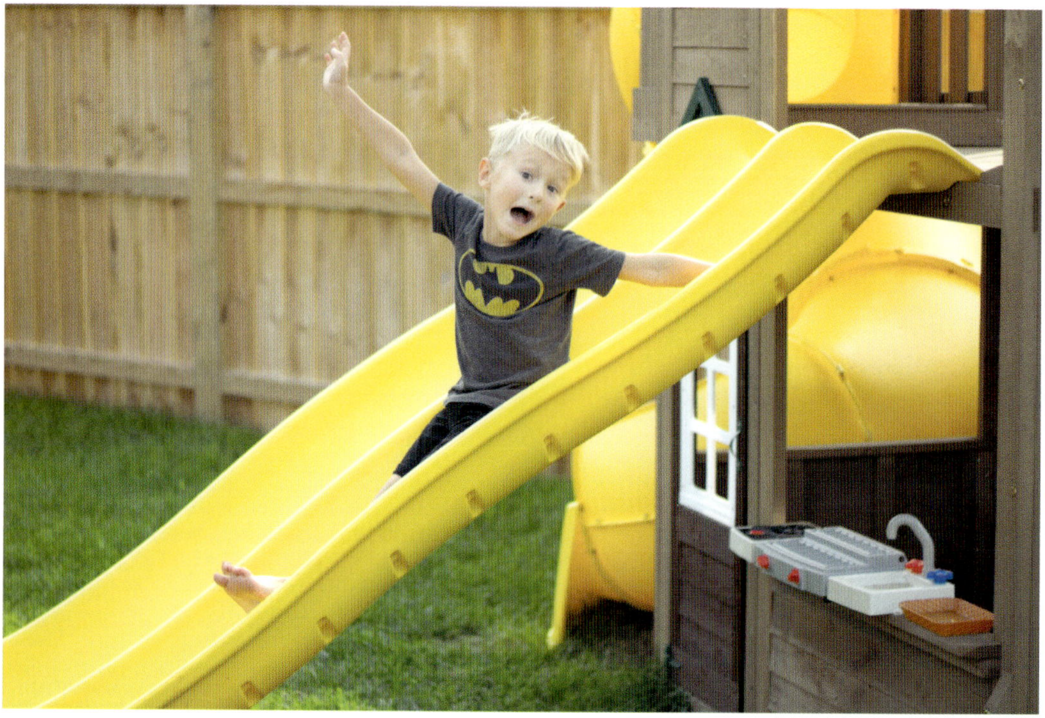

This shot has his motion perfectly frozen and sharp. That's because the faster you shoot your shutter speed, the better job it will do at freezing the motion. So many of my students tell me their cameras take blurry photos. In the wise words of the world's greatest assistant-to-the-regional-manager Dwight K. Schrute, "*False!*"

Really, the problem is that they are not shooting in manual mode and taking control of their shutter speed to shoot fast enough to freeze the motion of their subjects. Frequently they are also shaking the camera slightly, which shows up in the image as what we've been calling camera shake. It can be slight, but enough to make a photo unusable. So here's a rule I've set for my students in The Photo Mentorship that I'd like to offer you as well:

Do not shoot slower than 125 miles per hour when hand-holding your camera.

If you do, you're probably going to have motion blur of your moving subjects and you're highly likely to have the crazy camera shake as well. So don't shoot at 1/100 of a second. Not 1/80 or 1/60 either. Not slower than 125. *Don't do it!* If you don't follow this advice, I'll have to hunt you down and set you straight. *But*, you might be wondering, *what about shooting long exposures of the night sky or waterfalls?* Here's the deal: I don't want you to shoot slower than 125 miles per hour *unless* you are using a tripod to stabilize your camera. If you are using a tripod, you can shoot the longer, slower exposures required to really show motion flowing through your images. This waterfall photo was shot with a tripod and at several-seconds-long exposure.

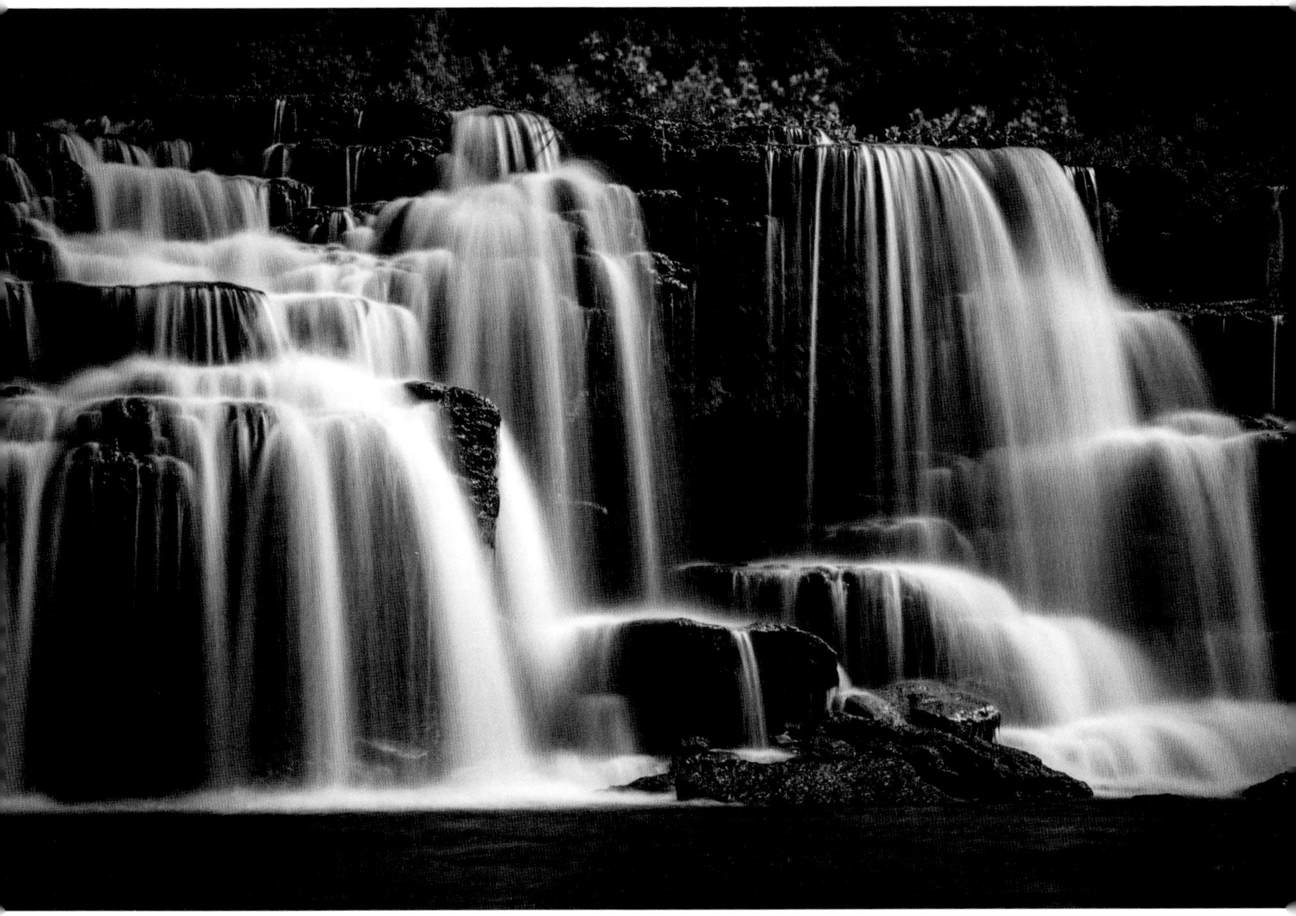

When photographers say shooting "fast," it means a very short duration of time. For instance, the shortest duration of time reflected in the cheat sheet below is 1/1000 of a second, or 1000 miles per hour. This will let the least amount of light into your camera to expose your image sensor, but it will do a better job at freezing motion. The slowest shutter speed represented in the cheat sheet is half a second, which is actually a very long time. This means that it will let the most amount of light into your camera's sensor (of the example shutter speeds), but it will allow a lot of motion to be displayed in the image. And of course, it's way too slow to hold the camera still without a tripod.

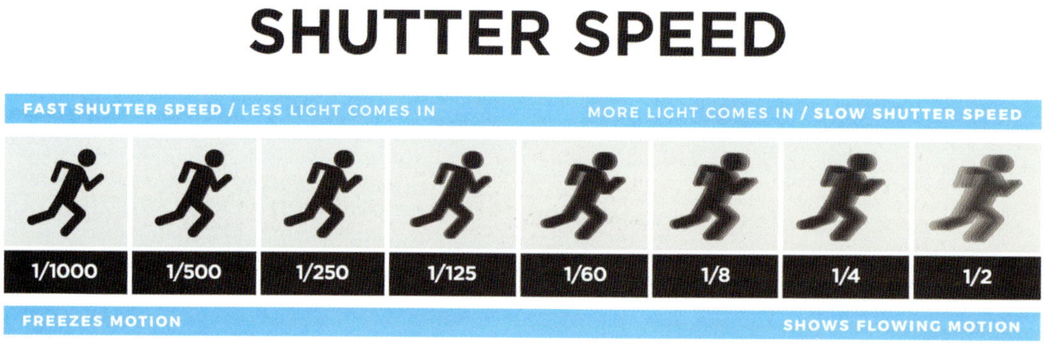

A longer duration of time (slower shutter speed) will allow *more light* to hit your camera's sensor *and* it will allow more motion to flow in your image.

A shorter duration of time (faster shutter speed) will allow *less light* to hit your camera's sensor *and* it will freeze the motion in your image.

Longer time = more light and flowing motion
Shorter time = less light and frozen motion

SHUTTER PRIORITY MODE

There's a learning curve in understanding how the fractions work and how they affect your images. I totally get that. That's why I'm excited for you to try out another semiautomatic mode called *shutter priority* mode. This mode is fantastic for learning how shutter speed affects your images without having to change all the other settings in your camera. You can set your camera to the "TV" mode if you have a Canon or the "S" mode if you have a Sony or Nikon camera.

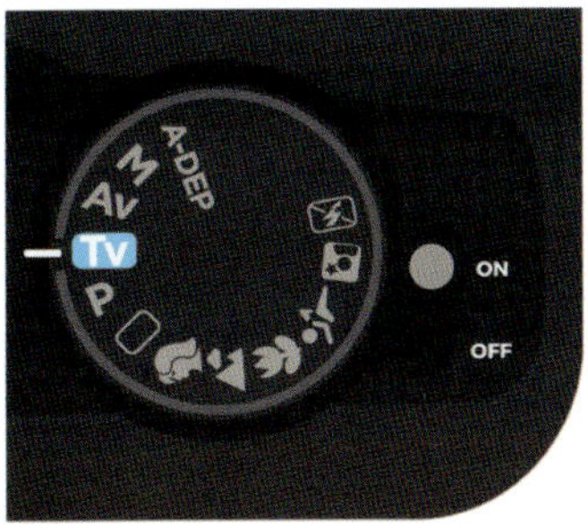

CANON

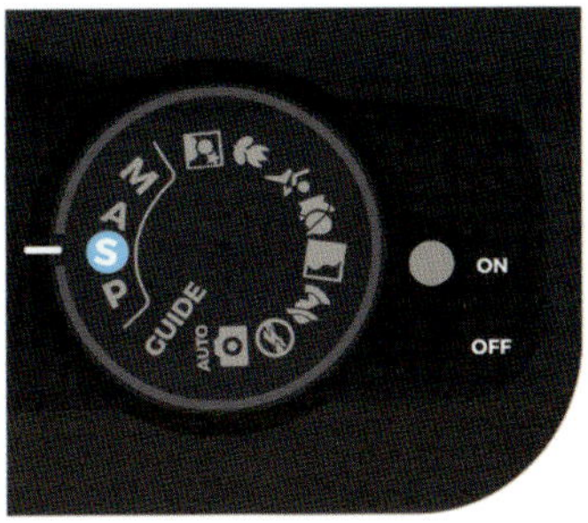

NIKON

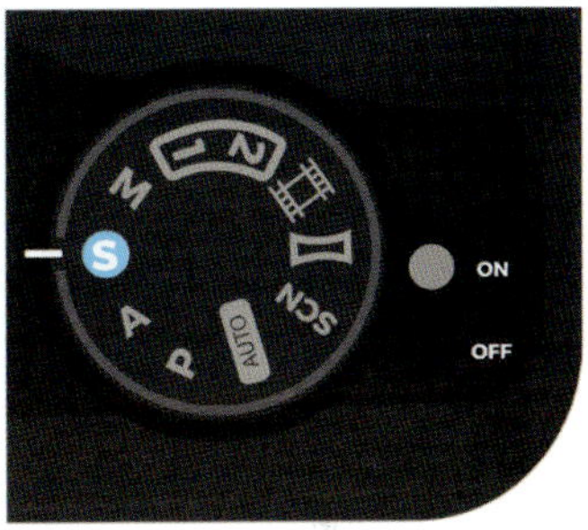

SONY

Once you're in shutter priority mode, you can set the shutter speed to whichever speed you want and your camera will automatically set your aperture and the ISO for you (we'll talk about ISO next). That way you're not having to worry about changing the other settings to get a decent exposure. You can then experiment with the different shutter speeds and see how they freeze or allow motion in your photographs. If you have a willing kid, friend, spouse, or fur baby, have them run in front of the camera while shooting at a fast shutter speed. Do the same with a slow shutter speed. You'll notice the difference.

ISO and Light Sensitivity in Your Image Sensor

ISO is the light sensitivity of your image sensor. The higher you raise the ISO number, the more sensitive your image sensor will be to recording light. This means that you'd need to raise your ISO to a high number to shoot in low-light situations, such as indoors or at concerts.

"That sounds great, David. So what's the catch?"

Raising your ISO increases the sensitivity of your image sensor, but it also degrades the quality of your image. The higher the ISO number, the more grain and noise will be noticeable in your image. If you've ever taken images with high grain or that look like they are low quality, it might have been because your ISO number was set too high.

As a general rule, set your ISO first, and set it as low as possible. Why? Because the lower the number, the better the quality of the details in your image, and the photo will be less grainy.

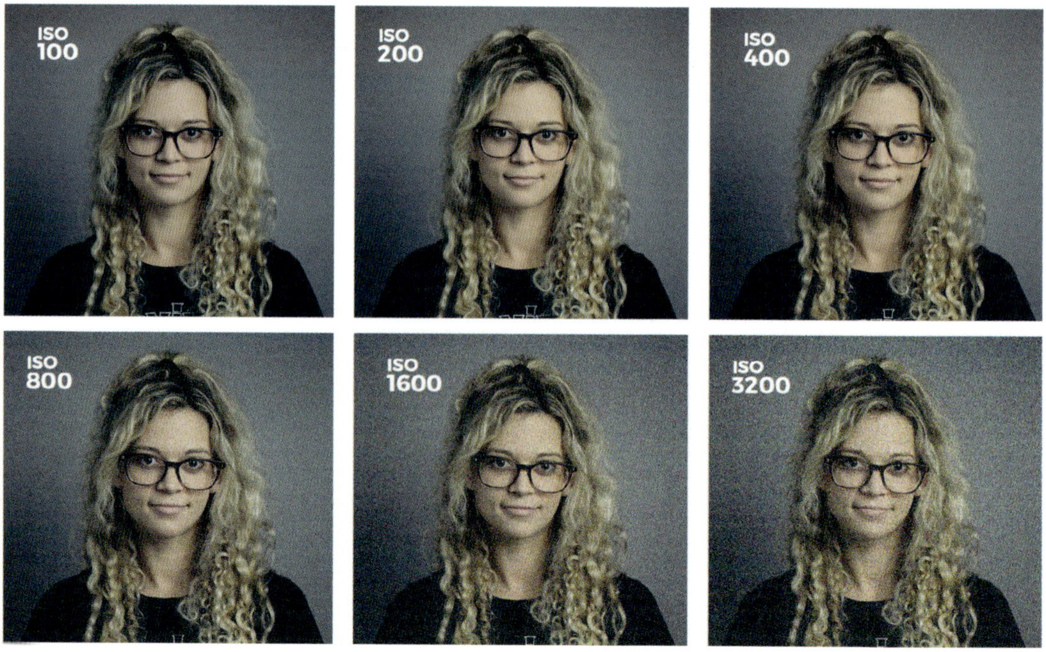

The lower ISO numbers are for shooting in brighter situations and will produce the least amount of grain and the highest quality. You can shoot as low as ISO 100 on bright, sunny days. When it starts to get cloudy you might have to bump your ISO to 200. No big deal. When you are in a low-lighting situation, like indoors without bright lights or outside at night, you might have to bump your ISO to 1600. Thankfully, if you have a modern camera, this still won't be too big of a deal and won't add too much grain.

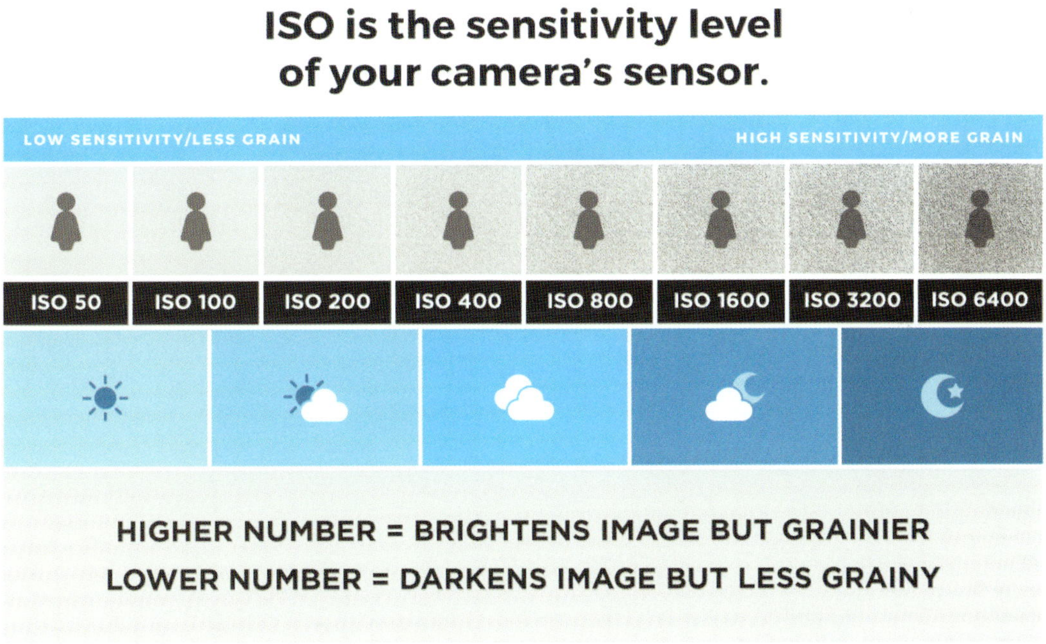

Most cameras won't show any noticeable grain in your images until you get above ISO 1600. You have it great with cameras these days—trust me. When I was starting my career, the cameras were terrible and would show horrible grain at ISO 400. But now many cameras are of such incredible quality that they barely show any noticeable grain even as high as ISO 6400, and sometimes higher. So while I still recommend shooting at low ISO numbers for bright situations, if you have a camera that's come out in recent years, you shouldn't have too much of an issue with grain. You lucky duck. You have it so much better than I did when I was a young Padawan photographer trying to learn this stuff.

Manual Mode

Now it's time to set your camera to "M" for manual exposure mode. In this mode you can individually set all three of the factors in the exposure triangle. When you set all three, keep a few things in mind.

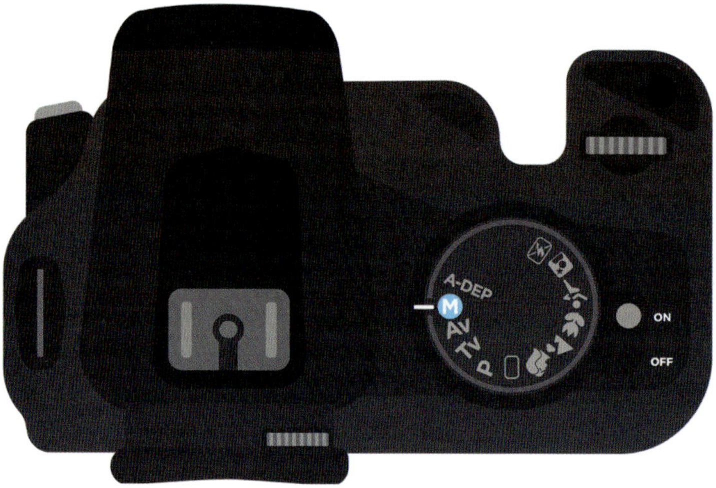

Set your ISO first according to your lighting scenario. And for the most part, you don't have to change your ISO again unless your lighting situation changes. For example, if you're outside shooting at ISO 100 and you step indoors, you might need to change your ISO to 800 because there typically isn't a lot of light indoors. That's fine. But don't keep adjusting your ISO just to change your brightness. That's what the other two factors—shutter speed and aperture—are for.

Next I want you to think about the type of shot you're going for. For example, if you want to shoot a portrait with a blurry background, you'd need to set your aperture next. Set your aperture to a large-size hole, which creates a shallow depth of field. Then focus on getting the correct exposure by compensating with your shutter speed. In the portrait example, if you're letting a lot of light in with the large aperture hole, then you would want to compensate with a fast shutter speed so you don't let in too much light.

If you wanted to shoot a waterfall and show the motion flowing through the scene, you would probably set your ISO to 100 since it's outside; then you might want to set your shutter speed next to a slow speed. Of course you'd need to be stabilized on a tripod for this, but you could set your shutter speed to something slow like 10 miles per hour or 1/10 of a second. This would let a lot of light in with the long duration of time. So you'd want to compensate by setting a very small aperture hole. Get it? Some of this is hard to put into words, which is why you'll want to be sure to watch the video lesson that comes with this book at PhotoMentorship.com/LTS. There's a step-by-step video on the lessons in this chapter that you won't want to miss. That said, you have the basics now, in terms of shooting and composition and understanding the various tools at your disposal. Now let's look at what you do after you've set up the shot and taken a great photo. It's time to get into editing.

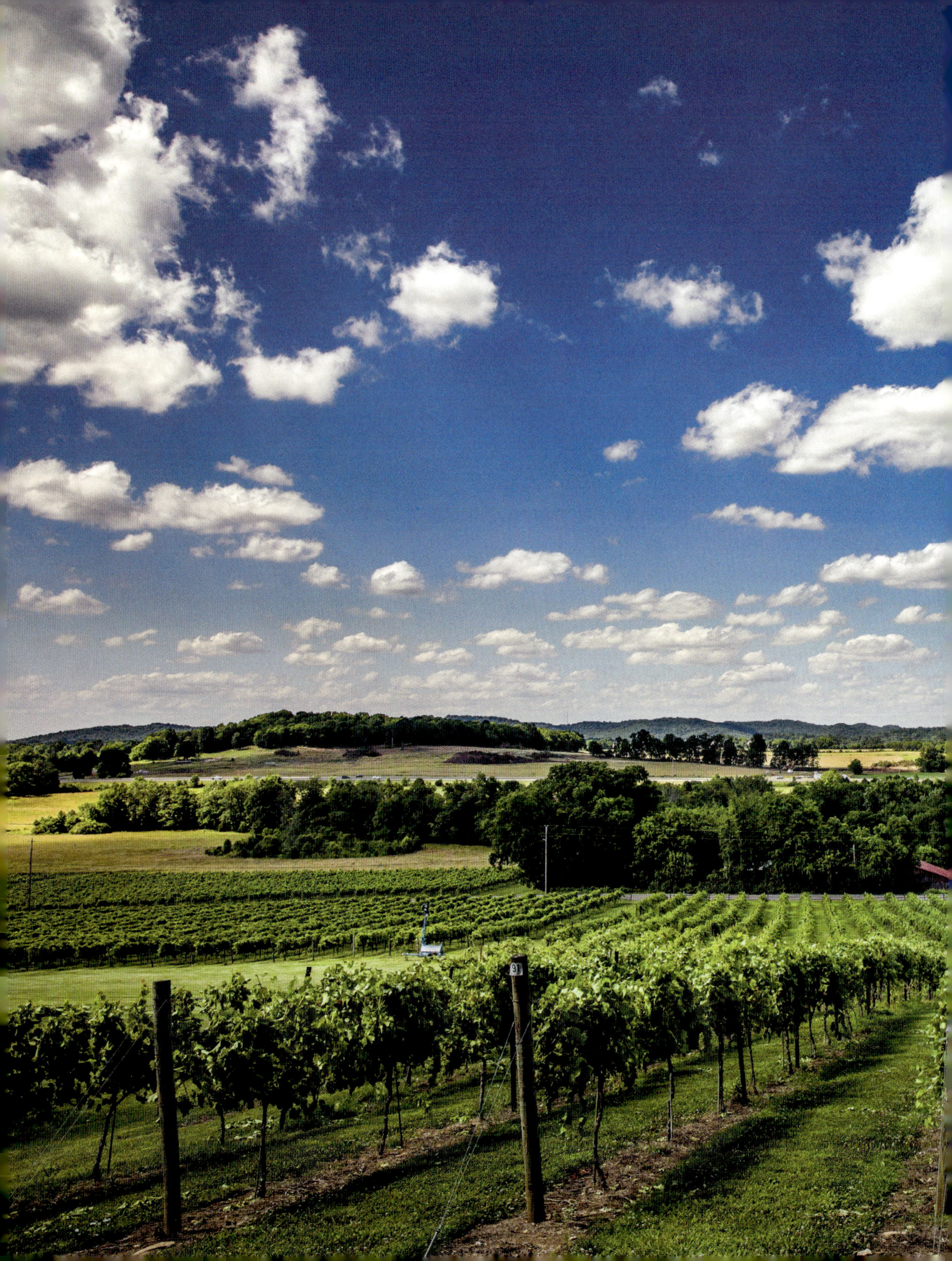

PART 3

EDIT

This section is all about editing and organizing your photos, which is not typically a photographer's favorite part. Most people I meet, especially early on in the process of picking up a camera, just want to go out and shoot. They want to use their cameras, create beautiful photographs, and tell amazing stories. Editing is often the part of the process where they stall out. They get stuck or discouraged because it can feel overwhelming and aimless. In this section, though, I'll teach you a method for editing and organizing that will simplify and clarify all that for you and won't have you glued to the computer screen for hours on end every weekend. It begins with understanding why we edit in the first place. It has nothing to do with adding in bells and whistles to your images or making them look unrealistic. It's simpler than that. Editing is about recreating the emotion you felt in the moment the picture was taken.

CHAPTER 8

Edit Like a Pro

HOPEFULLY BY NOW, YOU'RE EXPERIMENTING WITH YOUR CAMERA. ONCE you start seeing like a photographer, it's hard not to envision every scene in your life as a potential great photo. But shooting alone doesn't necessarily make your photos great. When my photography students first start taking photos, they almost always feel the photo is lacking something. What they see and what they are able to capture do not seem to be the same thing. Whether it's birds along the highway, a stunning sunset on a vacation, a beautiful day with your family, or watching a friend get married, like any good photographer, you snapped the shot to capture the moment; and of course, you told your friends all about it:

You've got to see the light in this sunset.

You've got to see the expressions on my kids' faces.

You've got to see how lovely the bride looked that day.

But as you pull the image up on your screen, you're let down by what you find. The image just doesn't do justice to your memory of the scene. It doesn't capture the way it really felt when you experienced it. It's not the story you remember seeing when you shot it. Of course not; this is normal. Sadly, this is where a lot of would-be photographers get discouraged and quit, thinking they'll never have what it takes to be a pro. But the truth is we all start here; we all struggle to communicate the emotion of the moment with a still-frame capture of it. That's why we edit.

Why We Edit

As I've said before, your camera can't capture what you see with your God-given eyes. You can see all the details in the highlights of the sky and, at the same time, the subtle details in the shadows beneath the horizon. Our eyes are amazing pieces of biotechnology. They can reconcile the many different shades we see, and our brains can show us a beautiful blend of brights, darks, midtones, and vibrant colors. Our cameras, as amazing as they are, can't even come close to that.

But this is exactly why we edit. *We edit to recreate that emotion we felt when we were viewing the scenes with our own eyes.* We edit to tell the most accurate story we can—to finish the story. We edit so we can let our viewers feel the same "*Wow!*" we felt.

The goal is not to make the scene look cheesy. We aren't editing to make our photos unrealistic. But too often that's exactly what happens—especially when photographers are just starting out. They'll go back and forth and spend way too much time worrying about a photo, then ultimately end up over-editing the photo and making it look bad, like the one below. They go too far.

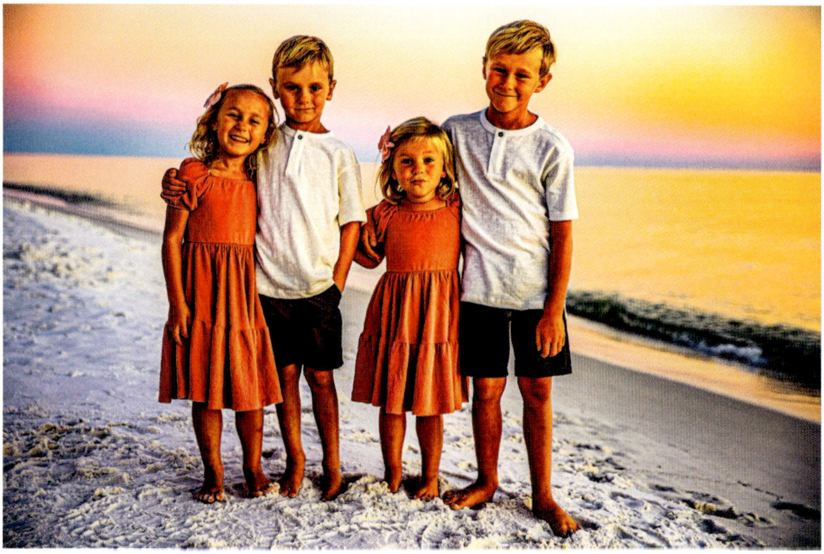

The Different Types of Editing

What about adding a fake sky and a unicorn baby standing on my shoulder pooping out rainbows? That's called *compositing*. And compositing in a program like Photoshop, combining a ton of different layers and elements to look like one surreal image, can be awesome and fun when it's done well. This incredible composite is by Kevin Carden, who teaches our Photoshop compositing courses included in The Photo Mentorship.

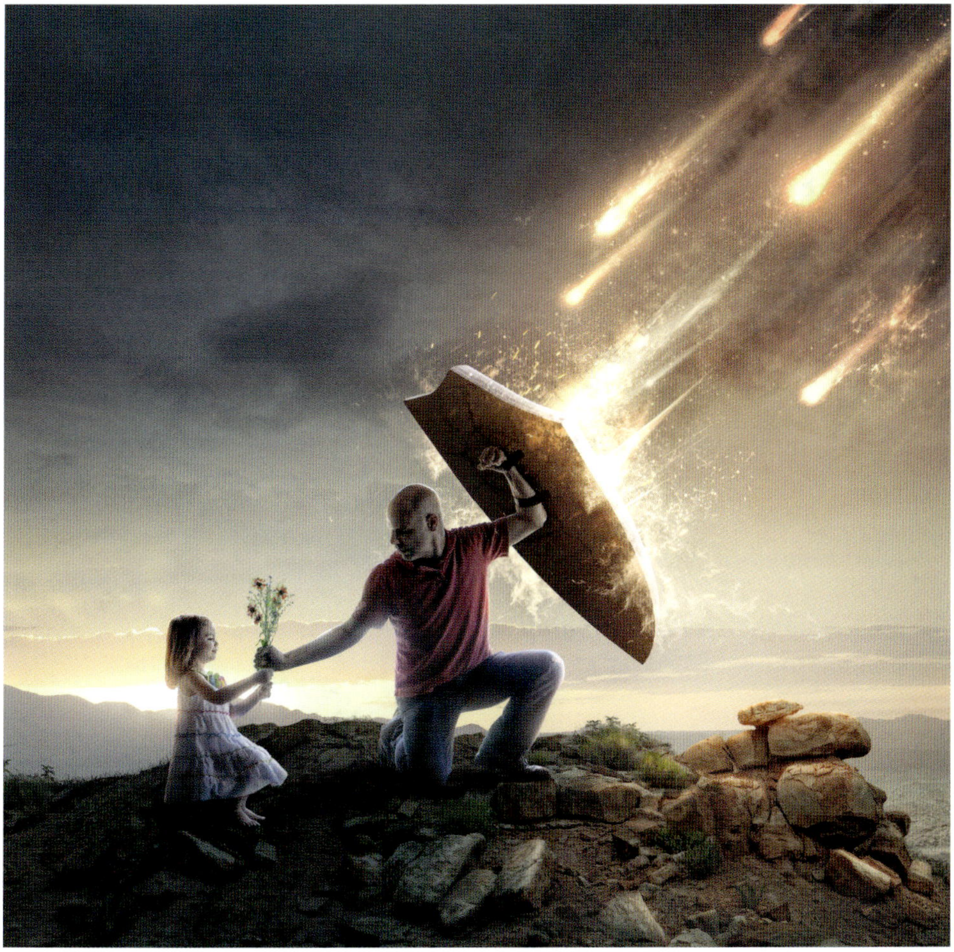

There are many types of editing. There is individual photo editing in a program like Photoshop, where you go deep in trying to perfect an image and do advanced things like skin retouching, head swaps, adding in a new background, and so much more. The idea here is to do everything possible to hone in and perfect the image before it "goes to print." For example, I would do that for the images my clients picked that were going to be on an album or magazine cover. Sometimes I'd spend eighteen hours editing one image before it went on an album cover.

"Okay, but David, what would I do for the other thousand photos that are not going to print or going to be featured somewhere important? Should I spend eighteen hours per image?"

Heck no!

What do you do with the rest of the photos from a photo session? And how do you pick just one of the best photos to finalize? Great question. This is where workflow editing comes into play.

▶ You can find a list of the best current programs at PhotoMentorship.com/LTS.

In a workflow program, like Lightroom Classic, you can choose your favorite images, organize them in various ways, and then edit many photos at once with presets and filters. This is the type of software program where you would essentially process 99 percent of a photo shoot. You'd do the bulk of the work on many photos, often thousands at a time, and then export them to send to your clients so they can choose their favorites. Once they've chosen their favorites, then and only then do you start the individual retouching and finalizing the images in a program like Photoshop. I personally don't even think about doing in-depth retouching of an individual photo until my client has chosen it as one of their top ten images.

I have an extremely efficient process you can follow to feel confident that you are processing your images correctly, choosing the right number of images, and of course editing your photos to look professional instead of amateurish. I use a framework for editing that I think every photographer should know how to apply to their own work. Following it will not only help the end results of your shoot turn out amazing, but it will make the process much smoother, less painful, and heck, even a lot of fun. In addition to being fun and easier, it'll help you keep track of where all your photos are. This might not be a problem for you yet, but believe me, it will be. If you're serious about photography, you'll accrue thousands of photos. We'll also cover how to back them up safely. And most importantly, we'll discuss how to know when you're done editing.

Most photographers have no idea how to tell when they're done with an image. They don't even know if it looks good or not. They just spin their wheels and waste time creating copy after copy of the same image, getting more insecure about whether they have what it takes as a photographer. Let's not do that.

This editing framework is typically for when you are shooting a larger format type of photo stored in a digital file type called RAW. I only shoot RAW images with my professional cameras, as opposed to JPEGs. The only exception is when I shoot on my phone, because RAW typically isn't an option. Serious photographers prefer RAW images because this format will record more information than a JPEG and is generally better quality. RAW images give you better and more information to alter in the editing process. Simply put, if you are serious about photography, you're going to want to start shooting in your camera's RAW format, which is an easy adjustment in the menu settings on whichever camera you have.

The Framework

The framework we're going to use follows the acronym DICEE:

D: Download
I: Import
C: Cull
E: Edit
E: Export

DOWNLOAD

Our first step is to *download*. You want to download the images onto whatever device you're using to edit. Sounds simple enough, right? Get every single one of your images off your camera and onto the device you use to edit. I also recommend downloading your images to an external hard drive. And then immediately to a duplicate external hard drive as well so there is a copy in case one of your hard drives fails. It happened to me once and cost me $2,500 to repair the hard drive. *Yikes!* Thankfully, they were able to recover it, but it was a costly repair.

IMPORT

From there you're going to *import* your raw images into a workflow program like Lightroom Classic so you can begin processing the shoot. Simply take your photos and import them into the program you use to edit and organize your photos. Sometimes this can take a bit of time, so you can grab a coffee while it's importing and building previews of your unedited images for you to sort through.

CULL

Now it's time to select the best images to tell your story. And that happens in a process called *culling*. To cull simply means to choose. So when we say we're going to cull images, what we mean is we're going to pick the images to keep, the images to throw out, and the images we love the most. We're going to narrow them down to the ones that best tell the story we want to tell.

I used to open up all my photos from a shoot and start looking for the bad images to take out. I'd sit down and do my best to figure out what I could get rid of. It felt impossibly overwhelming, especially when I was trying to cull down a wedding where I shot more than three thousand images. It was a brutal process. I would end up depressed after going through thousands of shots I took, realizing many of them weren't that good. It would also take me *for-ev-errrr*. To top it off,

I'd end up with a ton of images that practically looked like duplicates because I couldn't decide which ones to throw away. Then I would just start editing images to see which ones I liked. It was a miserable, inefficient process. Sometimes it would take me weeks of debating to decide which images were the bad ones. The whole experience felt paralyzing and depressing and made me want to quit photography.

But then I learned a secret when I took a workshop from an amazing photographer, Jared Platt. He taught me how to look at the positive side. Only look for the good images and don't stress, worry, or even think about the bad images. Just choose which images are great and that you are excited to show your clients (or friends). Don't worry about the rest.

This changed my life.

I went from it taking me weeks of editing per shoot, to being able to edit an entire five-thousand-plus-photo wedding shoot in a day or less. I could edit a portrait session from start to finish in less than an hour. And deliver the type of professional-quality images I was proud of.

I know so many photographers who approach culling by thinking about the bad images first. But if you do that, it'll lead you to a lot of self-doubt and frustration.

So can we make a pact right now? Never look for bad images again. Instead, let's approach culling by finding the good. Trust me—this will make the process so much more enjoyable. Because now you're not focusing on the negativity. You're not looking for your mistakes or mess-ups. You're looking for what you did well. You're finding your best work. And not only will it help you feel better, it will make the process of choosing images go *a lot faster.*

When we're culling, we're focusing on finding the good in our work first. It's a great motto for both photography and life, really. I mean, who wouldn't be a little sad if all we did was look at our work through the lens of what was wrong? Thinking that old way made me feel less like a world-class photographer and more like a straight-up failure. This simple shift in approach to the process of culling allows me to enjoy this part of the story more. So how exactly does this work? Let's break it down.

The Culling Process

We're going to follow my one-third-times-two rule. Here's how it works. First, you want to narrow down your shoot to about a third of the total images. We'll call those the "keepers." So let's say you shoot three hundred photos total in a family portrait session (this nice, round number makes for easy math). Then you look through and search for your top hundred or so keepers. Remember, you are only looking for the images that would make for good final photos. Then put the other two hundred unused photos in a "Delete" folder and forget about them for the next six months until you are ready to delete them. They will never see the light of day and don't deserve your attention, but you may not be ready to completely ditch them just yet. Just don't focus on them. Hang on to them until you have the nerve to delete them forever. You won't ever show them to your client unless they ask to see them, which has happened to me maybe once in twenty years. I do this as a sort of backup plan. After the client is happy with their photos and has moved on, feel free to delete those leftover images.

Of the keepers, you'll narrow those down to one-third again and call those your "choice" images. Now you have thirty-three-ish of the hundred keepers. You'll take the remaining sixty-seven or so keeper images and place them in a folder called "Extra."

▶ So how do you do this exactly? Workflow programs have features to help you sort. There are several great programs out there. Visit PhotoMentorship.com/LTS for a free video tutorial on how to do this.

Most workflow programs have a rating system where you select a photo, press the number 1, and it will give the photo a one star rating of a possible five stars. The more you like the image, the higher you could rate it. For instance, you could press the number 5 on your keyboard to rate the image as five stars if you really love it. But remember, you're only looking for the good. You're only starring the images you want to keep, so don't spend time 1-starring all your bad photos.

Cutting your total images by two-thirds right off the bat, and then doing it once again, may sound daunting. But trust me, it's not. When you're looking for images you want to get rid of, it's much harder to make a decision. But when you're flipping through and looking for images that you really love, it becomes easier. And mathematically, you're making fewer decisions. You only have to choose one hundred good images rather than two hundred bad ones. It's less time, less effort, and less frustration.

Those thirty-three choice images will be the ones you put more editing time into. You'll give them a little more effort in storytelling, separating them as your primary images to show your clients or friends. You'll say, "These are the best images from your shoot. These are the ones I'd recommend you frame or feature." Of course, you'll provide them with the extra keeper images too. You'll give them the option to view the extra sixty-seven images, but first showcase the best thirty-three.

To review, here's what a three-hundred-photo family shoot would look like once it's culled:

- 33 in the Choice folder
- 67 in the Extra folder
- 200 photos in the Delete folder, eventually to be purged

Using this process for culling helps you focus on your best work, and it will help you craft a better experience for your viewers. You aren't necessarily trying to shoot more than you need. It just happens. Some photographers can shoot way less, which is less work in the end, but that just comes down to the style of each photographer. Ultimately I end up shooting way more than I need, and so do most professional photographers; but it isn't necessarily true for everyone. The point is you are going to have to learn how to decide what to keep and what to toss.

Culling your photos will make you look more professional and teach you to be pickier in your craft. Bonus: your clients won't be overwhelmed with too many images to pick from either.

EDIT: THE FIVE-STEP RECIPE

Now that you've got your best images selected, it's time to get into editing. We're going to use my Five-Step Editing Recipe to recreate the emotion we experienced when viewing the scene with our own eyes. What follows is not so much a tutorial for photo editing software but a description of the kinds of adjustments you can make to your photos. Lightroom Classic is the application I currently use, but many professional apps will have the same or similar editing options.

I was once visiting a stunning city in Switzerland. There was a lake behind the city and the foothills of the Swiss Alps sitting in the distant background. As I stood there, the sun started to set. It was the perfect golden hour. The light looked incredible as it was flooding through this historic city all over the cobblestone streets and old buildings. It was a truly stunning scene.

Or so I thought. Because this is the picture I got back.

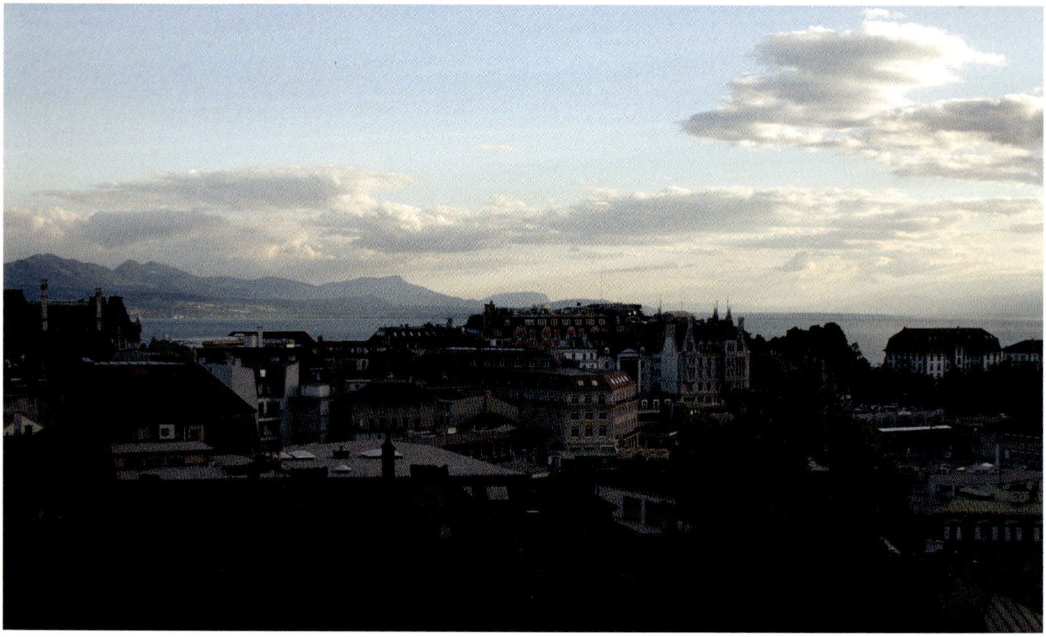

Trust me, this picture really does not do it justice. It's not even close to conveying the emotions I felt when I was viewing the breathtaking landscape with my own eyes. It doesn't represent the real-life experience at all.

Before we jump into the five practical steps, let's talk about the problems in this photo.

1. The landscape itself is dark. You can't see the details of the city.
2. As I remember it, the sky was radiant, vibrant, and full of golden sunset hues. But that isn't shown here.
3. The scene was popping like crazy. The city below was vibrant, but you can't tell from this photo.

So want to recreate that emotion, the pop, those colors, and those details that we lost when shooting the image with the camera, which is much lower tech equipment than our God-given eyes.

▶ If you get stuck in this section, be sure to visit my website at PhotoMentorship.com/LTS for bonus video tutorials that make all this stuff way easier.

Step 1: Adjust the Highlights and Shadows

The first thing we're going to address is balancing the exposure of the image. As we know, it's kind of dark. We lose some of those details beneath the horizon. But we cannot just simply brighten the whole image in this instance. Because although it may fix the problem of brightening the darker areas, it will also cause another problem: making the sky too bright and losing those precious details.

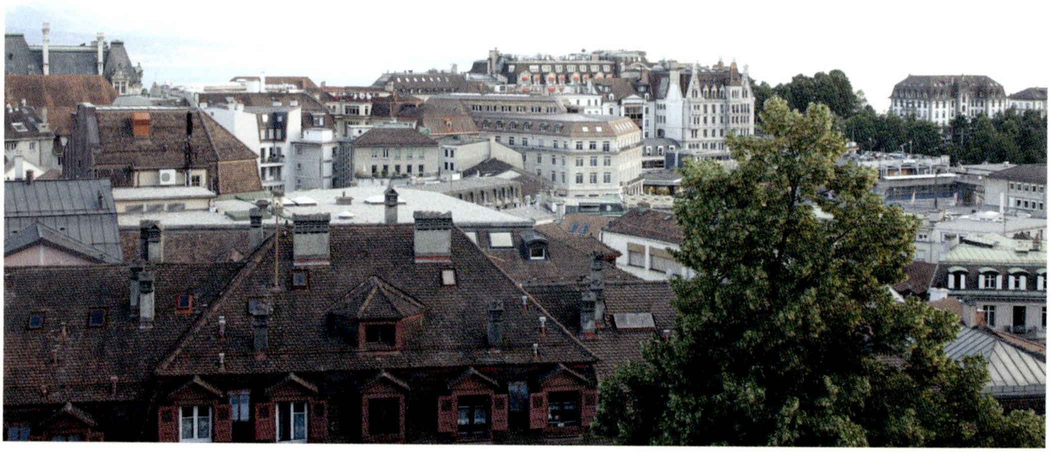

See what I mean? This doesn't work at all. Where is the vibrant sunset? Where are the clouds? Heck, you can barely even see the mountains. Don't worry; that's why we have the powerful tools of adjusting the highlights and shadows, which some people call "fill light."

Adjusting your highlights and shadows can be a powerful game changer. I don't want to cast a *shadow* over the rest of the book (heh, heh), but I think this may be the nugget people remember most. It's one of the most underutilized tools in editing. In every decent editing app out there you can adjust the highlights of the image to be brighter or darker. The highlights are the brightest part of the image.

Most editing apps are also going to allow you to change your shadows. You'll be able to make just the shadows brighter or darker as well. If you raise the highlights, it's only going to brighten the highlighted areas, or brightest parts, of the image. It's not really affecting any other areas. But I want to make the highlights a little more dramatic. I want to bring out the details in those almost-blown-out parts of the sky to make the clouds more dramatic. So to do that, we'll reduce the highlights.

Then, once you've set the highlights, you'll move on to the shadows, also known as fill light. As you increase the shadows, it will brighten up only the areas in the shadows. The reason this technique is powerful is because you're selecting a specific type of tone to alter—the shadows—while leaving other tones as they are. Unlike when we previously brightened the whole image and it made the sky too bright, this way you're only brightening the dark parts of the image and filling in the light in the shadows. By doing this you don't accidently make the sky too bright.

In this image I was able to max out my options of bringing back the highlights and raising the shadows to the extreme. As you look at it, you'll see all those details in the historic buildings themselves because we've brightened the shadows. You'll also notice that we haven't lost the details in the sky but have drawn them out and defined the clouds.

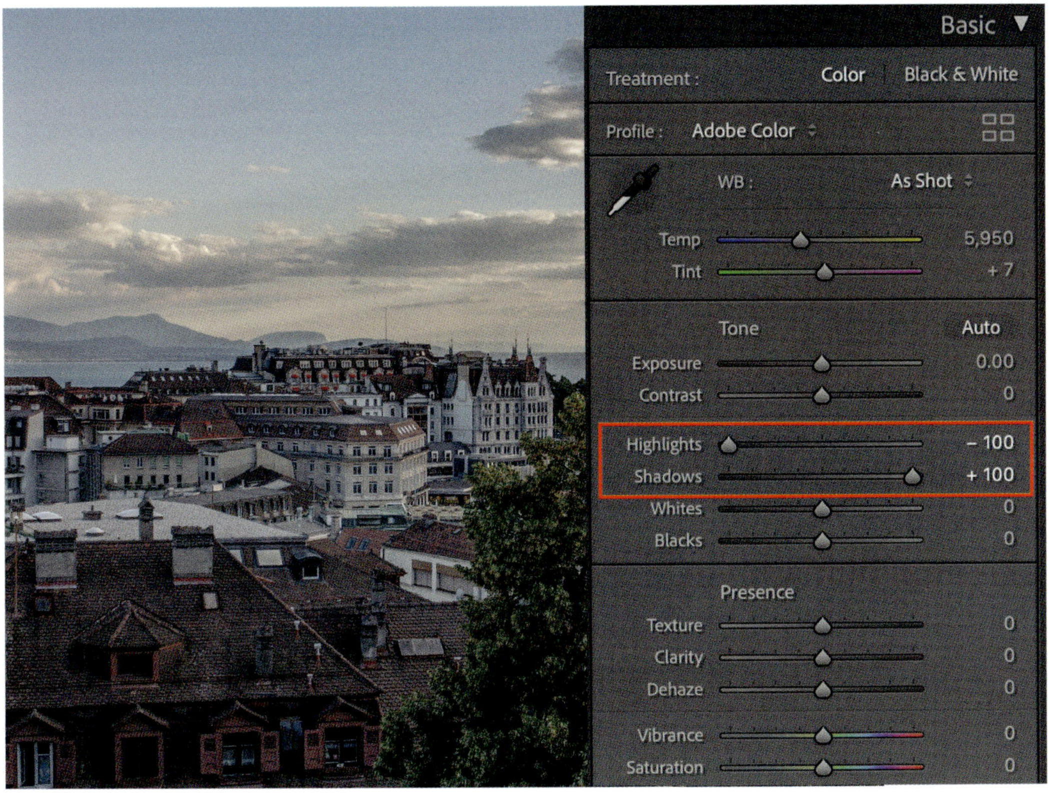

The image is starting to come to life. It's still a little dark, a little flat, and doesn't quite pop yet. But don't you worry, buckaroo, we can see a lot more details—and still continue to edit with confidence now that we know which details we have to work with. We'll be able to focus on recreating the emotion now.

Step 2: Adjust the Exposure

In the previous step, we adjusted the brightness of the shadows and highlights uniquely. In this section we are going to adjust the overall brightness by changing the exposure. As I've already explained, exposure is the brightness in your image. If you raise the exposure, you brighten up the image. If you lower it, you darken the image. This can be a tricky thing because, as I showed you in step 1, if you change

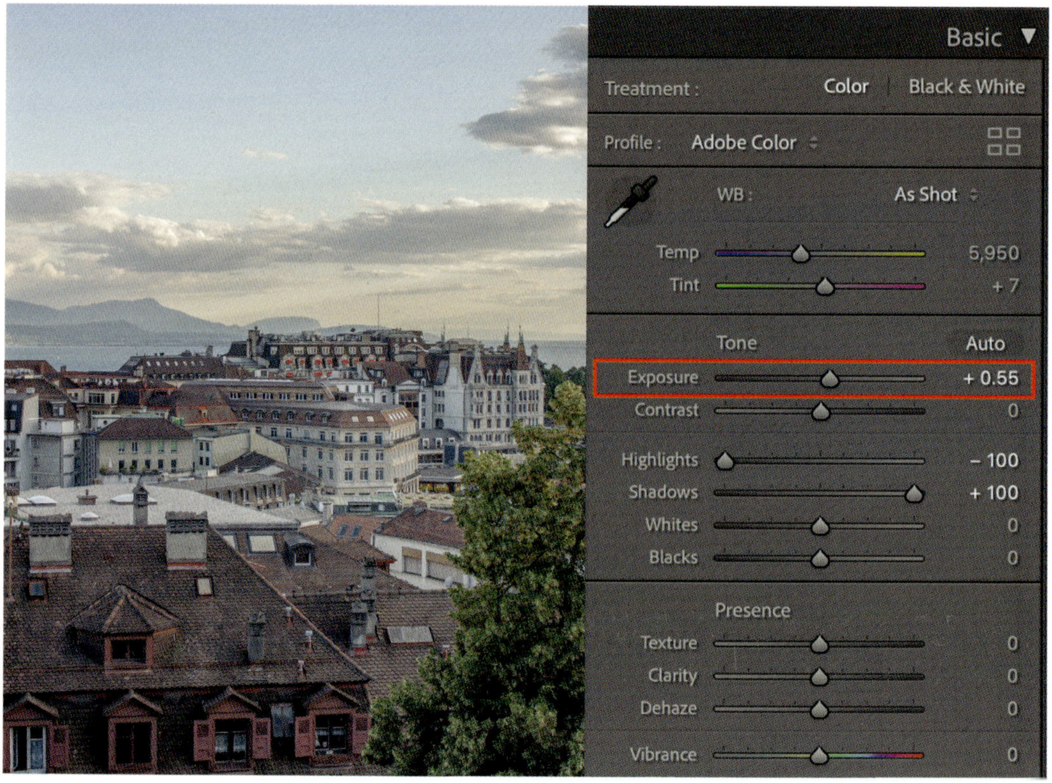

the exposure too much, it can fix one problem but cause others elsewhere. In this instance, since the image is still a little darker than I want, I'm going to raise the overall exposure just a little bit so that the brightness looks right to me. As I do this, it's starting to look the way I remember it.

Step 3: Adjust the Contrast

Step 3 is adjusting the contrast. When you add contrast to your image, you'll be making the black parts of your images blacker and the white parts whiter. It shows a starker difference between the bright and dark areas. Contrasting to 100 will make your highlights go more toward white and your shadows more toward black.

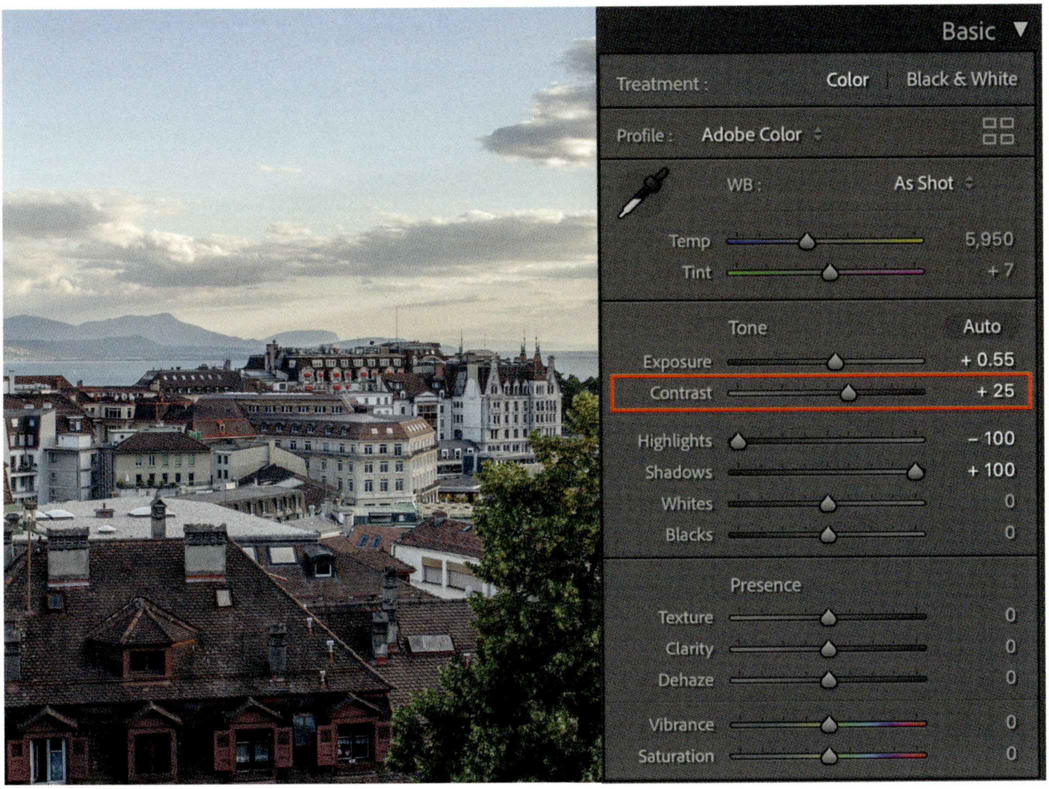

If you reduce the contrast to negative 100, you get the opposite effect. It makes those whites and blacks almost even with each other, almost taking out contrast altogether. It makes the image look really flat. It mixes the lighter and darker parts of the image and goes toward gray. You want to find the right contrast to make sure you're highlighting your darks and lights properly. In this photo I ended up doing about 25 percent contrast. That didn't make my image look completely amazing, but it's getting there.

The image is starting to pop a little bit more. Here's a word of caution though: try not to overedit with any type of editing, especially not with contrast. It can make your photos look cheesy and intense. Less is more. As with almost any editing trick, I recommend you adjust the slider to where you think it should be, then slide it back about 30 percent and see how it looks. It's easy to overdo this stuff, so a little moderation can go a long way.

Step 4: Clarify the Image

We've got a couple of steps left. Step 4 is to clarify your image. Many workflow programs will have an adjustment called *clarity*. If you reduce the clarity, it's going to make the image almost hazy. If you increase the clarity, it's going to make the image become super clear—almost pop! But be careful here, again, not to overdo it, because adjusting to add too much clarity can make your images look cheesy super fast. Essentially, adding clarity will make the details more defined. Sometimes at this point I'll give a 10 to 35 percent increase in adjustments like *vibrance* and *dehaze* if they are available in the app I'm using, which can add a slight additional pop. But definitely only a slight adjustment to avoid the image looking fake or cheesy. See the difference in the next photo?

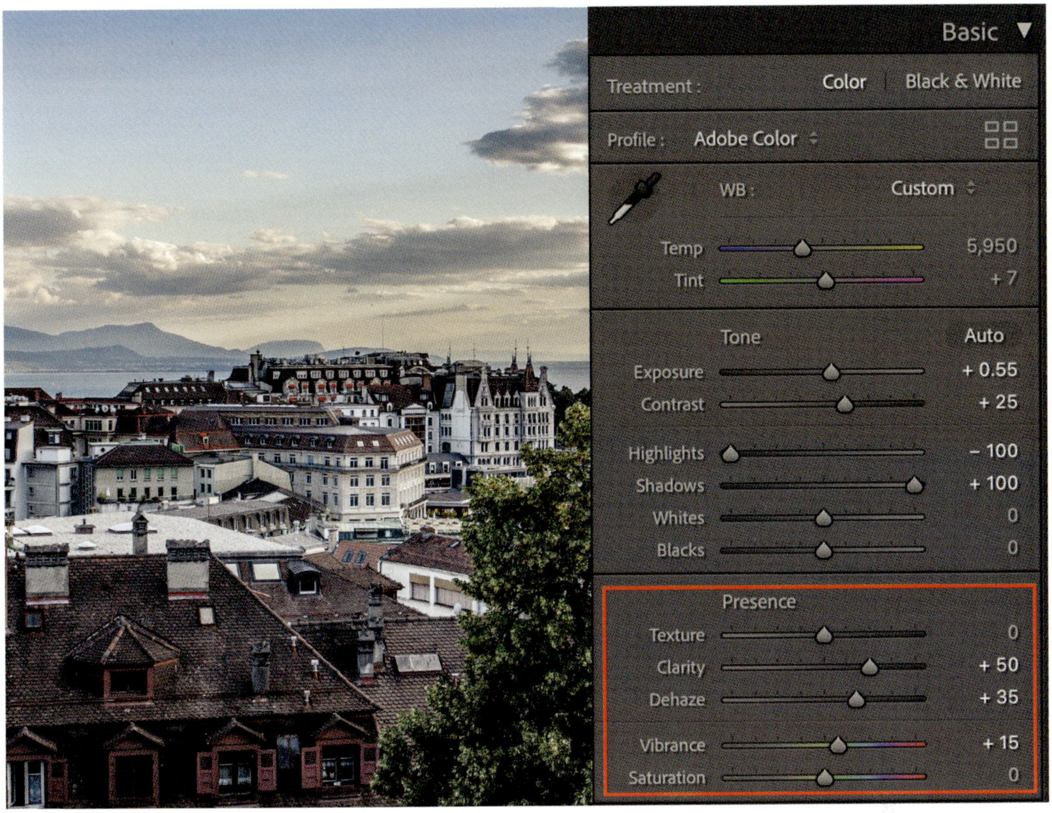
Basic
Treatment :
Color
Black & White
Profile :
Adobe Color
WB :
Custom
Temp
5,950
Tint
+ 7
Tone
Auto
Exposure
+ 0.55
Contrast
+ 25
Highlights
– 100
Shadows
+ 100
Whites
0
Blacks
0
Presence
Texture
0
Clarity
+ 50
Dehaze
+ 35
Vibrance
+ 15
Saturation
0

Step 5: Set the White Balance

Step 5 is to set your white balance to recreate the color and emotion of the original scene. White balance—the balance of color in your images—has two different adjustments, which are the *temperature* and *tint* of the image. The *temperature* is the scale of blues (cold) to yellows (warm). You might hear someone say, "Can you warm up that image a bit?" They are asking you to change the temperature adjustment to add more yellow. The *tint* adjustment is changing the scale of greens to reds. If the image is feeling too green, you can adjust the tint toward red instead.

How does this play out, practically speaking? To cool down an image, add more blue and green tones to give it a more wintry or night feel. To warm it up, add some yellows or reds to give it a more sunset feel.

In Switzerland, the light was getting low, the clouds were lighting up, and there was this gorgeous sunset. It was a reddish-yellow, super-warm feeling in the golden hour of the day. To convey that feeling, I need to warm up this image pretty significantly. I need to add some yellows from the temperature adjustment and some reds in from the tint adjustment. And voilà! The image now captures what I felt when I was there in person.

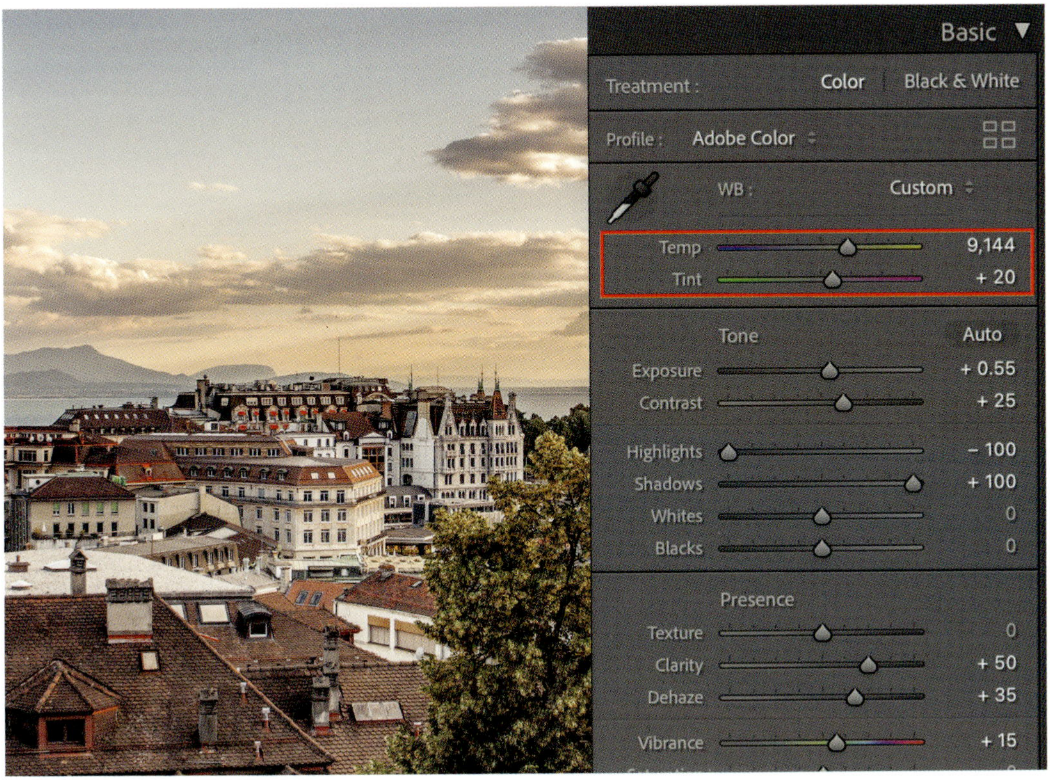
Basic
Treatment : Color Black & White
Profile : Adobe Color
WB : Custom
Temp 9,144
Tint + 20
Tone Auto
Exposure + 0.55
Contrast + 25
Highlights – 100
Shadows + 100
Whites 0
Blacks 0
Presence
Texture 0
Clarity + 50
Dehaze + 35
Vibrance + 15

Let's take a look at these photos. Below is where we came from. This is the photo I took straight out of camera.

BEFORE

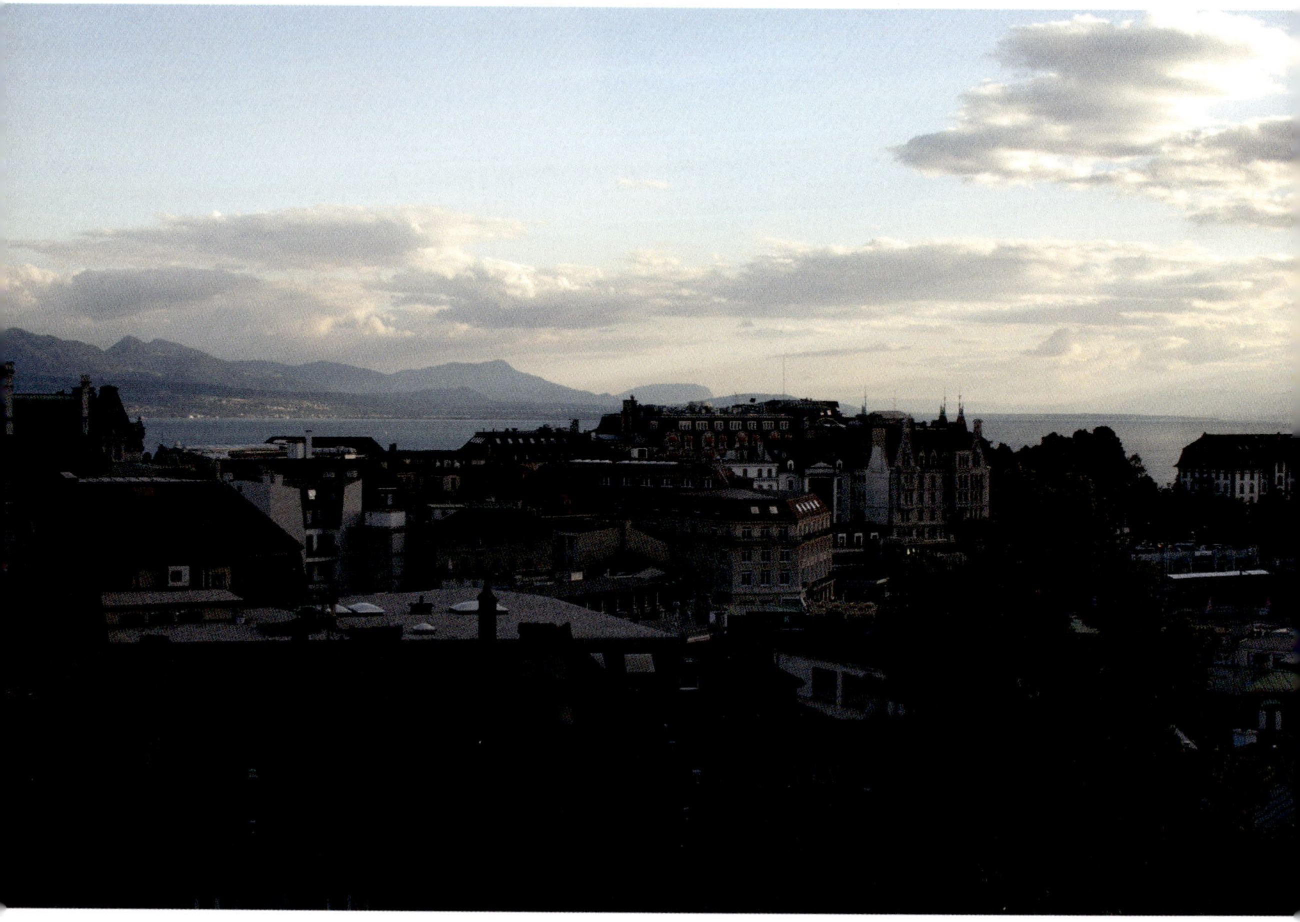

And the following photo is where we are right now. This is what it felt like when I was there in real time.

AFTER

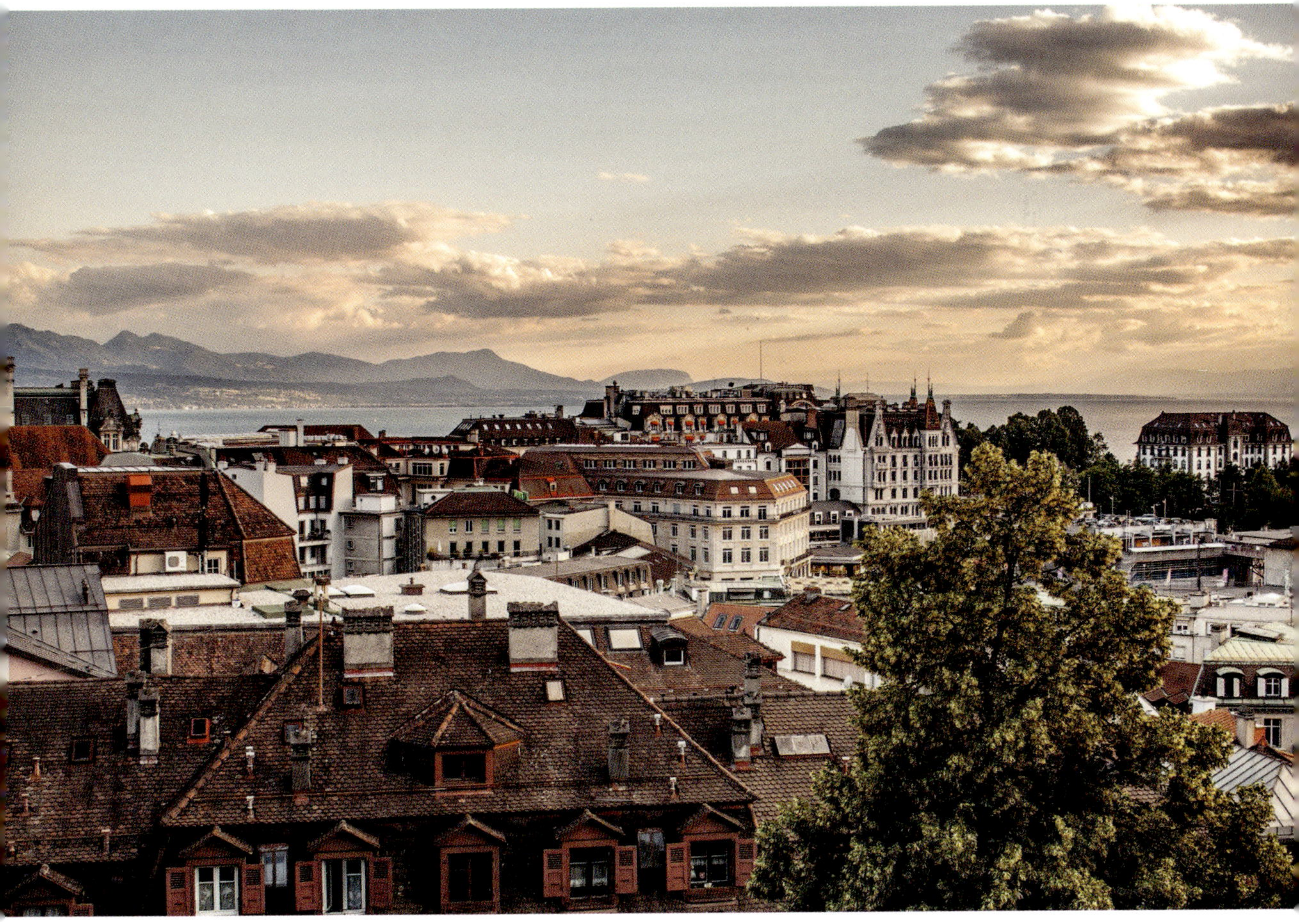

The way it made me feel when I was there in person was so powerful. But unfortunately, what my camera captured didn't tell that story. And this is why we edit! It allows us to recreate the emotion we felt when we snapped the shot. Now you can see, and hopefully feel, the same feelings that I felt that day.

Editing in One Click with Presets

The Five-Step Editing Recipe can be used in any situation to edit your photos from scratch, but is it the most efficient way to edit? What if you could edit faster? You can. You can edit your photos from *blah* to *amazing* in one click, using professional photography recipes that we call *presets*. Once you've downloaded and added presets to a program like Lightroom Classic, you can then use the presets to edit your photos in one glorious click. The best part? Presets can be used simply as a starting point. You're not stuck with the settings it applies, the way a filter often forces on you. Generally speaking, you can't adjust the settings of filters. You can either use them or not. With presets, though, you'll start with a set selection of your editing sliders, but you can alter them afterward if you'd like. In a way, a filter is like a mask, whereas a preset is like makeup. You can keep trying different ones until you get the image as close as possible to what you want, then alter the settings to get it perfect.

▶ For more help on this, you can go to PhotoMentorship.com/LTS to download some free presets to get you started.

BEFORE PRESETS

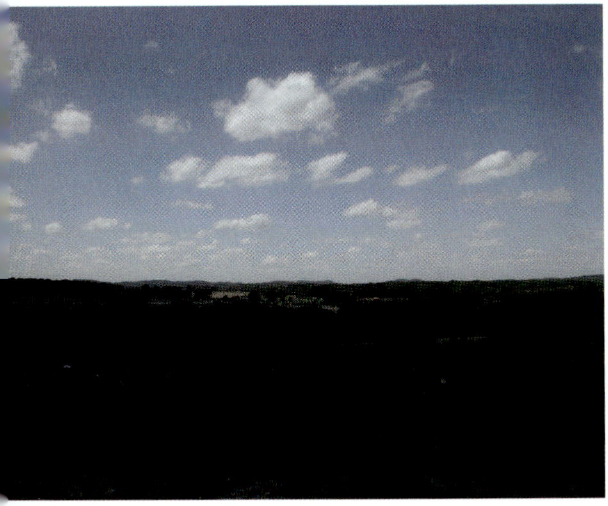

AFTER PRESETS

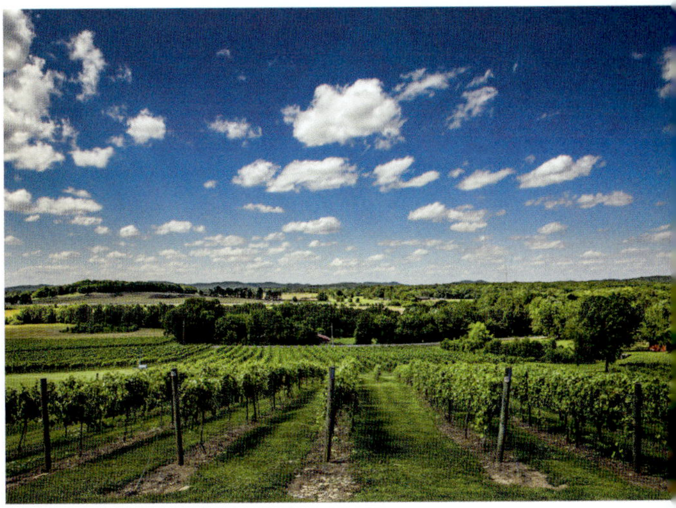

EXPORT

All that's left now is to *export*. When you are shooting your photos in RAW format you need to export the images to JPEGs. JPEG is the most common and universal file format in the world. Most of the images on the internet are JPEGs, and it is our go-to file type when we share images via text, email, or social media. In contrast, the RAW format is horrible for sharing because only certain programs can read and display it. What this means is when we are done using the editing superpowers that the RAW format provides, we export the images to JPEGs, which makes a universal copy we can share everywhere. You can easily export your edited photos to JPEG using your workflow program and start sharing your photos with the world. Get your finalized photos exported and out there to tell the story.

And that's the goal, right? If we edit to recreate the emotion we felt to share with our viewers, we're always thinking about the story we want to tell, the experience we want to share, and the feeling we want to recreate. Following this process helps us do that quickly and successfully.

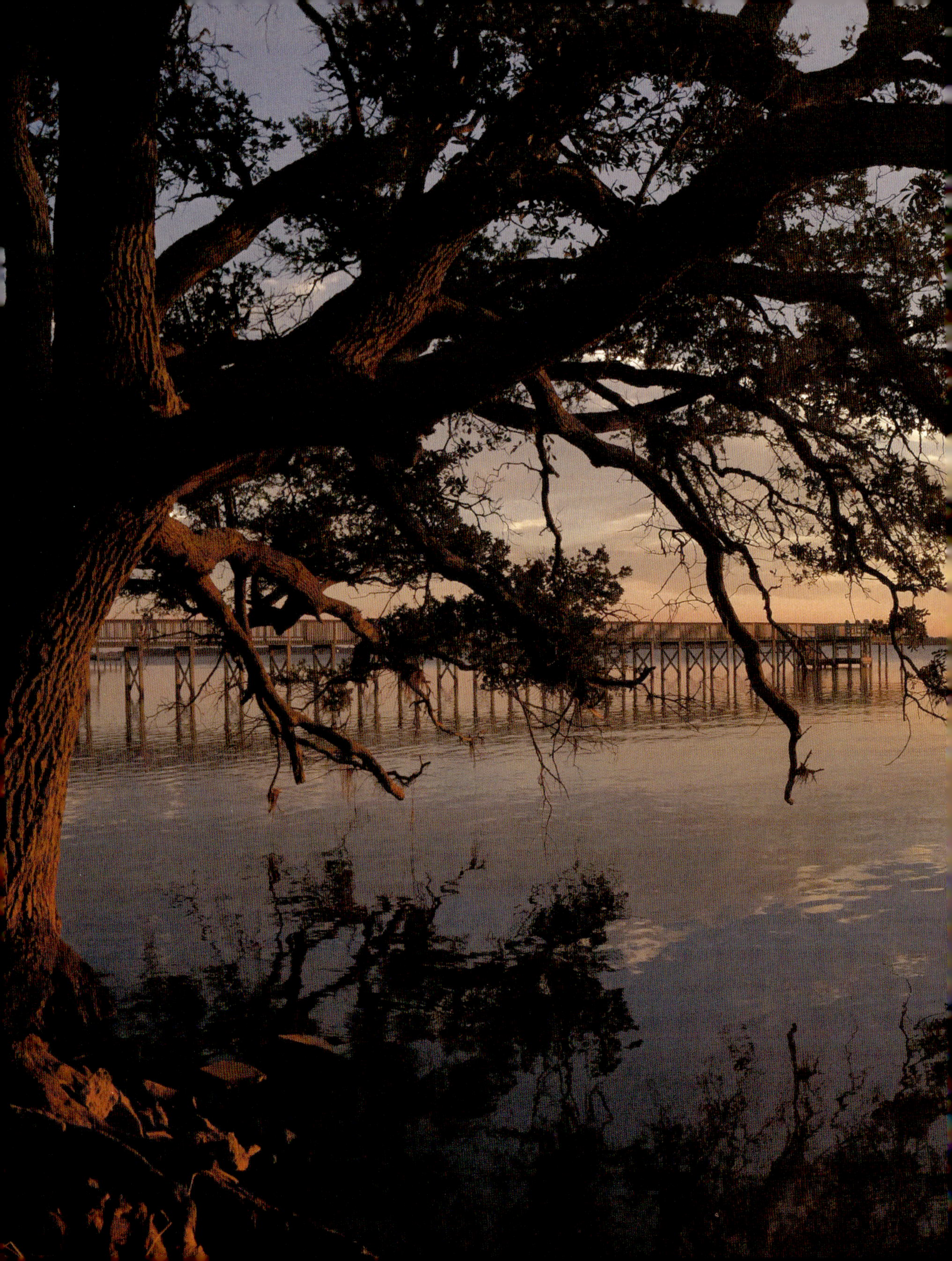

PART 4

DEVELOP

This part is about deciding what kind of photographer you want to be and developing the skills to become a great photographer. After you've mastered the fundamentals of photography, but before you actually begin earning money, you need to decide what your photography path will be. This means you've got to focus. You can't shoot everything and everyone and be successful. This is not about deciding your future forever but rather about moving in a certain direction. Even photographers who shoot for fun need to decide where they will focus their efforts—if they want to be amazing.

Your niche will almost certainly change as you grow, but you can't pivot if you aren't already moving toward something. In this section I am going to challenge you to do some introspection about what you want your business and life to look like. Taking your time to really design and develop your photography business is essential to long-term success. Earning money is fun, but these decisions will set you up for years to come.

CHAPTER 9

Pick a Path: Developing Your Specialty

IF YOU'VE EVER FOUND YOURSELF LYING ON AN OPERATING TABLE IN THE hospital, you know just how important expertise is. Nobody wants a heart surgeon who splits his time working as a part-time plumber. No one wants to hear, "I'm dabbling in surgery; it's my side hustle right now, along with cryptocurrency and longboarding." If your life is on the line, you want it in the hands of someone who has chosen their path deliberately and mastered it. You want someone who studied to become an expert in a particular focus. You want a specialist.

The same is true for photography. Okay, so maybe the stakes aren't as high as they are for a surgeon, but the dilemma is the same. You wouldn't hire a photographer who specializes in landscapes to shoot your wedding. You wouldn't ask someone who focuses on newborn portraits to take action shots at a football game. You'd turn to the pro in that field—the person who has studied and worked to become an expert.

Picking a path and developing a specialty will help narrow your focus and hone your skills. It will make you more competent and confident in your work. Eventually that will translate into the ability to market yourself as a specialist in your field. Your work in your area of focus will speak for itself.

And, perhaps most importantly, narrowing your focus will begin to attract your ideal clients to you. What is the first thing a newly engaged woman does when planning her wedding? She googles "[location] + wedding photographer." Brides only seek out wedding photographers, and high school seniors specifically want senior portrait photographers. We'll talk more about this in a later chapter, but hardly anyone seeks out a photographer who shoots anything and everything. Which is why if your goal is to develop your skills and eventually make a little (or a lot) of money as a photographer, it's important to go deep in one area and become well-known as a particular kind of photographer.

Maybe a full-time, booming photography business isn't what you want. That's okay. For some people, learning to see, shoot, and edit like a photographer is enough to take your hobby or passion to the next level. It's enough to help you tell the kinds of stories you want in your images. But if you want to turn this hobby into a business, part-time or full-time, picking a path is essential. Learning to use and understand your camera is a great step, but it's not the whole journey. If you want to take professional-quality photos—the kinds of photos you can build a business on—finding your focus is key.

The Different Paths

While there are a number of paths you could choose as a photographer, the biggest thing you have to decide is if you want to turn pro and make money from your passion or keep photography as just a hobby. Both are noble. There is no need to monetize every passion. Your skills and interests are no less valid because you don't make money from them. A student of mine is more fulfilled than he's ever been and only does volunteer photography. There is no wrong way to use your art.

On the other hand, there is absolutely nothing wrong with wanting to make money from photography and provide for your family doing what you love. If anyone calls you a sellout, send them over to me and I'll give them a talkin' to for you. Just kidding (kinda). But seriously, one of the greatest joys of my life is making a living from something I love doing. Don't let anyone cause you to feel shame for being successful at something they couldn't do. Because that's what criticism often is: jealousy.

I want to focus on some of the most common career paths photographers can pursue to turn pro and make a decent living. These paths are proven—they are tried, market tested, and true. So often we hear from people who want to develop a niche that's incredibly unique, and as an artist, I get it. But when I hear someone say, "I really want to photograph tattooed whales in Antarctica," I'm like, "That sounds really cool, but how are you going to make money doing that? Who really wants that? Will anyone actually pay?" If your specialty is your hobby, then those tattooed whales are a great focus. (And send me some pics, 'cause I want to see that!) But if you want to make money, then you need to choose a more marketable path that you know many other professional photographers are using to make a full-time living.

We won't talk about every kind of professional photographer here. There are so many niches and specialties to make a fantastic living. Instead, we'll talk about the most marketable ones. Not all paths are created equal, and the ones included below are some of the most lucrative in the industry—so choose wisely.

WEDDING PHOTOGRAPHY

Perhaps the most common and popular path that always comes to my mind is wedding photography. Wedding photography is how I went from broke to making over $100,000 per year. You probably don't need me to tell you that working in the wedding industry is one of the most common ways to build a lucrative career as a photographer. For better or worse, people are getting married all the time, and they're willing to pay good money to make sure those memories are captured. It's an achievable path because the market is there. It's a sure bet.

Let's do the math. If you put in the work and practice, it's reasonable that a good, established photographer could book thirty weddings a year at $3,000 each. That means by the end of the year, you've made $90,000. The bottom line is, if making money is your goal, shooting weddings as your specialty isn't a bad path to pick.

NATURAL-LIGHT PORTRAITS

Another common and easily marketable path is shooting natural-light portraits. This could mean shoots that are indoor, outdoor, or whatever. It just means the photographer is using natural light instead of supplemental light from speedlights and/or strobes. Natural-light portrait photographers can pick from a variety of categories. They can shoot family portraits, senior portraits, engagement pictures, newborns, or even maternity photos. The list goes on and on—this one is not exhaustive. These can all be great specialties for a photographer to make a living. If you want a lower-pressure lifestyle than the life of a wedding photographer, this is a great path to pursue, and there are tons of opportunities. People are constantly looking to have portraits captured of their loved ones to preserve moments in time.

My wife will beg me to agree to another family portrait session. My mom will say it's the only thing she wants for her birthday from our family. If I've learned anything from married life, it's that mama bear will get what she wants, one way or another. Happy wife, happy life, right? You can either be right, or you can be happily married. But sometimes not both. Choose wisely. Women are always getting pregnant, babies are always growing up, and seniors are always graduating. Change is always happening, and their mamas want those pictures.

Here's my point: natural-light portraits will always be in high demand. That's why specializing in and developing an eye for natural-light portraits can be very lucrative.

STUDIO PHOTOGRAPHY

Studio photography is another great option, particularly studio headshots. Both companies and individuals are regularly on the lookout for a photographer who can give them consistently great-looking professional headshots for websites, social media, directories, profile pics, book projects, speaker profiles, and more. This path is ideal for a photographer who wants to meticulously dial in their light to get exactly what they want in a controlled environment. The great part of studio photography is that if you can leave your lights set up, you can dial in the settings and have a more streamlined process for your next shoot. I know headshot photographers who will rotate in a new client every fifteen minutes!

REAL ESTATE PHOTOGRAPHY

One niche that has grown more and more in recent years is real estate photography. I mean, who hasn't spent hours scrolling real estate websites in the night, dreaming of buying that multimillion-dollar mansion on the beach? Or getting design ideas for their own home. Real estate photography helps fuel those dreams. With more and more of the housing market being pushed online, the market for a photographer who understands what to shoot in a home, and how to shoot it, is growing. That makes this path in the industry a marketable, money-making choice.

SOCIAL MEDIA PHOTOGRAPHY

Next there's the developing field of social media photography. Every business needs to be on social media these days and needs new and fresh content consistently. I know many photographers who are on retainer with coffee shops, restaurants, and social media influencers and shoot a set amount each month. It's great for both parties because the photographer has consistent, predictable work and the business knows they are going to have a certain number of solid photos coming in to post to their social media channels.

This is a great path for any photographer looking to create a diverse portfolio of content and make money in a field that's booming right now. As a social media photographer, you could be shooting anything from still life and product imagery for stores and restaurants to curated content for influencers or major companies. This path provides a great source of predictable income in a field where that can be hard to come by.

FOOD AND PRODUCT PHOTOGRAPHY

Food and product photography is traditionally used for commercial purposes. Restaurants, cookbook publishers, brands, and companies all need photos of their food and products to market them. Like social media photography, these images are used on social media, in print, in marketing materials, and in campaigns to sell goods and services. Though the path isn't quite as direct as weddings or portraits, this is also a good way to build a lucrative career in photography. Many of these companies have money to spend, and they understand what good photography can do for their brand.

LANDSCAPE PHOTOGRAPHY

So let's talk about the elephant in the room, shall we? Many aspiring photographers ask me how to make money shooting landscapes. And the truth is, you can make a full-time living shooting specialized landscapes. But it's hard and not nearly as common as other niches. Rich Coleman, my colleague, tells the story of his college professor who was critiquing one of his landscape photos:

> **PROFESSOR:** "You want to know how to make money with that beautiful landscape photo of the mountains?"
>
> **RICH:** "Yeah, that would be great!"
>
> **PROFESSOR:** "Put a bride in front of that mountain . . ."

Rich got it. He started a wedding photography business and started making six figures.

I'm not saying not to go for it. My friend Jonah Allen makes a fantastic living selling his landscape photography. But it's my job as your self-proclaimed photography mentor to be honest with you: this is a harder path. People who shoot landscapes do get commissioned for certain projects, but the most popular income stream comes from selling their prints. Jonah has a high-end photographic print gallery down in

Florida near where I live. You may have to get more creative here, and be resilient, but it's certainly not impossible to make a living shooting landscapes.

WILDLIFE PHOTOGRAPHY

Wildlife photography is similar to landscape photography in that it's a less obvious path to make a living in, and can take a lot of time to start getting paid. *National Geographic* won't be knocking on your door immediately. But that's not a reason not to go for it. It depends on your motivation, but most wildlife photographers choose to shoot wildlife as a hobby or passion. And if they want to make a living they will shoot another genre for that. While it's possible to lean out of your car window occasionally for a shot, you may need to learn some survival and adventuring skills to really get the shots worth publishing. You also have to be very patient to shoot wildlife. You can put people where you want them, but you can't make a great blue heron fly where you want it to get just the right light. As difficult as people can be, nature can sometimes be even more frustrating. Loving the outdoors is essential for this path. Heck, you could just shoot wildlife for fun and then list your images with a stock photo agency and see if they sell. You might be surprised and make some fun money back to pay for your equipment!

How to Choose

Maybe you're reading this and thinking, *This is great and all, but I still have no idea what my specialty could be. I have no clue what path to pursue.* It's rare to know your path before you start walking it out in this industry, as with most creative endeavors, so this is nothing to worry about. If you know photography is the business for you, you just have to start somewhere.

Start moving in the direction that sounds the best to you right now—any direction—and course-correct as you go. You can't get off the ground if you don't start. So pick up the camera and go for it. You might find the right path right away, or you might have to shift and pivot as you go. Either way, you'll never know unless you begin. When a plane takes off from New York traveling to LA, it rarely points directly at Los Angeles. The pilot has to correct the course while en route. But the plane has to take off first and start flying in order to do that. You don't have a hope of getting from New York to LA if the plane never takes off. Here's the point: you have to start. Because you can't change course if you don't get off the ground.

In most areas of business, it would be strange and ill-advised to start a business before you even know what you want to sell. But with photography, that's often what we do. The trick, though, is to try to be intentional and focused at the outset, knowing at least where you want to begin. But the good news is, nothing is wasted. If you begin working as a family portrait photographer and realize over time you'd rather work in the wedding industry, you didn't lose anything in the time you spent working with family portraits. The skills you developed can be applied in the wedding industry. You're shooting bridal parties, families, and various groups of people as a wedding photographer the same way you did when shooting family portraits. Don't be afraid to discover and course-correct as you go. We all do.

So how do you know where to start? How do you know which path might be right for you? Start by asking yourself a few simple questions.

1. **Do you want to shoot people?** Do you want to work with other people? You may not know if you want to work with a wedding party, a pregnant mother, a family, or a high school senior, but usually you do know if you want to shoot people in some capacity.
2. **Do you want to shoot things?** Do you want to work with still or inanimate objects? Again, this has a range. "Things" could mean mountains, homes, food—literally anything. If you know people aren't your thing, you probably know shooting something else is a better place to start.
3. **How hard are you willing to work?** Building any business is going to take work, and a lot of it. But if you choose a specialty that isn't as easy to market, you're going to have to work a little harder. Maybe you don't feel that wedding photography is your passion, but you don't have a ton of time

and want something that's easy to market. It's important to know how much time and effort you're willing to put in at the beginning. Take Jonah Allen, for example. As a young photographer, he set his sights on a specific specialty: seascapes. At first glance, I wouldn't say there's a major market for photos like these. But Jonah figured out how to make his work actually work for him. Where so many photographers who choose landscape-type work as their specialty might end up only with a hobby, Jonah has a full-blown career. He worked hard to develop and market his skill on his chosen path, and it paid off. He now sells his work to an exclusive group of clients willing to pay a higher amount because they know his work is exceptional. He does great work, and that's allowed him to turn his passion into a profession.

The same can be true for you. Whether you're looking to hone in on a hobby or build a booming business, the first step is to determine *what* you want to shoot, at least for now. You may not be sure, but I promise, if you commit to picking up your camera and start shooting, you'll find your path along the way. The important thing is to get moving.

CHAPTER 10

The Four Levels of Photography

AFTER YOU'VE CHOSEN A PATH TO START ON, YOU HAVE ANOTHER IMPORTANT question to consider: What kind of photographer do you want to be? This is different from picking your specialty. This is about your lifestyle and goals for how much money you want to make from this work. And it's all about time.

How much time do you want to give to this work? Be honest about this. If you can take great photographs and deliver a good experience to people, the amount of money you can make in the industry is limited mainly by how much time you're willing to put into it. And how much time you're willing to put into it both determines and is determined by your current lifestyle, or the lifestyle you're looking for. Are you looking to build a part-time business to serve as a side hustle? Are you hoping to make this your full-time career? Or is your goal to turn this into a six-figure, booming business? Your answers will determine the way you chart your course from here.

This isn't just about working hard. You can work very hard at this on a part-time basis. This is about your lifestyle. Are you working a full-time job already that you simply can't or don't want to walk away from? Are you a parent who has to factor in not just how to support your kids but also how to be present to take care of and nurture them? Are you willing or able to give up your nights and weekends to make this work? Are you prepared to charge what you need to so you can make the money you want to make for the amount of work you want to do? Are you comfortable with your income being a little inconsistent at times?

All that and more can make the difference in whether you choose to be a part-time photographer, a full-time photographer, a six-figure-earning photographer, or the creator of a "just for me" passion project.

The Part-Time Photographer

Let's take a wedding photographer, for example. Say you've chosen to specialize and market yourself in the wedding industry. Maybe you're a busy parent, or working a "day job" you aren't ready to leave yet, or just have a few weekends a year to give to photography. That probably means a part-time business is your best bet.

What does that look like, practically? Well, you'll simplify your offerings to maximize your time. As a wedding photographer, this probably means you'd determine the number of weddings you have time to do each year. Then you'd deliver your clients a simple package for a simple fee. Say, for example, you're going to charge about $1,500 to shoot a wedding. At that price, you just need to book about fifteen weddings each year to make around $22,500, which is a solid part-time take. In that pricing, you're only going to include edited images. No extra upsells or specialized albums or packages. It's a simple, straightforward fee that delivers what the client needs while covering your time and giving you a part-time side hustle.

The Full-Time Photographer

Or maybe you opt to go the full-time route: you want this wedding photography business to be your go-to gig all the time, and you're going to raise the stakes on time, money, and offerings. Let's say you book around twenty weddings a year at $2,000 apiece. That's $40,000 for weddings alone. The more serious and established the photographer, the higher she can raise her prices. But to make a little more money to support yourself, you also need to offer a few add-ons to your services. Maybe you offer engagement sessions, customized albums, printed announcements or thank-you notes—the list could go on and on. Let's imagine you sell a $500 album to each wedding client for those twenty weddings. That adds $10,000 to your $40,000, bringing you to $50,000 for the year. And that's just one add-on. The more additional services and products you offer, the more additional income you can make when booking clients. Just like that, you can move from a good full-time salary to a far better full-time salary.

The Six-Figure Photographer

And finally, maybe you want to pursue the path of a six-figure photographer. Again, you have to consider the time you want to give and the price you want to charge for it. So here, you could still be shooting around twenty weddings a year, but at about $5,000 each. What allows you to do this? You have more confidence as a photographer now, and you're more established, with word-of-mouth referrals coming from the work you're doing. It's actually not hard to get to this place after a few years of shooting. It just takes a little time and dedication. If you do a good job, stick around, and keep raising your rates, you can make this kind of money. Charging this much allows you to make a $100,000 base salary just for weddings alone, but again, remember that the add-ons and upcharges come into play here, helping you earn more. You start tacking on extra photo shoots for family members, customized albums and canvases grandma can also purchase, bridal portrait sessions available before the big day, and more. And with each client saying yes to a few of those things, you're not only able to move up to that six-figure situation, you're building a clientele who will come back to you again and again.

The Passion Project

I don't want to move on here without addressing another very valid path for your business. Maybe you've found a specialty you love. And maybe you even want to make a little money shooting in that field. But at the end of the day, this is really just a passion project for you. You're seeing and shooting like a photographer—maybe you're telling stories through images—simply because you're passionate about it. That's just as worthy a path to pursue as any other.

The goal in making photography your business isn't to make as much or even more money than the guy next to you. It's choosing the path that works best for you. The path that inspires you.

My fellow photography mentor Zach Gray told me that he often asks students in his workshops to take time to reflect. Maybe it's just twenty or thirty minutes where they sit down, get quiet, and ponder a little bit about their journey to the business side of photography. In this time, he encourages his students to think about who they want to be. Not who they *think* they should be, but who they *actually* want to be when it comes to their lives and work.

I love the distinction in this question. Because isn't it easy for all of us to set our goals and attempt to carve out our paths based more on who we think we should be than who we actually want to be? We follow all these people on social media and get the highlight reel of their careers coming in through our social media feed. And we start to think, *That's what my career should look like. That's what life as a photographer is supposed to be.* But the truth is, the reality isn't pictured there. We're setting goals for our real lives based on someone else's highlight reels, but are those highlight reels even what we really want?

The goal in choosing your path in business should simply be this: Choose what's right for you. Not what others think you should do, not what looks great on social media, not even what will make you the most money. Base your decision on what's really right for you. And nobody can tell you that but you.

I know this may sound like a bunch of fluff, but trust me, it's important. It's real life, and that can impact your business for better or worse. I know because

I've been there. This is the time to start making decisions, even if you aren't quite sure of the best direction for you. That's fine; you just need to begin and take this time and focus to get good. So let's pick a path and start practicing. You can always change directions later.

CHAPTER 11

Just Get Started

ONCE YOU'VE PICKED YOUR PATH AND DECIDED ON WHAT KIND OF PHO-tographer you want to be, it's time to start practicing—and practice some more. You need to get as much experience as possible right now. You learn, you shoot, and you keep learning and shooting. Ask for feedback, study your specialty, take photography courses, find the right coaching. Look for what you like and shoot it every opportunity you get.

Yes, this takes time and dedication, but as you've seen from some of the stories in this book, the payoff can be worth the hard work. Eventually you'll grow in confidence and competence, and down the line you'll find yourself saying, "I'm really good at this." *That's* when you know you've hit your stride. *That's* when you can start growing a business and charging a solid fee for your work—but we're getting ahead of ourselves here. What does it take to grow as a photographer, and what kind of professional do you want to be? Logging hours behind the camera is certainly part of it, but there's more to becoming a pro than just shooting a ton. You've got to build your portfolio. And how you do that just might surprise you.

Getting Started

When I was twenty-one, a few years after my car accident, I was drowning in debt, had no job, barely knew anyone in Nashville, and didn't have leads on photography gigs. I was newly engaged to Tammy, and we were in the thick of planning our wedding in my hometown. About this time I read a book called *Through Painted Deserts* by Donald Miller about an incredible road trip he took.

"Hey, baby," I said to Tammy one night when I was feeling particularly overwhelmed, "I'm going to take a two-month road trip around the perimeter of Mexico. Don't worry, though: the drug cartel hasn't been *super* active lately. Anyway, it's gonna be an epic guys' trip. I'll spearfish for dinner, surf every day, and camp on vacant beaches for free whenever possible . . . while you work and plan our wedding in a town where you've never lived. Cool?"

It was going to add thousands of dollars more to my already-overcharged credit card. We were planning the wedding in North Carolina, which was twelve hours away from Nashville. My fiancée's only connection there was me, and I was going on a two-month surfing trip. Pretty sensitive of me, huh? Don't blame me. You can thank Donald Miller for giving me the idea! Anyway, I did it: I left my fiancée to work her full-time job and finish planning the wedding with my mom while I racked up more debt and had one more bachelor adventure. Yes, I was an idiot, and I can't believe she stayed with me. Thank God he gave her peace to still marry me. Her friends and family were shocked as well. And yet, good came of it. During one moment on the trip, I was feeling the weight of my financial situation and realized I needed to grow up, that I had to figure out how to provide for my future family and take more responsibility. I was feeling conflicted, anxious, and aimless at the time and needed a revelation.

Walking down a beach 1,300 miles south of San Diego somewhere in mainland Mexico, I saw something incredible. Right then and there, as I was feeling scared and stressed about the future, I turned to face the ocean and saw hundreds of humpback whales jumping in the air and playing. I didn't know this at the time, but apparently they migrate to warmer climates in the Pacific during the winter—which it was.

Now, let me tell you. This was a spectacular sight to behold. The whales were jumping, scratching their bellies on the sandbars in the eight-foot-deep waters, and just having a good ol' time. It was beautiful and mesmerizing, but even with the stunning display of nature, I still couldn't shake the anxieties I felt about money. Alone with my thoughts, I couldn't pretend it would go away. I began to pray, or perhaps more accurately argue, with God. *What should I do?* And very distinctly, I heard God "speak" to me more clearly than I've ever heard in my life: *Shoot weddings.* It wasn't an audible voice, but I swear to you, it was real. At that moment, the message was as clear as day: *David, you need to start shooting weddings.*

Here's the truth, though: I didn't love the message. I didn't want that path. It wasn't the vision I had for myself as a photographer. I'd just made the move to Nashville at the time. And with that move, I had this idea of what I *thought* a successful path for myself as a photographer would be. I was sure I'd be shooting things like major musicians, concerts, album covers, and all the cool stuff my hero photographers in the area were doing. I wanted to do exactly what they were doing. I'd even had a glimpse of success before with Switchfoot and was beginning to see myself as a concert photographer. I knew shooting weddings could be a respectable path for a photographer, but it didn't inspire me like the commercial photography my heroes were producing. I loved the idea of shooting album covers and advertising campaigns that millions and millions of people would see. Weddings just didn't excite me in the same way.

Remember, I was recently engaged. All the money I had to my name was supposed to be going toward getting married and setting up our life together. But instead I was racking up more debt on this two-month trip to Mexico. I had a lot of debt from failed investments, a contract on a house, and literally had no job (just a few freelance photography assistant gigs at the time, which hardly paid the bills). Was it the best time to empty out my savings and put money on a credit card for a trip to Mexico? Looking back, the answer is most definitely . . . *yes*! Was it the most responsible? No. No, it was not. The trip was amazing and I don't regret the adventure or what I learned. It was worth the pain, the debt, and the fear. It was a coming-of-age experience. But nonetheless, I found myself on that beach in Mexico, considering my life, my future marriage, my career, and just exactly how I was going to be able to support my wife and our future family. I didn't know till then. So far, I'd been piecing together gigs assisting other photographers, but the work was inconsistent at best. It wasn't enough to build a life on, and that's when I heard the word: *weddings.*

I'm a guy who goes 100 percent into everything I do, so I knew that if I was going to walk the path toward wedding photography, I was going to be all in. There would be no room for album covers, concerts, and all the other things I *thought* should be the path for me at the time. It felt like saying yes to that voice there on the beach would ultimately mean saying no to the vision I had for myself. Instead of becoming some big-shot celebrity photographer, I was going to be the photography equivalent of the Wedding Singer.

So like any hard-headed, stubborn guy at the outset of his career, I argued. There, in my mind, I pleaded my case to God for a different path. And then, as clear as I've ever heard anything internally, I heard God say, *Hey, David, you're going to give 100 percent to this. You're going to be committed and focused, and it's going to pay off. And if you can do that now, I promise you, it won't be for the rest of your life. This is just a season. I want you to give me five years and commit to shooting weddings. And if you do that, I'll fulfill dreams you don't even know you have.*

This started to sound agreeable. It started to sound a little better. Not so much the idea of shooting weddings but the thought that it wouldn't be my forever path. This allowed me to say yes, even if it was a little begrudgingly. Now, this sounds a little contradictory to what I said before, which is to focus on what you want and go after it, and of course, I think that's the way to go. But I also subscribe to the philosophy of Lewis Schiff, who writes in his book *Business Brilliant*: "Do what you love, but follow the money."[1] That's what I was doing. Concert photography was not a viable career option for me, nor did I see much of a future in photojournalism or some obscure kind of art photography. I knew I needed to go where the money was, at least to get started, and find a way to love it.

The reality is I didn't have the slightest clue what it even meant to be a wedding photographer. At that point in my life, I had only ever been to small weddings in boring church gyms with brown-carpeted walls and high-maintenance people. You know the type. I didn't realize you could make more than $500 on a full Saturday shooting weddings. And with that number in mind, I thought I was going to have to

---

1. Lewis Schiff, *Business Brilliant* (New York: Harper Business, 2013), 28.

do at least sixty weddings a year to even hit a moderate $30,000. That didn't sound great or even feasible. But still, it felt like a clear message and a clear path. So that day on the beach, I decided to do it. I committed to pursuing the business of wedding photography with all I had. This is what you need to do at this point in the process: pick a path, any path really, to get started, and begin to work the system. It'll pay off; I promise. I mean, you might want to travel thousands of miles to stand on an empty beach and plead with God to hear what you should do next, too, but I can't guarantee the same results.

Shortly after that, a friend reached out and asked me to shoot her wedding. Was the price great? Not so much. But at the time—back in 2006—$500 felt like a small fortune. I went out there and gave it my all, researching and studying shots ahead of time, tearing out images in bridal magazines and pulling together ideas of how I could arrange my shots. My wife and I drove all night—from Nashville to a small town in Virginia—to shoot it. It was my first paid wedding, and I was doing everything I could to make it a success.

Truth be told, I crushed it. I didn't give 100 percent—I gave 190 percent. The photos turned out great—even better than expected—so I kept working. Kept studying. Kept preparing. I kept building my name and confidence as a wedding photographer. I started proclaiming that I *was* a wedding photographer; it was a thing I began to call myself. Because as we've learned, how you see yourself affects how others see you.

I booked eight more weddings that year, then started traveling more to shoot them. One good gig led to another, and so on; when you get out there, people start noticing you and recommending you when they see you do the work. It only takes a little time before all this attention turns into a solid business. Soon I was booking weddings all around the world, something I never dreamed was a possibility at the start of this path. By the following year I was making six figures shooting weddings in places like Greece and Switzerland. All because I had made a commitment.

All I had to do was be faithful to the path in front of me. In my mind, it didn't look like the path I wanted. But it turned out to be even better. I would've missed it if I'd tried to keep walking a road that was not meant for me at the time.

You Can Always Pivot Later

But, of course, that's not how the story ends. Fast-forward years after pursuing weddings with everything we had, and now my wife and I were in a much different place. At this point, I'd built a career that allowed me to pay off all my debt, travel the world, and create enough financial stability to allow Tammy to "retire" from her day job and join me full time in the business as a husband-and-wife photography team. Making more money than we ever dreamed possible, we decided to take the winter off and spend two months on the beach in Hawaii to celebrate. We were living the life!

One day, while we were out driving around the lush island of Oahu sightseeing, we were looking over the stunning views of the Pacific Ocean, and I noticed a ton of whales jumping, and water coming out of their blowholes. It was spectacular. I remember thinking at that moment, *That's cool to see this phenomenon again. The last time I saw that was in Mexico about four or five years ago . . .*

Holy frick, I thought. *It's been almost exactly five years—to the month—when God told me to shoot weddings.* With tears in my eyes, I realized God had fulfilled dreams I didn't even know I had. We had traveled the world, got featured in major publications, made enough money to pay off our debts, pay our bills, and thrive.

Holy crap. I'd done it. We'd made it. It had been a long, hard road, and I felt a sense of satisfaction, smiling to myself as I held my wife's hand while we watched humpback whales dive in the distance. And that's when a thought popped in my mind. It wasn't a thought as much as a familiar voice—one I'd heard my whole life, guiding me when I didn't know where to go or what to do. It said: *You've been faithful. Your time is up. You can transition out of this season of shooting weddings now and pursue your dream.* At that moment, I knew exactly what it was about. It was that same voice that had spoken to me five years ago, giving me permission to shift my focus. Now it was time to once again be faithful on a new course. To shift the focus of my business.

So I did. I started moving away from weddings and into commercial photography. I brought the same energy, the same drive, the same dedication to this path. Only this time, I had more to offer. I had five years of experience, expertise, and finances to bring to the table, all thanks to the time I spent developing and growing as a wedding photographer. That freed me up to do things like buy new equipment, have the experience of building relationships, market myself, and confidently position myself as a commercial photographer. I was ready. And my commercial photography took off beyond my wildest dreams.

My point is simply this: You have to pick the path that's right for you right now. You have to build the business that your life needs *now, not later*. You have to follow your gut toward your calling but also be sensible as you do. Even if the business you begin building isn't the one you imagined it would be, build it anyway. Start part-time and grow to full-time. Learn the ins and outs of portrait photography and bring that expertise to wedding photography one day, if that's your path. Give your *all* to shooting landscapes and apply those skills to your work as a real estate photographer. Yes, we all have dreams of making it big, but we all start somewhere. Big dreams take time, experience, and trust. All that is built slowly, but you can start sooner with entry careers like natural-light family portrait photography. It doesn't have to be forever, but it does need to be for now.

Decide where your focus will be as a business, and then go for it. Commit to giving it your all for a season. Stay faithful and focused to the work you've set out to do, and I promise you: the work will not be wasted. In fact, it will be the foundation on which you build the business you've always dreamed of. It'll only lead to better things later. The point of this part of the book is to help you understand what's ahead of you if you are willing to make some choices. They don't have to be the "right" choices, per se; they just need to be the right ones for right now. When in doubt, choose a path that appeals to you and see where it goes.

In the final section of the book, we're going to bring it all together and talk about how to make this whole thing work as a career, whatever that may look like for you. So what're you waiting around for? Let's go!

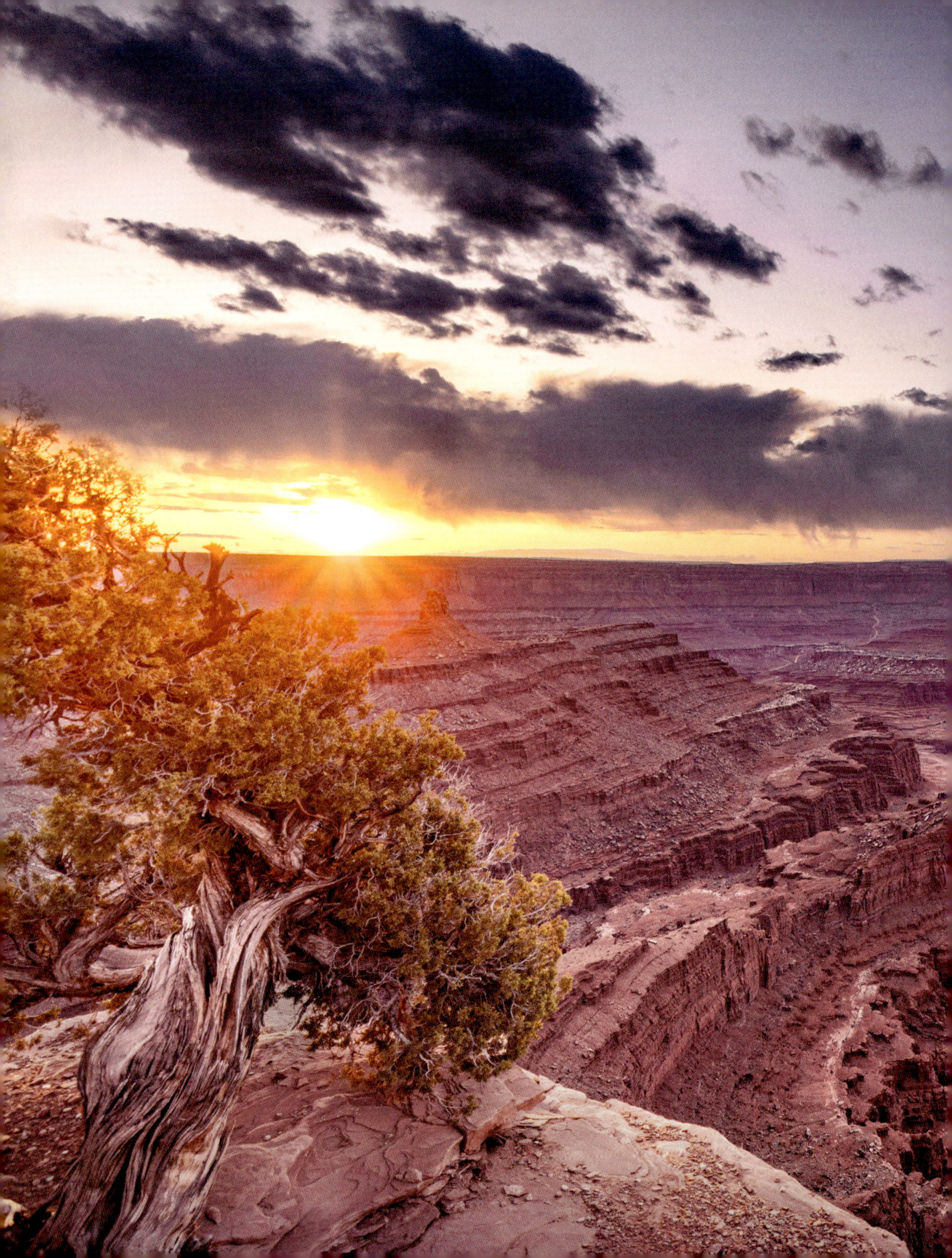

PART 5

EARN

So you've learned the technical skills to make a living as a photographer. But how do you take your passion and turn it into a purposeful business that could change your life and the lives of others? Now that you've started learning, how do you *really* start earning?

Imagine what it would look like to get up every morning and, instead of rushing off to a job you hate, you step into a vocation that gives you the freedom and space to do what you really love. What would that feel like?

In part 5, we'll get into how to create a legitimate business, book your first client, and, most importantly, offer a great customer experience so people keep recommending you. All this will create the momentum you need to get your fledgling business off the ground.

This is what we've been building toward; this is where it all comes together. Creating a photography business can change your life and livelihood, and this is where we'll explore the details of how to make it happen.

CHAPTER 12

Start a Legitimate Business

AMONG THE MANY MISTAKES I MADE AS A FLEDGLING PHOTOGRAPHER, ONE of the greatest was not establishing a legitimate business early on. I picked a path, narrowed in on a specialty, and got pretty dang good at taking pictures. I even started making money—but I didn't have anything formal set up that allowed me to serve my clients in the long-term. I took it seriously, I was trying my best, but I didn't know what I didn't know. It took me a while to figure out how to set up a legitimate business because I had to figure it out on my own. At one point, I'd done a lot of work and had a great year, having built up a small fortune in savings, only to have to pay it all to the government. Because I wasn't paying quarterly tax payments, I ended up having to pay everything I thought had been profit. After my first six-figure year, I literally had nothing left after taxes.

Unfortunately I see this happen with a lot of photographers. They act like a hobbyist, treating something they're doing for money as a diversion. Here's the thing: if you want to get paid hobbyist rates, act like a hobbyist. If you want to get paid like a professional, you have to act like a pro. In my case, I didn't know anything about the financial side of things. I was mostly winging it, like so many areas in my life at that time. When I started making money from photography, I didn't have a clue what I was supposed to do with it. If this was my business—if I was building this brand—there were probably things I needed to do. I instinctively knew I ought to be handling my money, marketing, and every aspect of my brand in a way that was reputable. Above board. Lawful. Scrupulous. You get the picture. I wanted to do good work and to be paid well for it. I realized that making it up as I went along wasn't going to work long term. Eventually I figured out how to build a legitimate business, one that looked and felt—to me and to my clients—like something worth trusting. But I could've saved myself a lot of stress and hassle if I'd set myself up this way from the start. So why don't we learn from my mistakes together?

The biggest question most photographers in this stage of business have is this: How do I book my first paying gig? And trust me, we'll get there. But before you take that step, you want to have all the ducks in a row for your business. You want to be building what we'll call your *beta brand*. Think of this as the beginning of your brand—the beta version that you're testing and building as you develop. I use the word *build* deliberately here. Because as you start out, that's exactly what you're doing. You're *building* something. You're not going to get it all right from the start. You're not going to get to the finish line right away. Rather, you're going to pivot to keep building as you go.

Remember, I wanted to be a rock and roll photographer. But where did I start my business? As a wedding photographer—because that's where the money and opportunity was. I built my beta brand there, and then, with time and experience, I shifted. I changed the focus of the business I was building. I pivoted my brand. The point is, I had something to pivot because I'd been building it the whole time. I didn't do everything right, but one thing I'll always be grateful I did was that I kept moving forward.

Focusing on building your beta brand gives you a direction. It gives you confidence to say you're a working photographer with a growing business. You've gone through the work of learning the foundations. You've started putting what you've learned into practice. You're growing into a pretty proficient photographer in your field. Taking steps to set up a business and build a brand shows the world (and yourself!) that you're serious enough to make this your work. It's an important and crucial step to take in the process.

So where do you begin?

Naming Your Business

Start by choosing a name for your business. This may not sound all that exciting, but I recommend going with your own name. I know, I know. Calling your business "David Molnar Photography" doesn't look great on paper, but the value isn't really in the "cool" factor. It's in the possibility for others to recognize and know your brand. In other words, to know *you*. There are so many different people working in this industry. And to be honest with you, so many of them are nameless brands. They come in, do the job, and go home. And while there's absolutely nothing wrong with that, it leaves little room for clients to remember *you*.

When you go in with your name as the brand, people know immediately who they're getting. You build a reputation attached to who you are. They won't just remember the images you shot; if you do your job well, they'll remember you. The way you made them feel, the work you did to take care of them, the personal touches that set you apart. And the next time they need a photographer, your name—your brand—will be in their minds. That's why simply sticking with your name for your brand is not only the simplest route but the one that can help you be recognized and remembered.

Of course, there are other things to consider when naming your business. Are you trying to build a brand that's bigger than just you? Do you want to hire a team of others to work with you? You can be specific or stay generic. A personal brand, more often than not, is going to sound warm and inviting, whereas something more generic is going to feel impersonal. Of course, you can succeed with a name that isn't necessarily your own; it's often just easier and more straightforward to market your name. However, if you feel strongly about a more artsy brand name, it can work well too. My friends Michael and Amy Headington, who own Images of Grace Photography, have built a fantastic business and reputation. Whatever you pick, just make sure it's something that's easy to remember and unique. As you begin building your business, the best you can do is focus on a clear promise that gets clients excited to work with you. That's what a good brand does.

Building a Website

And as soon as you decide on that name, you'll want to head to the good ol' interwebs and reserve a website domain for your brand. This is huge, because if that domain name isn't available, you're going to have to rethink your name. Your website is the digital front door of your business, right? So you want to make sure the name on the sign, figuratively speaking, matches the name you've given your brand.

This is why having a cohesive brand is so critical. An old-school marketing adage is, "The average customer needs to see a brand [at least] seven times before they trust it," so naming your business with your actual name, and having that same name anywhere someone can find you—from a business card to your social media handle—is crucial to building trust with customers and getting your business started the right way. Of course, you can always play around with the name based on availability. If DavidMolnar.com isn't available as a domain (I'm pretty sure it isn't), you can try something like DavidMolnarPhotography.com (don't you dare!). Simple changes like that can open up a world of possibility for you.

Think *clarity* in terms of brand name. For example, if your last name is difficult to spell, you might want to simplify your brand name so people can find you more easily. Maybe I'd want to go with "David M" if I was worried about people misspelling my name. Not only does it sound cool, but it's easy to remember and find online. Another trick would be to use a middle name or some abbreviated version of your last name, like "EmmaJay" instead of "EmmaJaworskinioplis.com" or "SaraJane" instead of Sarah Jane Beatrice Constantinople. If your last name was MacIntosh or something similar, you could abbreviate it to Mac. Anyway, you get the idea; use your imagination, and you'll find something that works.

Next, get to work building your site. There are a million routes you can take for this, depending on things like timeline, expertise, and budget. Many website-building platforms are easy to use, affordable, and provide a lot of templates that work well for displaying images and portfolios. You also have the option to hire someone to build your site for you, which will guarantee a unique and professional feel but with a heftier price tag. There are fairly cheap, great places online to look for freelance services for things like graphic design and logos. And gallery software programs can help you host and even sell your prints online. But the next step is to build your first photography portfolio to display on your site.

In The Photo Mentorship, we have a custom website builder that photographers can use, so it takes out the guesswork and allows you to get right to work.

▶ Visit PhotoMentorship.com/LTS to learn more.

Building a Beta Portfolio with Free Gigs

In the next chapter I'm going to teach you how to book your first ten paid gigs, and it's gonna rock your socks off. But before you do that, you first have to have photos to show those would-be clients. Chase Jarvis, whom we'll be hearing more from later, once said to me, "A portfolio is worth a thousand cold calls trying to get people to think of you as a [photographer]. Just doing the work and spending your own money and time and energy to create the work that you eventually want to get hired to do is a requirement."

Before anyone will hire you, they'll want to see what you can do. This is true of amateurs and professionals alike. No matter how much experience you have, clients will rightly always want to see proof that you can handle the job. It's really hard to convince anyone to pay you for a photo shoot if they haven't seen any of your work yet.

I know this is probably a confusing piece of advice, but it's a good idea to start with some free practice gigs to build your portfolio as a photographer. If you're trying to get paid, the word *free* doesn't sound all that appealing. But if you want to get the kind of work that pays, you have to have some work that shows you're capable of good work. You have to have a portfolio to present to those clients who might be willing to open up their wallets for you in the future.

So shoot a few gigs for free in the area of photography you want to focus on. An old adage says, "Only show what you want to sell." This is so true for photographers as well. Only show the type of work you want to get paid for eventually. Don't feature rock concert photos if you're trying to convince brides to book you to shoot weddings.

If you're trying to grow as a headshot photographer, shoot some headshots for friends and family. If you're wanting to do portraits, offer your services to newly engaged couples or growing families you know. If you're aiming to shoot weddings, ask a photographer you know to let you assist and second-shoot at a wedding for free. If you have a friend who is a recent or soon-to-be bride, ask her to dress up in her wedding dress to do a bridal portrait session. Her family would probably love the extra shots! Not only is this giving you practice and building your portfolio, it's projecting to the world that you're a photographer. And you'll be building a portfolio of the type of work you want to get paid to shoot.

A little pro tip here: When you do these free gigs, create an invoice to go with the images you pass on to the clients. Put your price on that invoice and cross it out to zero. This little trick serves a double purpose. First, it shows them your value. It helps prove you're a professional. And second, it makes them feel special. It allows them to feel like they're getting a real deal. It's a win-win.

And, of course, it helps you build your beta portfolio. Why do I say "beta" portfolio? Because it's just version one. You're going to keep on improving your portfolio with new photos over time. In fact, you're going to hate most of these photos in your beta portfolio a year or two from now. You'll be embarrassed of them and you'll probably have switched out your portfolio with newer, better work. This is completely normal, and it's also great because you don't need to stress too much about your first portfolio. It's just temporary. And it's easy to swap out photos on your website and update it with newer, more beautiful work when you create it. So just get your best photos together and start.

Once you have some decent photography skills, you should be hyper-focused on building your portfolio to showcase what you can do. You want your website to be a place where potential clients can find you, learn more about you, and see your best photos in your portfolio. But keep in mind: it took me years to build my portfolio. This is the time when you're gaining experience and really getting the ball rolling. Find opportunities to shoot whatever you can in your niche and work on developing a portfolio over time. Add the photographs you're most proud of and that showcase the best of what you have to offer. Showcase clients who are the exact kind you want to shoot more of. As you shoot more regularly and improve, you will be updating your portfolio all the time.

If you're just starting out, you may not have a ton of quality images to showcase yet. That's okay! This is where "practice" gigs come in; you're doing these so you can get enough material to showcase on your website. Remember: this is just to get started. Like so many steps in this process, you are simply doing this to move on to the next one. In photography, especially at the beginning of your career, the biggest enemy you'll face is inaction. Just start moving, start making some choices, and you'll be surprised where it takes you. In the case of this step, just start shooting and building some assets (your portfolio, brand, website, etc.). These are how you'll start getting known; they form the foundation for everything that will come. Take this time seriously, but don't overthink it. Nothing is permanent; you can always change things later, but you don't want to be in this exact same place a year from now. So what're you waiting for? Just make a move.

IDEAL CANDIDATES ATTRACT MORE IDEAL CANDIDATES

My friend and photographer mentor Michael Gomez asked me when I was twenty-one: "Do you want to know the secret to having everyone think you are an amazing portrait photographer?" Of course I said yes. He then said something that surprised me: "Shoot beautiful people. If you do that, everyone will think you're a great photographer and will want portraits just like the ones you have in your portfolio."

So when you are doing portfolio shoots, find ideal candidates for your work. If you want people to think you're a world-class portrait photographer, find people to shoot who make it easier for your photos to look good. If you want people to think you're an amazing food photographer, find the best-plated meals. If you want people to think you're an impeccable real estate photographer, find the most perfectly manicured homes that you can get access to. Even if you shoot them on a crappy iPhone, those people, places, and things that exude natural beauty are going to look good in a picture. So as you're building a portfolio that's going to get you paid, look for the kind of candidates who will make your work look good.

To be clear, I'm not saying you have to find models to shoot, although many photographers do that when building their portfolios. Just find what feels beautiful to you; look for the types of clients and work you want more of. Because whatever you shoot and share, that's what you are naturally going to attract. When you are trying to create a portfolio you will use to bring in more paying clients, here's a simple rule: *don't share images your ideal client wouldn't want*. Set yourself up to win. If you shoot people who look good in beautiful locations, others will want to hire you to make their photos look the same.

Think about it: if you're a food photographer, you'd shoot beautifully plated food in a high-end restaurant with beautiful lighting—or do your best to make it look that way. The same is true here. You want to set yourself up to win with the easiest type of already-put-together content. Properly exposed photos don't make people hire us. Photos that move an audience, that make people *feel* something, are the greatest influences for why someone would hire us. You should, therefore, do everything in your power to make your portfolio as beautiful and emotional as possible. It will not only make you more confident that you *can* take great photos, but it will also instill confidence in you from your would-be clients. What they don't know is that you picked a subject with great fashion sense—or a restaurant where the food already looked amazing. You used the "cheat code," if you will, and now you are getting paid well because of it. Nobody talks about this publicly, but I promise you: every pro I've ever met follows this rule.

CREATE EMOTION IN YOUR PORTFOLIO

People buy when their emotions and logic meet. If you can learn to create emotion in your photographs early on and represent that in your portfolio, clients will be much quicker to book you. The photographers who charge the most are master storytellers who create powerful photos that convey an emotion. A desire to see more. A desire in clients to have similar photos taken of themselves.

Customers don't pay a premium for amazing photos (with great lighting, perfect framing, and good color editing, although all those things are important). They pay for content. What I mean is, how does the photo make them feel? Almost all photography that sells is based on the emotional connection a customer has to it—the story it's telling. That's why we spent so much time at the beginning of this book on storytelling and emotion. It matters. In fact, it's the most important part of being a great photographer. For example, let's say you're a wedding photographer. What portfolio image do you think would convince a potential bride to book you?

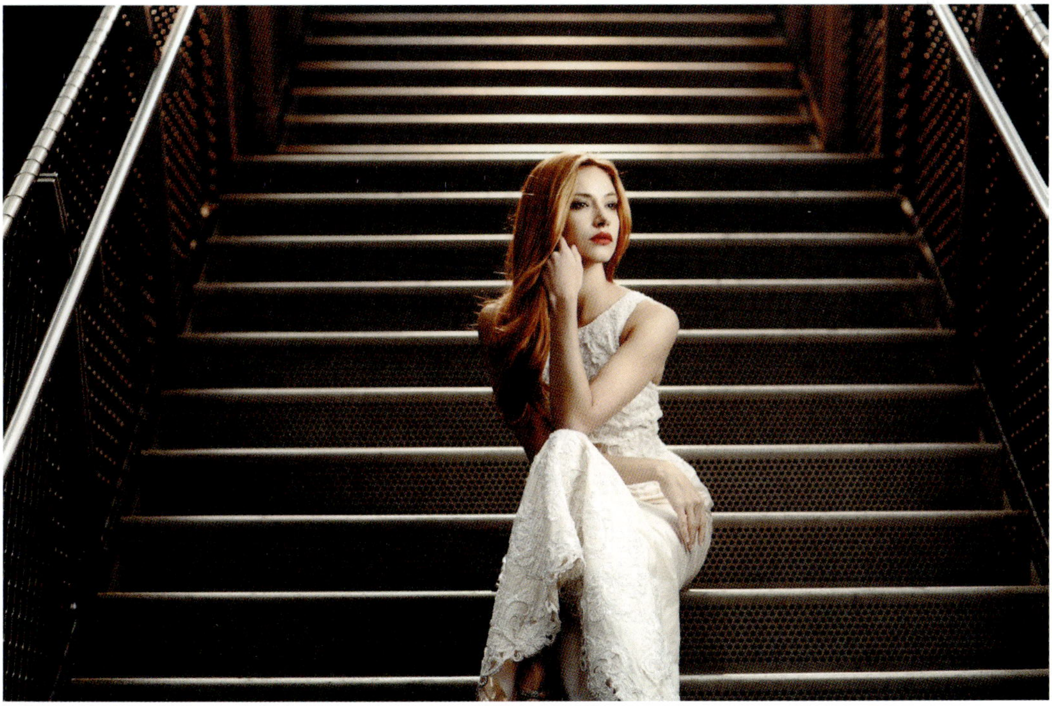

Credit: Zach Gray

This one of a bride sitting on some stairs, with really professional lighting, looking away from the camera, right? After all, it *is* a creative photo, and as photographers, we love these kinds of images. But a bride may be more interested in her story and how it makes her feel. And her sitting on some steps alone is probably not how she wants to remember the story of her wedding day.

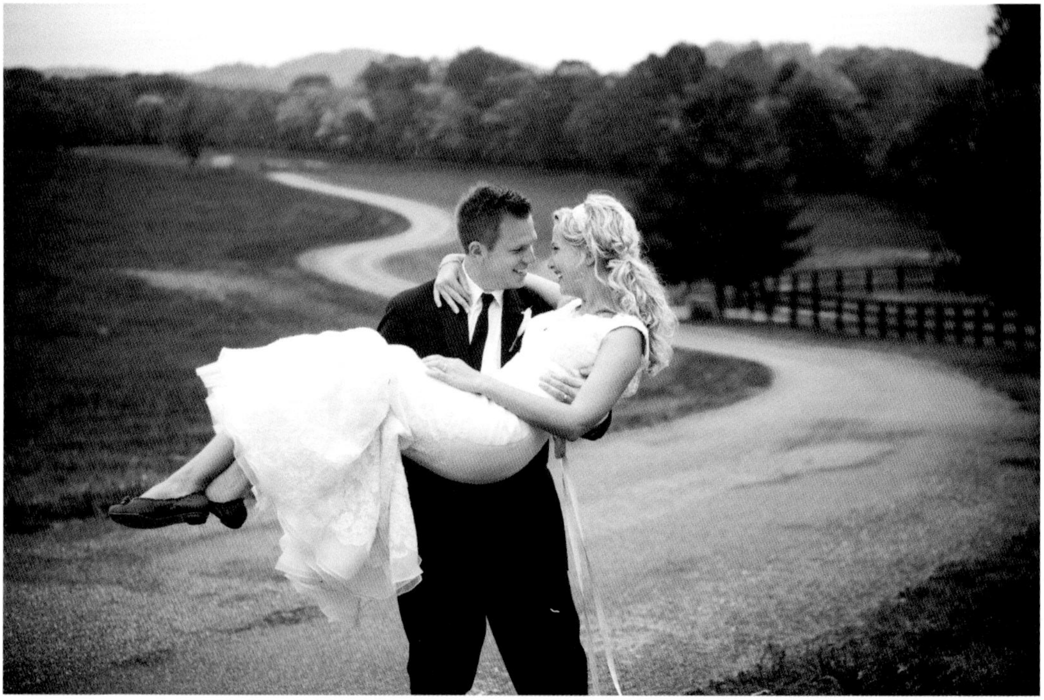

This photo is the moment right after they said, "I do." The groom picked up his new bride to carry her, so that she could keep that white dress clean. He looked into her eyes and she gently grabbed his neck, and they both smiled. The bride might be thinking, *The moment I have waited for is here, and he is mine, and I am his.* This photograph tells a story. It pulls at the heartstrings of what many brides long for: to be held, loved, and seen. Shooting images that tell stories like this should be priority number one. The more you include powerful, emotional images like this in your early portfolio, the quicker and easier it will be to book paid gigs in the future.

Your About Page

The About page is the most important page on your website, even more important than your portfolio or pricing page. It's a chance to tell a story that connects you to your customer, not just to talk about yourself. Clients don't care that you have loved photography since grade school. They don't care that you are passionate about taking pictures (isn't every photographer?). They want to know if they can relate to you and feel comfortable with you. If you're a family photographer, try putting a picture of you and your kids smiling on your About page and say something like: "I have three kids of my own. I know how fast they grow and how hard it is going to be to see them leave one day. All I will have left of these days are the memories in my photographs. This is what I do. I showcase you and your kids in their real environment so someday you can relive these stories." Find a way in. Find a way to connect.

Of course you can add some details about you. But clients aren't interested in your whole life story; they really want to know if you are a good fit for the shoot. They're asking themselves, *Would I like this person?*

A good digestible way to talk about yourself that makes you seem more relatable is to do a short list of fun facts. For example,

I love:

- My puppy
- Cookies and cream ice cream
- Sipping hot coffee with a good book first thing in the morning

I hate:

- Pickles and pickle juice on my fries (why do they do that?)
- Sitting in traffic
- Mosquitos

Picking things that are going to be funny, relatable, or good conversation starters may help would-be clients feel like they like you, just from reading little bits of information.

Granted, this has nothing to do with the photos you take, and that's exactly the point. Your client isn't hiring just your experience and skill; they're hiring you! They need to know they can trust you and follow your guidance in this experience. Getting them to feel excited about you and what you're all about will help them say yes to working with you and feel good about it. Another way to build connection is by making some statements that your ideal clients will resonate with, and make them feel like you are on common ground. Examples include:

- "I love seeing Marvel movies on opening night, but I'll choose eating dark chocolate with red wine and cuddling my wife on the couch while watching romantic comedies first."
- "I remember how vulnerable it felt to be in front of the camera for my first headshot, so I will pull out all my corny dad jokes to lighten the mood with my clients and make it a fun experience."

Some About pages are very chic and professional; others are incredibly personal and fun. That's fine; you pick what will attract the kinds of people you want to work with. This is *your* business; make it fun for you. Remember, like so many steps in this process, you can always change it later. Just create something that gets the information across in a way that represents who you are and what someone may be looking for.

Testimonials

It is critical to get some testimonials from people who have worked with you. When starting off, ask your portfolio-building clients to say something nice about working with you. You can use your mom if you have to. (I mean, not really, but if you do, at least don't make it too obvious. Also, thanks, Mom, for my first testimonial.) This is always great to do in the follow-up with clients after you've delivered pictures they love. It's a good time to capitalize on their excitement. Send each of your initial clients the questions below for them to answer on video. (Video testimonials are ideal. You can use parts of the transcripts as written quotes or the whole video on your site in different ways.) You can create an email template or form to send out every time.

1. What was the experience of working with me like?
2. If you were to tell a friend about me, what would you say?
3. What was your favorite part of the session?

Add their responses to your website as you go. Getting the first few testimonials may feel a little uncomfortable, but it'll get easier as you go. Don't be shy about giving clients an example of what you want them to say. A happy client is almost always willing to help you find more work.

Good testimonials do the talking for you, and you avoid having to tell people how amazing you are. All that does is make you sound like a salesman, and about zero photographers I have met got into photography because they love sales.

Real, genuine testimonials are what convince people you are legit. Most luxury items are purchased based on referrals, not some buy-one-get-one-free special you read about in the pennysaver. When you walk through the mall and the kiosk salespeople try to grab you and put lotion on you, your stomach drops because someone is trying to hard sell you something. *Yuck.* But when your friend says, "I just did this amazing photo shoot with David. It was so much fun and the photos are incredible! You should hire him!" you are very likely to trust that referral.

That is what a testimonial can do for you.

Inquiry Form

People need a way to get in touch with you, obviously. This could be a simple inquiry form or pasting your email address on a Contact page on your website. It doesn't matter. Just make it easy and obvious. It's also a good idea to place this form or contact button prominently on your website so people can easily book you. Don't make it hard for people to find you. Say it loud and clear. As Donald Miller says, "If you confuse, you'll lose."[1] Make it simple and obvious, and give people a way to reach you.

Should I Put Prices on My Website?

There is only one reason to put prices on your actual website: to filter out anyone who is looking for a different price. My friend Kevin Swan had a brand called Swan Luxury Weddings. He put his pricing on his website: "Starting at $7,500." He was making a statement. If you can't afford $7,500 to start, don't inquire. The opposite of that would be to show how cheap you are. Something like: "Dean's iPhone-Only Wedding Photography. Packages starting at just $500!" The iPhone-only is me being a little facetious (don't shoot weddings with just an iPhone), but you get the point. Most of the time I recommend waiting until you can connect with a customer before discussing prices. That way you get a chance to build some rapport, tell them a story, and then see if they value your price.

▶ Get our pricing cheat sheet and other business resources at photomentorship .com/LTS.

The Legal Stuff

Listen. My team and I are not accountants or lawyers, so we advise that you chat with both to successfully start your business the right way. But that said, there are things we see almost anyone who is successful do from the start—and if they

1. Donald Miller, *Building a StoryBrand: Clarify Your Message So Customers Will Listen* (Nashville: HarperCollins Leadership, 2017), 12.

don't, they regret it. Now that you've done almost everything else, you have to get down to the real business of building a brand. I'm talking about the nitty-gritty details of registering and legalizing yourself as a business entity. Here's what you need to do:

1. **Get your EIN, or Employer Identification Number.** Register with the IRS and get your own tax ID for your business. With that, you'll be able to open a bank account for your business.
2. **Set up your business license.** Register as an LLC or sole proprietorship so you can operate as a business on a state level. This might be the point where either your eyes start to glaze over or your heart starts pounding. Lots of people don't like this part, but I promise you it's easier than you think. You can start with a simple google "LLC + your state" or "sole proprietorship + your state" and see the differences between those two to make the best decision for yourself. That said, a sole proprietorship will most likely be enough to get you started. You can probably take care of this in an hour or two.
3. **Open a business bank account.** A business bank account keeps your business finances separate from your personal funds. The benefits of a business bank account are that it helps limit your personal liability and customers can pay your company directly.
4. **Open an income tax account.** Make sure you immediately set aside a portion of every dollar you make to give to the government, so you don't make the same mistake I once did. When you transfer money from your business account (where all payments made to you should go), and want to pay yourself, you have to pay income taxes. If you take 25 percent of whatever you pay yourself and move that into the account labeled "Taxes," then you will ensure you do not have a massive tax bill each quarter. Your CPA will help you determine the exact amount due, but in the United States, putting 25 percent away for taxes will ensure you do not have too little in that account.
5. **Find a CPA.** A CPA is a tax expert with extensive education, like an accountant on steroids. Beyond the requirements for a basic accountant, they must

pass an extensive CPA exam and meet continuing education requirements. This is not the place to cut down on costs and save money. You'll only be creating more work for yourself later on. Pay an expert to make your life easier, and they'll save you more money than if you didn't hire one at all.

6. **Charge sales tax.** You can get a sales and use tax permit on your state's Department of Revenue website. This is the only way you can legally charge your clients sales tax to pay the government. Failure to get the proper permits and pay taxes can result in hefty fines, legal battles, and even full closure of your business.
7. **Get liability insurance.** You may also want to purchase professional liability insurance if you do events like weddings or bar-mitzvahs. This kind of insurance protects you if you were to lose all the photos or provide incomplete service, for any reason whatsoever. Good photography insurance policies will cover your liability and also cover your equipment in case of loss, damage, or theft.
8. **Use a contract for your services.** A contract is a written agreement between the photographer and a client. The contract becomes a binding legal document once signed by both parties. This contract will protect both parties (making sure you are paid and they get exactly what they're paying for) and should lay out relevant information, including services to be rendered and products to be included, client information, and all fees. A good contract will ensure your client is informed and everything runs smoothly. Contracts are specific to the exact expectations of each client (and although you may have a general contract, you will likely send out one that is slightly amended based on the goods and services you are rendering to that specific client).

What is the real point of all this stuff? To create and operate a legit business. To build the brand you want for yourself and your work. To see yourself as a real, working photographer. And to encourage others to see you the same way.

And finally and most importantly, ask for help. Get the support you need as you get started. But no matter what, get started. You're building, and that means you have room to develop and grow as you go. That will never happen if you don't start.

▶ Lots of the technical details have intentionally been left out of this chapter because it doesn't really matter where you buy your domain name or who hosts your website. For information on the specific contracts we use and insurance companies and CPAs we recommend, visit PhotoMentorship.com/LTS.

CHAPTER 13

Find Your First Paying Clients

BEFORE THERE WAS EVER SUCH A THING AS AN AUDIOBOOK, IN THE YEAR 1956, Earl Nightingale recorded what would become the first of many self-help and personal development programs, a simple spoken-word record called *The Strangest Secret*. In this short recording he introduced a simple yet profound principle: "We become what we think about."[1] It is a simple and clear argument for how our thoughts create our reality and how we all need to focus on what we want—and that very focus turns us into the kind of person who can get what we want.

Becoming a professional photographer begins with your confidence and purpose. If you want others to see you as a photographer worth paying for, you have to believe you're that photographer. You have to call yourself a photographer in every sense of the word and with every opportunity you have. Early in my journey, I made a choice to articulate to as many people as possible that I was a photographer. I started a very basic blog and portfolio (remember Xanga? Myspace? No? Okay, cool; I'm just old I guess), and I posted my projects there. Then I talked about it. I shared it. I took my camera with me everywhere and took pictures at every turn. I was obsessed with taking shots, posting them online, and telling people about

---

1. "The Strangest Secret Article by: Earl Nightingale," Nightingale Conant, accessed March 16, 2022, https://www.nightingale.com/articles/the-strangest-secret/.

the work I was doing. Why? Because I saw myself as a photographer and I wanted other people to see the same thing.

I was confident, or at least I acted like it. I was becoming what I thought about, not just speaking it into existence but acting it into being. This, if nothing else, is the main thing I want you to take away from reading this book. Just like with the Switchfoot concert, I had to take a leap and proclaim to everyone that I was a photographer, maybe even before I believed it myself. There wasn't a person I came in contact with back then who didn't know I was working to become a photographer. I saw myself becoming world-class and had faith that I would "make it" before I ever made a dollar. But, to be honest, I was still scared and full of doubt, feeling a bit like that guy in the Bible who said, "I believe; help my unbelief!"[2] That was the truth: I believed I would become great, but I doubted my talents and experience. That's normal; we all have doubts. Success happens when you walk through the door anyway. That "do it anyway" mindset made way for the money to come. Earl Nightingale was right: we really do become what we think about.

So if you're asking how to book your first paying gig, start there—with your mindset. We began this book with the instruction to start with how you see yourself. And I will remind you again: start with yourself. Because until you're confident enough to project who you want to be and proclaim that to the world, nobody else is going to see you that way. It starts with you.

When you're focused enough on a specific goal, your belief becomes a part of you. It literally pours out of you. And that's huge. You can market your work and build your business on every available platform in the world, but if you aren't coming with the confidence that you *are* the photographer you say you are, you're going to stall out fast. When you exude confidence about who you are and what you do, people notice. They remember. They believe that you can do exactly what you're telling them you can do.

Sometimes I look back at my work from those early days and I'm shocked at how I ever thought those images were good enough to share, let alone get me paid

2. Mark 9:24.

work. But at the time, I was so confident that my work was good enough—I was so confident that *I* was good enough—that people were willing to take a chance on me. When friends heard that someone was looking for a photographer, my name popped into their minds. I truly believe that's simply because of my belief.

There's something infectious about someone who truly believes they're going somewhere. If you have a friend who plays guitar casually, you're probably not going to stake your reputation on recommending him to play on a friend's album. But if that friend were committed, confident, and totally dedicated to their craft, you'd be a lot more willing to get behind them and help them on their journey. They're going somewhere, and you want to help them get there because you believe in what they're selling.

The same is true for you. You might be wondering how this self-belief has anything to do with finding your first paying client. You probably want me to get into the actual techniques you came here for. And we will. But the most important point is that if you learn to see yourself as a photographer and project that with confidence into the world, opportunities will find you. When you decide, *I'm going to be a photographer*, suddenly you're going to start seeing opportunities to *be* a photographer. Your mindset will open your eyes and open doors to the work you want. It might sound a little esoteric, but I promise this is true. The world will meet you where you are, and you'll be amazed what comes your way.

Creating Momentum

Chase Jarvis is a famous photographer with a boatload of awards to his name. But back in 1990, he was just a kid with a dream. A week before his college graduation, Chase's grandfather died and left him his camera. Both his father and grandfather had been photography hobbyists, which sparked an initial interest in the craft. After graduation, Chase and his girlfriend (now wife) Kate went backpacking through Europe, where he taught himself how to take great photos with the inherited camera. They didn't have much money, so they would sometimes skip meals in favor of spending what they had on developing rolls of film. Those six months served as a self-taught crash course in photography for Chase. And it paid off.

When they returned from their trip, neither he nor Kate wanted to get "real jobs." They both had a passion for skiing, so they moved to Steamboat Springs, Colorado, where Chase worked in a ski shop and tuned skis for the US freestyle team. He was slowly developing an interest in outdoor sport and adventure photography and figured being right in the middle of the action couldn't hurt. In Colorado, Chase was surrounded by world-class skiers and snowboarders—willing subjects all around. All he needed was a shot.

Occasionally the ski shop would receive prototypes from a company for the US team to try out before they were available to the public. The fledgling photographer got an idea to photograph the team trying out this equipment and then show it to the marketing rep the next time they came through. To market the skis, they'd need marketing material and great pictures, which he knew he could do. He'd been to REI and looked around at the huge pictures on the walls of strapping men and women scaling mountains and racing downhill in the snow and knew he could do that—heck, he might even be able to do better.

So he went down to the community college and printed off several photos he'd taken to make a little portfolio showing off the fancy prototype skis that weren't available to the public yet. He knew the marketing team would be anxious to sell them, so presentation was everything. His opportunity came when a marketing person from the ski company came through the shop. He was there for a photo shoot for another product.

Boldly, Chase confronted the executive: "I thought you'd be interested in these photos I took of the Hart skis the freestyle team has been trying out," he said.

"Holy crap," was the reply. He loved them. The company didn't have to go to the hassle of booking a professional and paying thousands of dollars for a shoot. The pro had come to them. They offered to pay for the rights to use one of Chase's photos for their marketing materials, offering him $500 and a pair of skis, which he gladly accepted. It was his first paying client. Things didn't exactly take off from there, but it was a huge vote of confidence for Chase and helped him get his start.

Booking your first paying client, no matter how small, does something for you. "It's all about inertia and momentum," Chase later shared in an interview my team and I did with him. "When you get some momentum, that feels like a massive unlock. You're able to do a lot more when you start feeling like you're running downhill." As you begin to put yourself out there as a professional photographer, your self-belief will carry you far. And that kind of confidence plus actually being paid for your work? That kind of momentum is almost unstoppable.

By now maybe you're thinking: *That's great, David. But how do I actually make money? What are the practical steps I can take to actually book that first paying gig?* Good question. Let's get into that.

Booking Your First Ten Gigs (and Making Your First $1,000)

So now you're ready to book your first paid gigs. This is an incredible milestone. But if you're like me, it can be nerve-wracking to put yourself out there and ask for money. Don't worry, though; I have a foolproof method that even introverts can use to make their first $1,000. It's called the "Half-Off Portfolio Kickstart," which is, essentially, a limited-time deal that you're going to use to make people feel special, book your first paid gigs, get kick-butt photos for your portfolio, and book more gigs. If you do this right, the best part about it is your clients will be begging you to let them be one of your top ten, hand-selected clients for these shoots.

This method could be done for engagement shoots, family portraits, headshots, senior portraits, real estate, food photography, weddings—almost anything that pays. Keep in mind that this is assuming you already have some decent photos in your portfolio that you've done while practicing on your free shoots. You need some photos to represent what you want to do for other clients. It's possible to do this before you have your website finished, but you'll need to at least point people to a gallery of your best work on social media, send them a portfolio PDF, or share a private link to a file transfer site.

The secret to this method is all about how you present the information. Your goal is for it to feel special, inclusive, and available for a limited time. We talked earlier about having confidence. Now is the time to muster it. In this example, I'm going to talk about a straightforward type of shoot: family portraits. But this could easily apply to various types of photography.

Remember, only show what you want to sell. Go after and feature the kinds of clients you want to attract. This means if you want to shoot family portraits, don't bring in rock star clients (I mean, actual rock stars)—or vice versa. If you want to attract more clients with money, shoot people who look like they have money. Focus on the people you want to attract and keep in your business, because if you do a good job, they will likely want to hire you again and tell their friends. Like attracts like.

Here's how it works. You explain to your friends or acquaintances that you are now a professional photographer and you are really trying to step up your game and build a gorgeous portfolio of family photos to show off on your new website. If it's under construction that would be a great time to share that. Then go on to tell them that you are looking to handpick a few beautiful families to feature in your new portfolio. At this point you're making them already want to be one of the handpicked "beautiful" families. We're all a little vain inside; we all want to feel special and chosen and secretly believe we're better than someone. They'll be inspired by your definiteness of purpose if you portray all this confidently and clearly. People want to "hitch their wagon" to someone who is headed toward success.

I remember friends of our family, the Pisanis, who lived in Washington, DC, told me they wanted to get a shoot with me early on to have an "Original David Molnar" photo. I thought, *Wow. They believe in me. They think I'm going to make it one day.* They could see I was going to be a successful photographer, and that was so encouraging to me. All it takes is getting a few sets of people to believe in you early on to help encourage you to spread your wings.

So back to the half-off shoots. If you play this right, people will be waiting in line to be picked as one of the ten clients you invite. You explain to them that you have this awesome location that is perfect for shooting family portraits and the light is incredible. Maybe it's a secret spot at the beach or a park, or a wheat field. If you have examples from a free shoot that you are proud of, show them the photos at this location. Maybe you want it to be a style shoot where you're bringing a picnic or a blanket to wrap the family in. Mention if you have any props planned to promote the experience. And talk it up. The enthusiasm is important here and can be contagious. Tell them the shoot is going to be half off what you are going to be charging once your new portfolio is finished. And in this shoot everything is going to be included: all the editing and access to all the digital images of the final edited photos and the rights to use them for anything they would like.

Now here's the part that even a non-confrontational introvert can do: ask them, "Do you know any amazing families who are looking to get beautiful family portraits taken of themselves? Know any families that might be interested in shooting at my secret spot on the beach for half off my normal price? And get to keep all the images to use for whatever they want? Do you know any friends or family of yours that might be interested in that?" This is indirect and lets them be not interested if they are not interested. But if they *are* interested, they will say, "How about me?!" Then tell them, "Wow! For sure. I would love to shoot you guys for this!"

Or, you could add, "Of course your beautiful family would be a perfect fit for this, too, if y'all were interested in a half-off shoot, but I don't want to assume you're in the market for new family photos." It's the introvert's way to ask your perfect client in a non-confrontational and low-pressure way. It feels inviting and intriguing without forcing them to turn you down.

You don't have to ask people directly if they will book you. You ask your ideal client if they "know anyone" who wants one of your portfolio-building shoots for a 50 percent discount, and hopefully that person will say, "Heck yeah! I want one!" If they don't, they can recommend someone who comes to mind. Do you see how this is a no-lose scenario? They can say, "Yeah—my friends Bobby and Laura might be interested. Let me ask them for you." And then your contact doesn't have to deny you. They can refer you. Some people will be home runs and want to book you ASAP. They'll feel special that you asked them. Some people will just say, "Not that I can think of." And that's okay too. And some people might know someone who is the perfect candidate for one of your half-off portfolio-building shoots.

So let's get practical and talk about how this actually works. Make a list of people, with a goal of twenty-five to thirty-five names. This should include names of friends, family, businesses you know, organizations you work with, your dentist and doctor, artists and internet influencers—anyone you can think of—whom you can tell that you're building a portfolio of new work and who would fit your ideal demographic. Go to them and tell them you are building your portfolio and doing some amazing styled shoots for half off, and ask them if they "know anyone" they think would be interested to get one of these ten shoots.

Decide on the "standard price" for the shoot and then offer it for "half off." Don't say your fee is $20,000 and you're doing half-off shoots if that's not where you want to begin. Be realistic and don't be afraid to charge less than you'd like to eventually get paid. You're not going to keep your prices there for long. Do some homework, and decide what you think is a good average for your area of expertise. Maybe you charge more than the market rates, maybe less—whatever you do, just do it on purpose. If you have no idea what to charge and you are doing a simple shoot, you might say your one-hour rate is $250. And that these half-off shoots are $125. That's a good deal for the family if you provide great photos and it's not going to take too much time. If you do this ten times, you'll have $1,250, which may have paid for your first camera and lens!

The key is to make them feel special. Let them know this is *only* for a select few people, and if they refer you, those referrals will be billed the regular price. Ask them to share the photos online when you send them but not to tell people in the future about the amazing discount they got because it was only for these ten portfolio-building shoots.

When you've done them, you've gained a ton of experience and ended up with some amazing photos for your portfolio. That's a huge win. Making money while building your portfolio is great, but the ultimate goal is bigger than that. It's to create a photographic experience for your customer that is remarkable. These first few experiences customers have with you are crucial. You want these customers to be part of your initial marketing, telling everyone they know about what a great experience they had, in addition to how great their pictures are. We'll talk more about delivering a world-class experience later, but just keep that in mind for now.

Get Creative

All these things—the one-time freebies, discounts, and deals—are the pathway toward more sustainable paying gigs. They're building your portfolio, your reputation, and your business. And you need those things to book future real, solid, paying gigs.

Because—let's be honest—nobody is going to trust an amateur to shoot their biggest moments. Take a wedding for example. It's a tricky thing to book your first wedding. What couple wants to trust somebody who's never shot a wedding before to shoot the most important day of their lives? So you have to get creative. In his early years, my friend Zach Gray had some friends who were getting married and looking for a photographer. When he offered up his services, their response was simple: "We know you don't shoot weddings."

Instead of taking that no for an answer, Zach got creative. He offered to shoot their engagement photos for free. If they liked them, then they could hire him for their wedding. And if they didn't, they got some free photos out of the deal. There really wasn't a way for this couple to lose, and it gave Zach the chance to prove himself and his work. And guess what happened? He crushed it and got to shoot their wedding! As you're developing your skills and working up to more full-paying gigs, deals like this will be huge in building your confidence and your portfolio. And with each gig you do, your ability, your confidence, your business, and eventually your pricing will grow.

My first "real" paying gig was a wedding. I was twenty-one. Before that, I'd done two projects where people sort of handed me money on the back end, but this was different. This time my friend Sarah was getting married, and she'd hired me to capture it.

Sarah knew I was a photographer because, as a part of my life, she'd heard me talk about it. I came with that confidence, and she saw it. I used her as a test model for different shoots when I was getting started building my portfolio, and that experience was good enough for her to remember me when it was time to choose a photographer for her wedding. She believed in me enough to take a chance on me. To this day, that request remains a big deal to me.

Of course, I didn't tell her at the time that I didn't really know how to shoot weddings. I said yes, knowing I had about three months to figure it out. This was the wedding in Virginia I mentioned earlier. The one where my wife and I drove through the night and arrived at three o'clock the morning of the wedding. I left Friday afternoon after my wife got off work and slept barely a wink in a nearby hotel. I was an absolute mess of nerves. Up until that day, I spent time tearing sheets from bridal magazines. I didn't know how to pose brides, bridal parties, guests, or families. In other words, I didn't know anything. So I studied every pose in every magazine I could find. I even created a folder of poses and images to reference while I was shooting.

I gave it everything I had. Not only was this my first opportunity to really commit to being a wedding photographer; it was my friend's wedding. I didn't want to let anyone down, myself and Sarah included. Plus, $500 felt like a million bucks to me at the time. That wedding mattered to me for so many reasons, and I did whatever I had to do to pull it off.

That small paying gig led to seven more that year. I got my first referrals from some of her friends and bridesmaids. People saw the images from that wedding and found me online. It was only one gig, but it did wonders for my confidence and my business. At that point, I was a wedding photographer. I had a paycheck and portfolio to prove it.

Within a year's time I had booked my first international wedding. It was a gig in Greece and they paid me $2,000 to shoot it, plus the additional thousands in travel expenses to get my wife and me over there. All that growth happened because of the confidence to see myself as a photographer and the courage to post and ask for referrals. Because of my willingness to project that proudly into the world. Because of my pursuit of the work, sometimes even for free.

It paid off in ways bigger than I could've imagined. And I think the same can be true for you. I can't emphasize this enough: learn to see yourself as the photographer you are. Don't be afraid to put that message into the world. And when the time comes, say yes with the confidence that you deserve to be paid for the work you do. There are practical steps to take, yes, and we've covered them. But the most important part is to get out there with everything you are, and just see what happens.

Because you, my friend, are a photographer.

CHAPTER 14

Create World-Class Client Experiences

ONCE YOU'VE BOOKED ONE PAYING GIG, YOU'RE ON THE WAY TO BOOKING another. And another. And another. In short, you're officially a working photographer. The goal is to *stay* a working photographer. Besides being great at your craft, the other way to ensure you'll continue growing in business is to create a great experience for your clients. The goal is to go above and beyond their expectations. To do more than just meet their basic needs. To deliver the kind of customer experience that keeps them not just coming back to you but telling their friends to do the same. Treat those first few clients like gold.

Again, it's important to remember you're in the phase of *building* your client experience. In other words, this is your beta version, similar to your beta brand. At first, you're probably not going to be able to deliver albums in customized packaging that makes your clients feel like they're opening a Tiffany box. That might be a part of your customer delivery experience one day, but it's not the one you're building at the start.

Instead of focusing on the grand, expensive elements of your customer experience, focus at first on setting up standard systems that will give your clients a smooth process from beginning to end. Know what the client is expecting of you and set the standard of what you can deliver based on that.

Communication

The key to this process is communication. Up front, you want to communicate clearly to your clients what they can expect to get from you. My secret is simple: under-promise and over-deliver. Tell your customers you'll have their photos delivered to them in three weeks and then turn them around in three days. Promise them a small number of edited images and send in a few more without charge. Set realistic goals for yourself in terms of things like timeline and deliverables and then build in some wiggle room before you communicate them to your clients. That way, if you run into a roadblock and need the wiggle room, you're not apologizing or asking for an extension. You're simply meeting the expectations you set from the start. But if you don't need that wiggle room (and most likely you won't), you're blowing their expectations out of the water. You're giving them something to talk about—something to tell other people about you and your work.

Of course, communication isn't just about expectations. It's also about communicating in a way that is generally respectful and professional. For example, this includes responding to clients in a timely manner. In other words, don't "ghost" people, even if you make a mistake with their photos and want to hide your head in the sand. Treat your clients with respect even when they're difficult and may not even deserve it. This will all pay dividends later.

During the Shoot

Keep in mind when doing the actual shoot that your clients likely will have some anxiety about the shoot itself. They're likely wondering, *Will I look good? Will I feel comfortable? Will this be worth the time and financial investment?* It's your job as the photographer to recognize this and disarm them. It's hard to take great pictures of people if they are stiff and stressed out. Focusing on a few simple techniques will help them relax and help you knock it out of the park experience-wise.

TIP 1: STOP WHAT YOU'RE DOING AND CONNECT.

When a client shows up and you are holding a huge camera with a massive lens around your neck, already shooting, it can feel like a first date starting a little too fast. *Easy, buddy—we just met!* It looks and feels intimidating. Stop what you are doing, whether in the studio or on location, and take a few minutes to break the ice.

Look them in the eyes and ask some questions about where they're from or what their hobbies are. I like offering something vulnerable about myself, like how big of a geeky board game fan I am, to help let their guards down. This is especially important if you haven't met with the client before. Connecting personally with the person you're about to shoot can put them at ease. If they have kids, you could talk about your own children briefly. You can talk about how you changed the bed sheets for your three-year-old in the middle of the night or stayed up late to watch the game with your roommate. Whatever it is, the point is to connect and relate, to share a little humanity with them so they can trust you more.

If the client has kids who will be a part of the shoot, this is a great time to get down on their level and act a little goofy with them. Getting kids to cooperate during a shoot can be tricky, so it helps if they like you. Telling jokes to get the family laughing comes with the added benefit of helping the family connect with each other before being photographed, which of course is the story we want coming through in the photos. It's weird to show up and expect a stranger to photograph you, so don't be a stranger.

TIP 2: BRING THEM A MEANINGFUL GIFT.

I learned this tip from some old colleagues who used to shoot wedding clients. They would bring a book about the first year of marriage during the first interaction, which made the clients feel special. It also had the added bonus of getting their minds off posing and looking right. Think of something unique and small to bring each client when you first meet. Small touches like this go a very long way with clients.

TIP 3: COMPLIMENT THEM.

This tip is straightforward, but the key is to make it genuine. Early in your interaction, offer your client a sincere compliment. It can't be fake or feel forced. Most people can pick up on insincerity immediately, and in addition to being just plain wrong, it will probably make your subjects even more self-conscious than they already are. Find something about them that you admire: their eyes, their shoes, their hair, anything. Just make sure you mean it. This will disarm them right away, and you'll notice that they start acting more comfortable with you.

TIP 4: GIVE THEM SOMETHING TO DO AND GET OUT OF THE WAY.

Something else my friend Zach does is make the first setup a walking shot with a long lens. He would sometimes jokingly ask, "Are you pretty good at walking?" That usually got a laugh. It can be helpful early on in a shoot to give your clients something to *do*. Clients don't want to stand there, look at you, and smile, especially at first. Like a first date, it's good to have something to do to take the pressure off. It's always awkward to just sit and stare at each other and be forced to talk about the weather. But if you're bowling or playing Putt-Putt, there's naturally something to talk about and focus on. The same concept applies here. Have your clients walk, look at something, act something out, or do some other activity for your first set of shots. It'll loosen everyone up. You can even make up a silly scenario to throw at them, like, "Pretend he just gave you a pair of shoes you've been wanting forever." Get creative with it.

You can use this technique for family shoots, engagements, weddings, or any portrait session. Make up your own silly scenario or example to use. Once they feel good and realize that getting their picture taken can be easy and painless, you can then start moving in closer to do the more posed shots.

TIP 5: GIVE GOOD DIRECTION.

If a client doesn't know what to do, they tend to panic. If they have good direction from you, it makes all the difference. It can be confusing to say, "Move your left hand," or "Sidestep to the right." Everything is backward when you are facing each other. Is it their right or your right? See what I mean? It can be confusing. That's why I always use what I call the "mirror trick."

Tell them to treat you as a mirror, and do what you do. Show them "turn your head this way" as you turn yours in the direction you want them to mirror. If you need their body moved so they are leaning in a direction, lean yours in that direction, and so on. It is clear, simple, and lets them know that you are in control at all times, which makes a client feel at ease. They may have felt like they had no idea what to expect, but they will feel calmed by your confidence.

TIP 6: MAKE THEM FEEL BEAUTIFUL.

One of my cardinal rules of photo shoots is to never *ever* say anything negative about how the client looks in a shot. This includes things like "I don't like this angle," "This looks bad," "This isn't working," or even "Oops." Some of those things may sound more like photographer or camera problems, but they will make the client feel like they look bad. Which again will lead to our problem of making them feel self-conscious and vulnerable, which will lead to worse pictures.

Too many photographers spend too much time focusing on their settings rather than affirming or directing their subjects in a positive way. Regardless of what the last shot looks like, let them know they look awesome. This comes back to finding stuff you can genuinely compliment them on. Keep repeating that step throughout the rest of the session. When they feel like they look beautiful, they will look beautiful.

Even if you're not in love with the shot or their pose, tell them you love their outfit and how you loved it when they were standing at such-and-such an angle. Don't say, "I hate this angle on you," or "That dress makes you look fat." Always try to be encouraging and work toward a great shot. Even if you haven't achieved it yet, keep encouraging your subjects as you tweak the shot. Keep encouraging them until you find the gold.

TIP 7: HAVE A LIST OF JOKES HANDY.

Naturally, I am a cheesy joke collector, which has come in handy in my photography career. About a decade ago my friend Jeremy Cowart told me he actually writes his cheesy jokes in a note on his phone for easy reference, so I started doing the same. And let me tell you, the jokes I have in there are *terrible*. On their own, they're pretty bad dad jokes. But when I tell them, it feels natural and works with my personality. I also happen to think they're funny and always laugh the loudest. A huge bonus for me is that people will laugh at me laughing rather than at the joke itself. They'll shake their heads and tell me how bad the joke is. And find themselves chuckling. Which was the goal anyway!

If this isn't part of who you are, don't do that. Remember, clients can sniff out a fake. But keep a running list of jokes that work with who you are. Humor comes more naturally for some, so you may have to work on it. I don't consider myself naturally very funny, but since I've worked at it, I can disarm a room with a silly pun. Begin experimenting with humor in your shoots. It's the easiest and simplest way to connect and put your clients at ease. It's also great for getting a natural smile in a photo.

TIP 8: THANK THEM FROM THE HEART.

Your clients will almost certainly thank you at the end of the shoot. You did just provide a service for them, after all. But I like to offer back my genuine gratitude as well. I thank them for trusting me to do this. I tell them how much fun I had and what an honor it is to do this work for them. Never say anything untruthful, but it is true that without clients you wouldn't have a business at all. So thank them for choosing you and for the experience you had together.

These few simple techniques help the shoot go smoothly and make your client feel comfortable. It makes you very memorable, which in turn results in great testimonials and referrals down the road.

Management and Delivery of Photos

A huge part of the client experience is in the management and delivery of their images. Like we said, you may shoot three thousand images, but your client doesn't need to see every single one of them. That would be overwhelming—not the word you want in a review about their time with you. Culling the images and featuring only the best ones eases the customer experience and delivery process for your clients.

An online proofing platform that manages their images digitally is another great tool. Proofing software allows you to upload your photos online to a secure space where clients can view and download them. There, they can also select their favorites and order them right away. The selected images will be printed and shipped from a professional photo printing lab. Your clients get their photos in the mail and you get paid. It's a seamless process that ends in a win for everyone.

▶ Head over to PhotoMentorship.com/LTS for a current list of my favorite online client proofing galleries and a tutorial on how to make the most money with them.

The bottom line when it comes to creating a great client experience is to just keep it fun and easy. Put yourself in the shoes of your client. What would you like? What makes you feel taken care of or blown away? You can be the best photographer in the world, but if you don't treat people right or are a pain in the butt to work with, no one will want to work with you again. And they won't send their friends your way either. Which, at the start of your business, is everything. Be polite, overcommunicate, work hard, and deliver on what you said you would. It's that simple.

Conclusion

I WAS NEVER SUPPOSED TO BE A PHOTOGRAPHER—JUST A KID FROM A SMALL beach town who lost his big opportunity to do something great with his life. But, like I said before, almost dying changed things for me. When I woke up in the hospital from my accident, I didn't instantly have a moment when I knew what I was supposed to do, nor did I immediately have a brand-new outlook on life. I was depressed and confused. I wondered how my life was going to turn out and if I'd ever achieve the big things my parents told me I was destined for.

But it did get me thinking, and that was enough.

I started wondering what I'd do without my identity as an athlete and what would come next for me. In the depths of my own despair, I began to consider what made me truly happy. In those days only two things came to mind: photography and the ocean. Since I'd grown up on the beach, I never imagined I'd live away from the salt water for any extended period of time. But I was willing to sacrifice my love for the saltwater life for a little while. And at the time, photography seemed like it could be the way to a bigger, better life, and I was right.

After moving to Nashville and making moves toward my dreams, something still seemed to be missing. I was building a career that I never even thought was possible, but I was landlocked, and being away from salt water felt like life without breathing. I didn't just like the ocean—I *needed* it. I loved photography and it fulfilled a need deep in my soul, but I needed the beach just as much. I was never supposed to move away from the ocean.

Every moment of clarity I've ever had has come at the beach. I decided I wanted to pursue photography while living on the Outer Banks. I proposed to my wife and got married barefoot on the beach. God told me to pursue weddings for the next five years while walking on that beach in Mexico just before I got married. Five years later, during a dream vacation in Hawaii with my wife, I finally realized it was time to move on to something bigger and hopefully better—and that happened on the beach too.

Years later, while living in Nashville and after years of success as a celebrity photographer, I made my next pivot into teaching and mentoring others. I loved what I was doing. I felt so much life and excitement from this new kind of work. And yet, something was off; I didn't feel like myself. Something inside me craved the ocean and the adventure it brought. My life always made more sense while walking on sand; it was time to come home. It did, however, take an act of God to convince my wife to leave our dear friends and life in Nashville. God spoke to her and said, "Move here," of course, while at the beach. So we made the move to raise our kids in the crystal clear waters of the Gulf of Mexico and haven't regretted it for a second!

Recently I hosted a retreat for some photographers in my online community, and they all joined me in the beautiful panhandle of Florida. My photography dream has grown bigger and more fulfilling than shooting celebrities and multimillion-dollar marketing campaigns. Today I get to help other photographers fulfill their photography dreams; and yeah, I get to surf whenever I want, which is soul nourishing for me.

As part of this work, I get to host events and run online communities and continue to teach courses for photographers who want to improve their craft. During my most recent retreat, while sitting on the beach surrounded by an amazing community of photographers, I watched them take pictures and listened to their stories about booking their first clients. We laughed as we all shared our blunders and mishaps along the way. And that's when it hit me, staring off into the ocean, feeling the sand beneath my bare feet, feeling the excitement of these students all around me.

This is the real dream, I thought to myself. *This is the dream that, eighteen years ago, I hadn't even thought to dream.* And that's what a dream does: it keeps growing, keeps inviting others to join you along the way. This is what photography has given me: an opportunity to be the mentor I never had, to share what I know and see others come along for the ride and do the same. Today I get to work with an amazing team of photography mentors who love this work just as much as I do, and every year, we help hundreds of thousands of people achieve their photography dreams and impact the world around them.

I wonder what will happen in the next eighteen years?

At one point, not long after that workshop, I put on several warm layers, gloves, and a scarf and went to the beach. I couldn't believe it, but there were actual snow flurries in Florida. That's a rare occasion. Standing there in the cold with no other human soul in sight, I somehow didn't feel lonely. There was a purpose for my visit that day. On that empty white-sand beach, surrounded by a hazy mist hovering over the water, I signed a digital contract on my phone to fulfill a lifelong dream of authoring a book. I always dreamed I would have to take a fancy elevator up one hundred floors in a swanky tower in New York City, but somehow this felt more fitting.

I'm sure your dreams and goals look different from mine. You might not love the water or the ocean. You may enjoy surfing or riding around town on a bicycle for hours each day as I do. But the point is that photography can change your life, if you let it. It can open your eyes to incredible, beautiful new possibilities. It can introduce you to interesting people and bring you to amazing places in life that teach you things about yourself and the world you never knew. It can even make your financial dreams a reality.

So what's your *why*? Where are you headed, and how might this journey somehow surprise you? Everything I love came to me through photography: my wife, my friends, my dream home, my career, and just about every great experience I've ever had as an adult. I hope this book has taught you the infinite possibilities of pursuing photography both for passion and for profit.

No matter your goals, I'm cheering you on from sunny Florida—here to be the guide I needed but didn't have, sharing this hard-won wisdom I've learned through my own blood, sweat, and tears. I continue to learn every day how to be an even better photographer, and sharing this information is the most important work I've ever done.

I was never supposed to make it, after all—but thanks to God and the many mentors and helpers I encountered over the years, I did. And if I can do it, with the limited resources I had, you can do so much more. I'm rooting for you every step of the way, whatever your goals are. We all have something we want to accomplish, a vision for the future that we hope to see come true. And before we can do any of it, we first must learn to see. When we learn to see, we change the way we look at the world; and when we do that, anything is possible.

Credit: imagesofgracephoto.com

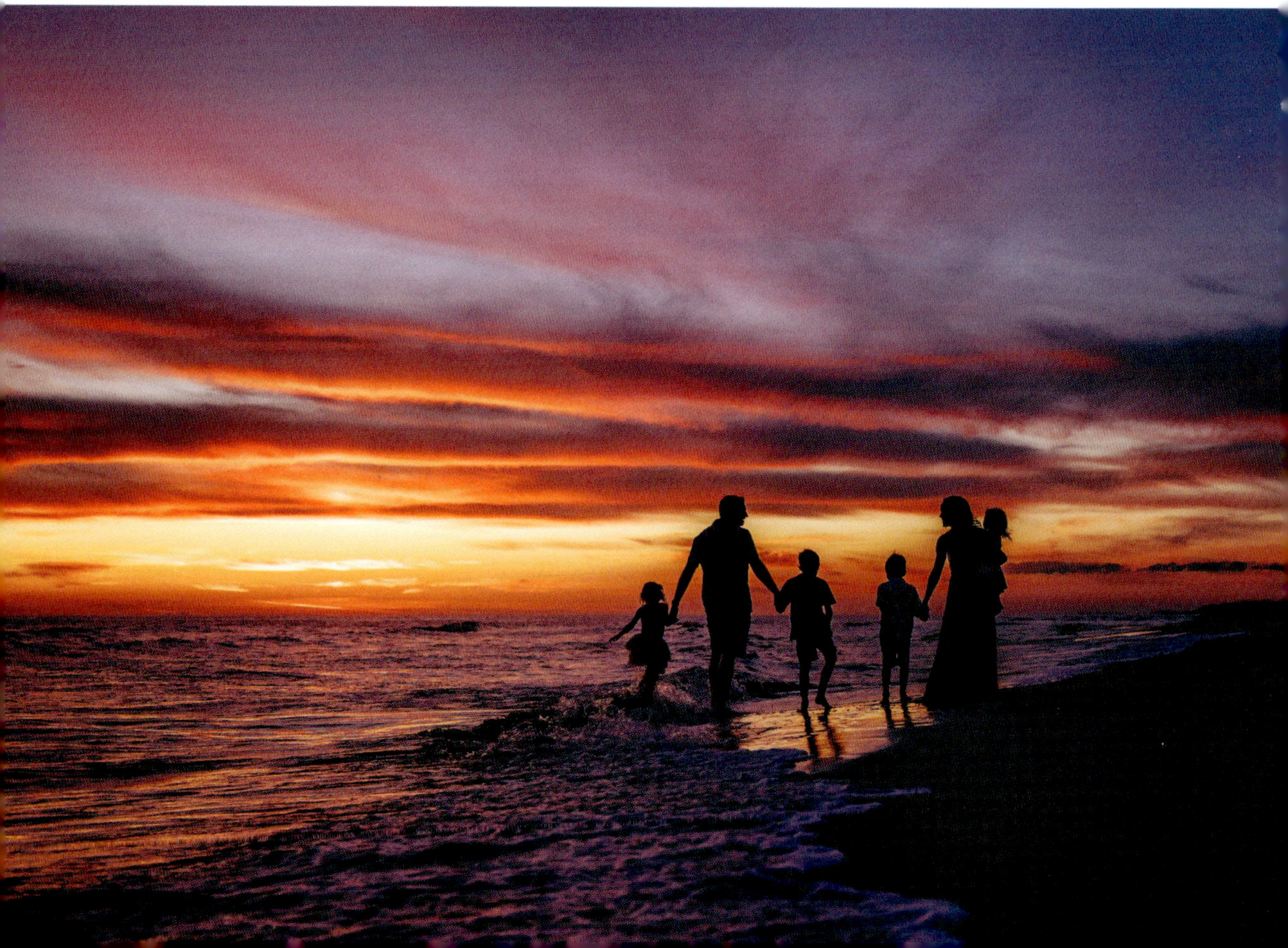

You're Invited!

Now that you know the five steps to photography success, you have everything you need to become a great photographer. But sometimes, even with the right tools and direction, we can find ourselves wanting extra help and support as we progress toward our goals. That's why I want to invite you to The Photo Mentorship, a program my team and I created to define the path to photography success.

It can be a lonely and confusing path without the right direction, but with the right mentoring, you can pick the path you need to help you succeed. In this thriving community of photographers, you will develop your unique skills and find a unique focus. It's where you can "level up" as a professional, learning what it takes to get serious about your art and grow a thriving business. Members get unlimited access to our step-by-step training courses, access to a growing, supportive network of photographers, and unlimited questions answered by our expert mentors.

If you want step-by-step help and personal feedback to help you move forward, we'd love for you to join us at PhotoMentorship.com/join. See you there!

Acknowledgments

I WOULD LIKE TO THANK MY LORD AND SAVIOR, JESUS CHRIST, FOR THE incredible gift of life I get to live. To the love of my life, Tammy Molnar, thank you for all your love, support, feedback, and encouragement over the years and especially while writing this book. This book is a million times better because of you! To our four kids, Judah, Christian, Rose, and Juliet: You inspire me daily to be a better man. I'm gonna win the next game of Catan! (Thanks for letting Daddy spend some late nights working on this thing.)

Thanks to my dear friend and writing partner, Jeff Goins, for encouraging me to write this book and for your abundant patience and diligent work in helping me navigate the writing process. I'm so proud of what we've created! To the best agent, Roger Freet, thank you for seamlessly guiding me through the process.

To my parents, Bill and Lynn Molnar, thank you for living out a great example of Jesus in our home and for your unconditional love and encouragement that I could be whoever I wanted to be.

I also want to thank my dear sisters and their spouses: Melody and Jason Morgan, Robin and Sam Brooks, and Esther and Forest Davis. To the extended Molnar, Farris, and Deveau clans—I love and appreciate you all.

To my dear friend and cofounder of The Photo Mentorship, Rich Coleman, thank you for all your support and contributions to this book, and for shooting the incredible book cover photo. I love creating with you! To Zach Gray, thank you for not only your invaluable contributions writing and creating the Earn section of the book but also all the things about business and marketing you've taught me over the years. I wouldn't be where I am without you! To Kristy Taylor, thanks for all your amazing design work on the cover and inside the book.

A *huge* thank-you from the bottom of my heart to all of our TPMers! Thank you for allowing me to be your photography mentor. You're the reason this book exists.

Thanks to Zach and Velvet Kelm for believing in an immature twenty-one-year-old and for sticking your necks out for Tammy and me to create life-changing opportunities for us. To the stellar staff at Horizon—Andrea Fleck-Nisbet, Amanda Bauch, John Andrade, Meaghan Porter, Jenn McNeil, Hannah Harless, Kristen Sasamoto, and the rest of the team: thank you for believing in me and helping me figure out the many parts of what it takes to make a book, as I couldn't have done it on my own.

And to my entrepreneur friends who continue to inspire me: Josh and Chelsea Axe, Michael Hyatt, Donald Miller, Dave Touhill, Dave Chesson, Bryan Harris, Evan Tardy, Grant Baldwin, Alli Worthington, Matt and Hilary Barnett, Dan and Joanne Miller, Brian Crist, Shaun Winn, Don Hejny, Bob and Linda Lotich, and TJ Varghese—thank you all for being who you are and teaching me so much with your words. Special thanks to Tim Grahl for challenging me to figure out my teaching niche and pivot early on.

Thanks to John and Korey Cooper for believing in me and giving me a chance to photograph the *Awake* album cover for your band, Skillet. It changed our lives! Thanks to my music industry friends like Colton Dixon, MercyMe, Matthew West, Newsboys, Jim Scherer and the crew at Big Daddy Weave, Tricia Brock, Thousand Foot Krutch, Hawk Nelson, Kristian Stanfill, Shelley Giglio and the Passion crew, Pat Barret, Dana Salsedo and Jeff Mosely from Fairtrade records, and so many others. Thanks to all the fabulous brides and grooms that trusted us with their wedding photography and gave us the opportunity to travel around the world.

And much gratitude to Nata Salvatori, Jonah Allen, Chase Jarvis, Michael Gomez, Jeremy Cowart, Russ Harrington, Roger Gibbs, David Bean, Paul F. Gero,

Kristin Barlowe, Biff Jennings, Kevin Swan, Shaun Gordon, Daniel White, Ashley Lurie, Jeff Carpenter, Billy Diggs, Mrs. Sawyer, Mr. Guiley, Jason Brieholz, and Ken Binkley for their stories and teachings that taught me so much about life and photography.

And of course, I couldn't have done any of this without the help of my current and previous team members: John Price, Kristen Cook, Josh Wood, Chris Ellison, Melanie Williams, Payton Miller, Betsy Finchum, Autumn Barb, Norma Tracy, Crystal Livesay, Matthew Shetz, Steve Wible, Dave Olsen, Kaci Moran, Reed Hewitt, Claire Gosteli, Kevin Carden, Joni Buyes, Jason Wain, Jim Cook, Philip Slowiak, Emily McGonigle, Brandon Chesbro, Amber Kelly, Cody Valenzuela, Kelly Corey, Crystal Min, Emily Alexander, Carol Fulton, Ashley Logan, and Kerri James.

Thank you to my 30A crew: Ben and Alexa Follas, David and Ali Jay, Josh and Liz Meeh, Matt and Misty Parenzen, Michael and Genevieve Howland, Ryan and Stephanie Langford, Michael and Amy Headington, Kyle and Alissa Aichele, JT and Ashlee Tollet, Kurt and Erika Buchert, Brett and Shannon Kozimor, Leslie and Trey Begin, Sarah Grace and Brandon Meckelberg, Mark and Kristen Foley, Steve and AJ Strout, Bryce and Hayden Russell.

Thanks as well to my Nashville crew: Brandon and Whitney Nall, Nick and April Ray, Josh and Morgan Thompson, Pete and Mary Camiolo, Nick and Tricia Baumhardt, Travis and Maggie Gravette, Andrew East, Franklin Cole, Michael Smallbone, Darren and Brandy Whitehead, Kyle and Kristy Chowning, Darren Tyler, Bryan Currier, Andy Traub, Isaac and Stephanie Meek, Will and Kristen Butler, Wade and Natalie Benz, Jaz and Anna Boon, Jeff Rose, Warren Barfield, Zach Prichard, Luke Stokes, Patrick Burke, and Nathan Oates.

Thank you to the fine establishments whose employees listened and encouraged me during the writing process and let me steal their WiFi: Bart, Kelli, and Victoria at Prema Café; Beachy Bean Coffee; Black Bear Bread Company; Shore Thing Cigars; Watersound Beach Club; Raw and Juicy Café; and Alan at MH Salon for the awesome haircuts.

About the Author

DAVID MOLNAR IS A CELEBRITY AND ADVERTISING PHOTOGRAPHER, believer, and family man. His work has been seen on millions of Pepsi cans, in *People*, on *American Idol*, and in the *New York Times*. His clients include March of Dimes, Google, Pepsi, and Sony, among many others. Feeling so blessed to be realizing his dreams, David is now focusing on being "Your Photography Mentor." He is helping hundreds of thousands of photographers pursue their dreams by creating world-class photo education, inspiration, and resources. Visit him at davidmolnar.com.